Justice, Migration, and Mercy

Justice, Migration, and Mercy

MICHAEL BLAKE

OXFORD
UNIVERSITY PRESS

OXFORD
UNIVERSITY PRESS

Oxford University Press is a department of the University of Oxford. It furthers
the University's objective of excellence in research, scholarship, and education
by publishing worldwide. Oxford is a registered trade mark of Oxford University
Press in the UK and certain other countries.

Published in the United States of America by Oxford University Press
198 Madison Avenue, New York, NY 10016, United States of America.

Library of Congress Cataloging-in-Publication Data
Names: Blake, Michael (Michael I.), author.
Title: Justice, migration, and mercy / Michael Blake.
Description: New York, NY, United States of America :
Oxford University Press, 2020. | Includes bibliographical references and index.
Identifiers: LCCN 2019035262 (print) | LCCN 2019035263 (ebook) |
ISBN 9780190879556 (hardback) | ISBN 9780197682432 (paperback) |
ISBN 9780190879570 (epub) | ISBN 9780190879587 (online)
Subjects: LCSH: Emigration and immigration—Government policy—
Moral and ethical aspects. | Refugees—Government policy—
Moral and ethical aspects. | Freedom of movement—Moral and ethical aspects.
Classification: LCC JV6271 .B53 2020 (print) | LCC JV6271 (ebook) |
DDC 325/.1—dc23
LC record available at https://lccn.loc.gov/2019035262
LC ebook record available at https://lccn.loc.gov/2019035263

1 3 5 7 9 8 6 4 2

Paperback printed by Marquis, Canada

Contents

Contents

Preface

On September 5, 2017, I walked into an auditorium south of Seattle, raised my right hand, and became a citizen of the United States of America. On the same day, President Donald Trump announced that the program of Deferred Action for Childhood Arrivals (DACA)—which protected the undocumented brought to the United States as children from deportation—would be abandoned, in favor of some ill-defined future replacement. I was waiting to take my oath when then-attorney general Jeff Sessions made public the administration's decision to rescind even the minimal protections offered by DACA. The decision seemed to me then, as it does now, both unjust and cruel. My pathway to becoming an American citizen has been lengthy, and laden with the usual bureaucratic hurdles, but went as smoothly as such transitions can ever be expected to go, and on September 5 it ended with my becoming a citizen. For a great many other people, however, September 5 represented a different sort of ending; a tool by which they were able to build lives of value for themselves had been taken away, and they have had to adjust to a new, more precarious reality. I came home after the ceremony and began to write this book.

Why am I acknowledging these facts? There are two reasons. The first is to acknowledge the simple truth that migration, and migration policy, are live topics for political controversy; the political landscape is different than it was when I began thinking about these topics, and by the time this book is published the landscape will be different still. I have tried to acknowledge these facts, to the extent possible, by seeking a moral story we might use to evaluate new forms of policy; the moral story, I hope, might give us guidance, or at least remind us of our best ethical values, even as the specifics of migration policy change. The second reason, though, is to acknowledge that I have a particular position within the world of migration: I am a migrant, but I have had a significantly easier experience of migration than a great many migrants throughout the world. I have tried to be honest, both about what I take to be the right sorts of ethical values, and about my own experience of migration. Migration policy, in states like the United States, has often been set up to protect people like me, at the expense of more vulnerable people—people without my (relative) wealth, my racial identity, or my education. Part of what led me to write this book is the thought that one need not think that migration is itself a human right, in order to think that we can and should offer moral criticism of migration policy. One does not have to defend open borders, in short, to be in a position to offer robust criticism of the ways in which borders are currently being closed. It is worth noting, though, that I cannot help but write as someone for whom these borders are considerably less violent than they have been for a great many others.

This book reflects several years' worth of thinking about migration, and I have been lucky to have had a group of colleagues and friends who have helped me along the way. It should go without saying, of course, that very few of them actually agree with everything I say; all of them, though, have contributed to making my views better, through their conversation, criticism, and care. My students Michael Ball-Blakely, Julio Covarrubias, Sean Haldeman, Stephen Blake Hereth, Mitch Kaufmann, Amy Reed-Sandoval, and Patrick Taylor Smith have been kind enough to listen to my thoughts on these subjects as they developed. The University of Washington has been an exceptional place to work and to teach, and I am particularly grateful to Stephen Gardiner, Jamie Mayerfeld, Michael Rosenthal, Bill Talbott, and Andrea Woody for their help and friendship over these years. A wide group of scholars and friends have helped me think about these issues; I am especially grateful to Gillian Brock, Joseph Carens, Luara Ferracioli, Javier Hidalgo, Adam Hosein, Stephen Macedo, Pietro Maffetone, José Jorge Mendoza, David Owen, Ryan Pevnick, Mathias Risse, Alex Sager, Grant Silva, Sarah Song, Anna Stilz, Christine Straehle, Laura Valentini, Christopher Heath Wellman, Shelly Wilcox, Caleb Yong, and Lea Ypi. Versions of the ideas in the final two chapters of this book were given at colloquiums at the University of Durham, the University of British Columbia, and Princeton University; I am grateful to audiences at all these universities. The structure of the book was first laid out in a summer school on migration hosted by the Ruhr-Univerity Bochum's Institute for Philosophy I; I would like to thank Volker Heins, Thorben Knobloch, Corinna Mieth, Andreas Neiderberger, Christian Neuhauser, Itzik Pazuelo, and Janelle Pötzsch for the conversation and the philosophical community. I am, finally, very grateful to Peter Ohlin for his support of this project.

Portions of chapter 4 of this book appeared as "Immigration, Jurisdiction, and Exclusion," 41(2) *Philosophy and Public Affairs* (Spring 2013); portions of chapter 4 appeared as "Immigration and Political Equality," 45(4) *San Diego*

Law Review (2008). I am grateful to these journals for permission to use these materials here. This book was supported in part by a grant from the National Endowment for the Humanities, through its initiative on The Common Good; I would like to express my gratitude to the NEH for supporting my work. This manuscript was finished, finally, while in residence at the Helen Riaboff Whiteley Center, at the University of Washington's Friday Harbor Laboratories; I am grateful to the staff of the Whiteley Center, for their creation of an ideal environment in which to study and to write. My most profound debts, as always, are to my wife Melissa Knox, and to my children Eloise and Gus, who continue to be the reason for whatever optimism I have left about the world and its future.

Justice, Migration, and Mercy

1

On Morality and Migration

When I set out to write this book, I wanted to write the definitive moral account of migration. I did not succeed. Indeed, it seems to me now that the subject of migration is simply too *big* to be adequately analyzed in any single book. When people move between countries, they create new things: new lives for themselves, new relationships with others, new norms in the market-place and in civil society, new ways of being in the world. Migration reflects the whole panoply of human experience, and the human experience itself is too complex for us to theorize about all at once. Consider, for instance, the many subjects on which a complete moral theory of migration would have to take a stand:

(1) **Migration and history.** The world is made up of countries whose wealth and power continue to be shaped by a shared legacy of colonialism and exploitation. We do not face migrants from hypothetical countries, but from specific societies born out of this shared and violent history. Many migrants, moreover, seek to migrate from countries that were once colonized, and seek to migrate to the wealthier societies that were once colonial powers. A full theory of morality in migration would deal with whether, and how, the colonial legacy creates particular obligations to allow such migration to occur.[1] To refuse to engage with these matters risks courting incoherence in one's views on migration; as Kishore Mahbubani put it, the citizens of the less developed countries

> are like hungry and diseased passengers on a leaky, overcrowded boat that is about to drift into treacherous waters, in which many of them will perish. The captain of the boat is often harsh, sometimes fairly and sometimes not. On the river banks stand a group of affluent, well-fed and well-intentioned onlookers. As soon as those onlookers witness a passenger being flogged or imprisoned or even deprived of his right to speak, they board the ship to intervene, protecting the passengers from

Justice, Migration, and Mercy. Michael Blake, Oxford University Press (2020). © Oxford University Press.
DOI: 10.1093/oso/9780190879556.001.0001

the captain. But those passengers remain hungry and diseased. As soon as they try to swim to the banks into the arms of their benefactors, they are firmly returned to the boat, their primary sufferings unabated.[2]

Citizens of the world's wealthiest countries—or, at least, political theorists from those countries—tend to think that they have some degree of obligation to help overcome our global legacy of colonialism, and they assume the right to criticize those who engage in tyranny or exploitation abroad.[3] They rarely ask whether they might help the global poor by bringing them to societies in which they might become less poor. A full theory of morality in migration would help us understand whether, and how, migration might be used as a response to colonialism.[4]

(2) **Migration and global economic justice.** The world right now has wide disparities of wealth and power among the states. For the past several decades, political philosophers have sought to bring philosophical concepts of justice and right to bear on the global gap between the wealthy and the impoverished.[5] Even if these inequalities are not produced by colonialism and its legacy, we might still ask whether or not migration law and policy have a role to play in overcoming global economic inequality. Migration might, at the very least, have some role to play in *maintaining* an unjust division of the world's wealth. The 1965 Immigration and Nationality Act in the United States, for instance, had the functional effect of cutting legal immigration to the United States from Mexico in half—at the same time as global economic forces made employment in Mexico more tenuous. These forces led to an increase in the number of Mexican citizens working without legal right in the United States.[6] The functional effect of the 1965 act, then, was to increase profits for American businesses, who were able to absorb benefits from a disposable workforce poorly positioned to demand workplace rights—with comparatively little economic benefit flowing to Mexico.[7] Being born on the "right" side of the Rio Grande, it seems, is something like the modern-day equivalent of lucky birth in a feudal society, an accident of birth that endows the fortunate with undeserved advantage.[8] A full moral theory of migration, then, would have to help us understand how migration policy might be constrained by the demands of global distributive justice.

(3) **Migration and domestic economic justice.** When people migrate, they often join the labor market in their new society; the effects of their doing so are complex and resist any simple description.[9] There are, however, some frequently encountered effects that might call for moral analysis. The first is that migrants tend to be viewed by the native-born, when economic conditions are poor, as the *cause* of those economic difficulties; as the US Commission on Civil Rights pithily put it, every generation of migrants ends up resented by the generation of migrants that came before.[10] The second, though, is the simple fact that the presence of migrants affects both what work is open to native-born residents and what wages will be provided for what sorts of work.[11] Many of these effects are beneficial to all segments of society; some, however, are not—especially for the least well educated, who may find themselves in competition with migrants for low-waged or casual labor.[12] If we are worried about economic justice between the rich and the poor citizens of a democratic state, we might have reason to ask about these effects— and about whether or not a full moral theory of migration would insist that we adjust our migration policy to address them.

(4) **Migration and racial justice.** Migration to the United States, after the 1965 act, does not explicitly reflect ideas of racial superiority or inferiority; migration policy, however, has the potential to both reflect and exacerbate ideas of racial hierarchy. Earlier American policy, of course, reflected racism in a fairly robust way. The Immigration Act of 1924 was justified with reference to the "scientific" racism of Madison Grant, who also fought for laws against miscegenation. Prior to this act, the Chinese Exclusion Act had explicitly precluded "any person of the Chinese or Mongolian races" from entering the United States for purposes of migration.[13] Modern forms of exclusion rarely announce their racism quite so neatly; they may, however, both stem from and exacerbate forms of racial animus that are worthy of condemnation. Sheriff Joe Arpaio, for instance, was convicted of violating a judicial order preventing him from targeting people of Mexican descent; the Department of Justice had found that Hispanics were four to nine times as likely as whites to be stopped by Arpaio's patrols.[14] Arpaio was, in the view of many, using laws against undocumented residency as a tool for the harassment and marginalization of people of Mexican descent— citizen and non-citizen alike. Migration policy, in short, can be a tool with which societies announce who is marginal and who is not; how

the borders are policed can be a way of announcing who is important within those borders.[15] Even the very notion of *illegal* migration can be a way of rendering the migrant something less than human; it is not an accident that the populist movements making headway in Europe and in the United States have tended to demonize the migrant as a bringer of disease.[16] The phenomenon which links race with migration, and then insists that the migrant is less worthy of respect in virtue of both race and status *as* migrant, is one that is found in any number of social contexts. Thus, Svetlana Alexievich describes the words of a Tajik activist in Moscow:

> Two young Tajiks were taken to the hospital in an ambulance from a construction site. . . . They spent all night in a cold waiting room, and nobody helped them. The doctors didn't conceal their feelings: "Why do you black-asses keep showing up here?" . . . I had this very long conversation with a police general. . . . He wasn't an idiot or some one-track-mind military type, he seemed cultivated. "Did you know," I said to him, "that you have a real Gestapo man on your force? He's a master of torture, everyone is afraid of him. Every homeless person and migrant worker he comes across ends up crippled." . . . But he just looked at me with a smile. "Tell me his name. Good man! We'll promote him, reward him. . . . We intentionally create impossible conditions for you people so that you'll leave as soon as possible. There are two million migrant workers in Moscow, the city can't digest this many of you suddenly descending on us. There are just too many of your kind here."[17]

The general is more honest than many, but I suspect the core of his view—*there are too many of your kind here*—is one that is not wholly unfamiliar to many people, even if we would hope few would be willing to use that view to defend torture. A full theory of morality in migration, though, might provide us the resources to effectively understand, and rebut, the worst versions of that view; or, failing that, at least provide us with the tools needed to understand how we might make our disagreement with them known.

(5) **Migration and moral phenomenology.** A full moral theory of migration would not simply be a theory of how politics might respond to the migrant; it would also provide us with the tools needed to understand what it is to *be* a migrant, and how the experience of migration matters

from the standpoint of ethics.[18] To be a migrant is to be a particular kind of creature: one who is committing to building a new life, in a new place, with new people. For every new possibility, however, there is a possibility foreclosed, and the price of a new life is that the old one is, to a greater or lesser degree, removed from view. This explains why deportation is as violent an act as is undoubtedly is. James Madison, in rejecting the Alien and Sedition Acts of 1798, wrote eloquently about the power of losing one's home:

> If the banishment of an alien from a country into which he has been invited as the asylum most auspicious to his happiness—a country where he may have formed the most tender connections; where he may have invested his entire property, and acquired property of the per-manent, as well as the movable and temporary kind; where he enjoys, under the laws, a greater share of the blessings of personal security and personal liberty than he can elsewhere hope for and where he may have nearly completed his probationary title to citizenship . . . if a ban-ishment of this sort be not a punishment, and among the severest of punishments, it will be difficult to imagine a doom to which the name can be applied.[19]

Deportation pains us, then, because it is the loss of something; a home, which is perhaps best understood as an aspect of the self that inhabits that home. In migrating, we enter into a world which requires us to acquire new ways of relating to the other members of our social world; this, in turn, may require us to be something en-tirely new, both to others and to ourselves. Jean Améry, living in exile in Belgium, described this well; what, asked Améry, does a *home* provide to us?

> Reduced to the positive-psychological basic content of the idea, home is *security*. If I think back on the first days of exile in Antwerp, I still have the memory of staggering on shaky ground. The mere fact that one could not decipher people's faces was frightening. I was having a beer with a big, coarse-boned, square-skulled man, who may have been a respectable Flemish citizen, perhaps even a patrician, but could just as well have been a suspicious harbor tough about to punch me in the face and lay hands on my wife. Faces, gestures, clothes, houses, words (even

if I halfway understood them) were sensory reality, but not interpretable signs. There was no order for me in this world.[20]

In emigrating, one must build a new self. And if many people do this voluntarily, it should still be remembered that this process is painful and necessarily involves profound forms of loss. If the emigration is involuntary, moreover, we should not lose sight of its origin, forgetting that this loss is forced at the request of another, who thinks this loss is more palatable than having to continue associating with the disfavored. Deportation, I will argue, is not always morally wrong; but it always entails a partial destruction of what the deported has made of her life. It is therefore not an accident that *deportation* is often metaphorically linked to annihilation. The Armenian genocide began with the promulgation of the Tehcir Law, which authorized the deportation of those Armenians engaging in "espionage against the state."[21] The Wannsee Conference, similarly, described the systematic murder of the Jews through the euphemistic phrase *nach dem Osten transportiert*— transported to the east.[22] A full accounting of the morality of migration would, we could hope, enable us to understand just how to make sense of what is at stake in migration: what is lost in emigrating, what is lost in refraining from that emigration, and how to understand the moral gravity of forcible removal from one's home.

A full account of the moral issues raised by migration would have to provide us with the tools needed to understand all these aspects and the ways in which they relate to one another. It would require a full account of the complex ways in which our world has been made in the past, and how it is being made in the present, by a shared legacy of evil and violence. I am not sure that such a theory is likely to be produced; I am, however, quite sure that, if such a theory is forthcoming, it won't be written by me. In this book, I intend to do something slightly more modest. I want to do only two things, with a due recognition that doing those two things can provide us with only part of the moral story we require.

The first thing I want to do is to lay out what I take to be the best justifying story for the state's right to exclude. This, I think, is what must be done before any of the more specific moral issues I have described can be adequately analyzed. If the state is going to prevent some people from entering onto its territory, that state will have to provide some story about why it is within its rights to do so. I want to give one version of that story in this book—one I think stands a chance of being harmonious with the ideals of justice that animate liberal political philosophy. I will begin with materials that I take to be, if not uncontroversial, at least potentially attractive, and I will use these to derive a particular account of what the state might say by way of justifying exclusion. Understanding that account, I believe, might go some way toward helping those of us who live in liberal political communities to navigate the difficult waters of our public debates surrounding migration. The account I offer is going to include both the right to exclude and—as importantly—limits on that right; there are persons that are not rightly excluded, and reasons that cannot be used in justification of exclusion. Understanding what the moral story I provide cannot permit is as important as understanding what it might permit. Even if I succeed in this task, though, I will have provided only part of the story. What I say here is, in principle, susceptible of being trumped by other particularistic factors; the individual history of a country might provide us with resources from which to argue that what is otherwise permissible might have become forbidden. Michael Walzer, in a similar vein, argued that the United States could not rightly exclude those turned into refugees by the American invasion of Vietnam; the military history of the United States had "effectively Americanized them even before they arrived at these shores."[23] On Walzer's account, political communities have the right to exclude a great many people—but they can, because of their histories, forfeit that right, at least as regards some people. I am open to such a possibility, too, although not without some worries about how to understand its theoretical basis.[24] In what follows, though, I will focus primarily on the right to exclude and its limits—and leave concerns about circumstances in which that right is forfeited for another time. This choice does not mean such particularistic concerns are not important; they are, I think, often as important as the broad moral right to exclude against which they are pressed. My task here, though, is to understand that latter right, and doing so is an important precursor to the larger moral conversation.

The second thing I want to do in this book, however, is to go beyond justice and open up space for alternative moral concepts to be applied to migration policy. The conversations we have about migration are often made with reference to competing ideals of justice. Those who disagree about the morality of migration disagree about who can make what claims of right as regards particular social institutions. These conversations—both in politics and in philosophy—are important and likely to continue in the near future. But they are incomplete. In ordinary life, we can be terrible people without actively violating rights. We can be cruel, callous, vicious, petty, and so on—and can do so without necessarily doing any actions rightly considered *unjust*. I will use the concept of mercy here as a way of getting at the distinct moral virtue involved in doing more than simply failing to violate the obligations of justice. An individual who fails to be merciful does not thereby wrong any individual person, at least in the sense of doing to her what justice precludes; but he can be said to be a bad example of what a person should be. As Jeffrie Murphy notes:

> [T]he virtue of mercy is revealed when a person, out of compassion for the hard position of the person who owes him an obligation, waives the right that generates the obligation and frees the individual of the burden of that obligation. People who are always standing on their rights, indifferent to the impact this may have on others, are simply intolerable. Such persons cannot be faulted on grounds of justice, but they can certainly be faulted.[25]

What I want to do in the later parts of this book is to explore these ideas not simply as regards persons, but as regards polities. I am going to argue that a state can be morally criticized, even when it doesn't trespass against the norms of justice, if it fails to demonstrate the appropriate virtue of mercy. States—like persons—have the obligations not simply to respect rights, but also to do some things that involve taking care of other people, regardless of whether or not those people have rights in justice to that sort of care. I believe that this sort of virtue can be an important supplement to conversations about justice in migration, for at least two reasons. The first is that there seem to be cases in which the best description of a particular piece of migration policy isn't *unjust*, but *unmerciful*; the policy isn't demanded as a matter of right, but reveals those who created it as insufficiently attentive to the sorts of moral values that ought to be taken seriously by those charged with the design of public policy. I believe those of us who care about political ethics have reason to defend the thought that there are ways of criticizing policy quite distinct from inquiring about its justice; and that the notion of mercy might be one important virtue that ought to be reflected and respected in public discourse about migration policy. The category of the merciful, I will argue, is capable of fitting into any number of moral frameworks as a distinct module; ideas similar to the one I discuss here can be found in Christian ethics, Kantian beneficence, and feminist ethics of care. The concept is powerful, both rhetorically as well as philosophically, and those of us who seek ethical reform of migration policy might find the concept a useful one in public advocacy. The second reason, more controversial, is that the idea of mercy might provide us with some way of defending policies that are also demanded by justice. There may be multiple ways of describing the evil of particular forms of migration policy; and there can be occasions in which the language of mercy might be more powerful than the sometimes arid notion of justice.

Some people will be hostile to much of this. When I first gave a talk about the concept of mercy, the first question came from an audience member who thought the very idea was disreputable; I would rather fight for justice, she said, than beg for mercy. This reaction is not entirely wrong; where justice demands the elimination of a particular policy, for instance, the concept of mercy is sometimes the wrong place for us to start. Those who sought to overturn Jim Crow would have been hesitant to couch their demands in terms of a request for mercy. (If those who passed the Civil Rights Act of 1964 described that act with reference to mercy, moreover, we might think that description vaguely obscene.)[26] To this, I can offer only two rejoinders. The first is that we impoverish the discourse of political ethics by insisting that only language derived from justice can be a part of our conversation. If, as I will argue, the liberal state has some right to exclude the unwanted foreign citizen, then we may have a need for ethical discourse in understanding how we ought to best make use of the freedom such a right affords us. To insist that fighting for justice is the only way forward is to ignore the wonderful complexity of our ethical vocabulary. The second rejoinder, though, is that sometimes the question isn't what we would rather do, but what will get the job done. We might want to separate the question of how we know what justice requires, from the distinct question of how we can convince others to go along with the policy justice recommends. The idea of mercy, I will argue, can both help us understand the ethics of migration policy and also motivate rightful policy in an increasingly nativist and hostile political community.

Some people, of course, will be hostile to a great deal more than the concept of mercy. Some will want to question whether there should be states or borders at all.[27] I want to push back against this sort of view, in two ways. The first is conceptual; I take the concept of immigration to have meaning only against the backdrop of the modern, Westphalian system of states. When I moved from Boston to Seattle, I did not migrate; when I moved from Canada to the United States, I did. Migration—as I understand and use it in this book—requires the crossing of the borders of a sovereign state; it therefore requires the existence of sovereign states. Not all uses of the concept have this entailment; Michael Fisher's history of migration begins by describing Gudrid the Traveler, who settled in what is now Canada in 1002 CE, as "an immigrant from Iceland."[28] For my part, though, I will insist that being an immigrant from Iceland only makes sense when there *is* an Iceland, and being an immigrant requires the existence of states *like* Iceland; thus, for purposes of the present book, I will assume that the state system, or something very much like it, will persist as the backdrop of our normative discussions. The second reason for my rejection of radical analysis, though, is more philosophically grounded; I describe myself as an institutional conservative—which I should note, is rather unlike being a conservative, full stop.[29] The institutional conservative begins with the institutional forms we have and asks what they would have to do in order to be justified. This is a rather different thing than insisting that the institutions we have already do a good—or even adequate— job of things. It is also a different thing than asking what forms of institutions we might have, were we beginning the enterprise de novo. The reason for my rejection of the latter question is simple: if we can adjust what we have and meet the tests of justice, then we should do so—where that *should* refers both to the conceptual difficulties involved in building new institutional forms and to the practical difficulties engendered by revolutionary changes in institutional framework.[30] If the task is hopeless—if the institutions we have cannot be made to do justice—then we have reason to seek more radical solutions. What I do in this book, though, is to see whether or not, in principle at least, those more radical solutions can be avoided.

At this point, though, I would like to acknowledge a few difficulties involved in the task I have given myself. The first is to acknowledge who I am; I am a migrant, as I have said, but a rather privileged one. I was born into a relatively wealthy society and emigrated to another relatively wealthy society; to be an emigrant is to be, if Améry is correct, vulnerable to some degree, but my vulnerability was and is reduced by the social power given to me by my wealth and social identity. I say these things because, while I am writing ideas I hope will be motivating to a great many readers, these ideas come from a particular person—and likely reflect, in ways I cannot anticipate, my own particularity. I have to acknowledge, further, that I am writing in a conversation in which American and European voices dominate; I am writing to academics, in response to a conversational agenda set up by other academics, and I must acknowledge that the people to whom

I respond tend to be rather privileged as well. I acknowledge all this because I think the dialogue we have built is one that would benefit from greater inclusion, of all sorts; at the very least, the arguments in this book would be better were they subjected to the sorts of critical engagement that could only come from those conversations our current philosophical world makes difficult. What I say here, then, is at the most a contribution to our ongoing debates about the morality of migration; it is emphatically not intended to conclude those debates.

Some final limits. I will be focusing on immigration—which I will take to entail crossing an international border, with the intention to remain in that new country indefinitely. This means that I will ignore, or treat in passing, some rather important political topics. I will not discuss, for instance, the possibility of partial membership, whether that concept is understood with reference to the rights of the resident or the duration of her stay.[31] I will also ignore the difficulties involved in understanding how we might condition the transition from such a partial status to the full status as citizen; are citizenship tests illiberal, or do they reflect legitimate interests held by the liberal state?[32] For that matter, what sorts of integration might be rightly expected of the one emigrating to a new society? These questions are important—but they will be dealt with only in passing in this book. I will also be ignoring, finally, the effects of migration upon distributive justice in the country to which emigration is sought—as well as the effects of that migration upon those left behind.[33] These are important topics—indeed, they form a central part of many discussions about the consequences of particular changes in migration policy. In what follows, though, I am concerned with what might justify the exclusion of an unwanted person from a political community; I will therefore be concerned with the economics of migration only to the extent that such factors affect the ability of a society to live up to the demands and guarantees of liberal political philosophy.

We can therefore transition to a discussion of what I take those demands and guarantees to be. I have, here, to assert some premises on which my later arguments depend. I take these premises to be defensible and have, in fact, sought to defend some of them elsewhere. In the present context, though, I want simply to offer them as starting points. One who disagrees with them will likely disagree with what comes after them. Explanations, though, must end somewhere; mine will end here, with five premises I will use to justify—and constrain—the right to exclude.

(1) **Autonomy.** I will assume that human beings have a right to the circumstances under which they live as autonomous agents—by which I mean nothing more metaphysically robust than that they are capable of building lives from which they are able to derive value, and in which their own agency plays a significant role in determining the activities and plans they pursue. I take this to be a cosmopolitan value, in that *all* humans are entitled to the circumstances under which such autonomy is possible; all individuals are entitled to that set of institutions needed to guarantee and fulfill such autonomy. Institutions such as states, then, cannot restrict their moral attention to the autonomy of their own citizens; they are commanded to work together to build a world in which all individuals are provided with the rights and resources needed to live autonomous lives. I will use a fairly thin notion of autonomy; it requires no more than that the individual in question be rightly understood, as Joseph Raz had it, as part author of her own life.[34] Even this thin notion of autonomy, though, can have some significant implications. I take liberal political philosophy, in at least the tradition in which John Rawls wrote, as being a way of working out what sorts of politics would best respect this sort of autonomy. Rawls took as a premise of his work that individuals are possessed of a particular vision of what makes their lives have value—what he called a conception of the good—and that politics must be justified to individuals with reference to how it enabled them to pursue that good in concert with others.[35] The notion of autonomy, I should acknowledge, is rather complex; I hope, for the moment, that these complexities may be ignored.

(2) **Planning.** I will assume, further, that the exercise of autonomy demands the ability to make plans.[36] This idea is also found in John Rawls; for Rawls, the good we pursue enables us not just to act in the moment, but to structure our agency over time. Thus, for Rawls, a person just is "a life lived according to a plan."[37] The notion of the plan is important, because it allows us to connect autonomy with our experience of time; had we no sense of memory or anticipation, we might still have a good, but it would not be the sort of good that animates humans lives as we know them. We remember value in the past and anticipate value in the future; we live in time, as it were, and know ourselves to do so—which differentiates the good for us from, say, the good of a goldfish. This means, though, that our autonomy can be frustrated, not simply by the denial of freedom in the moment, but by the denial of those

resources and rights needed to act over time. We have need, that is, of those circumstances required to enable us to make and pursue plans, while recognizing the limits on those plans that come from sharing a social world with others.

(3) **States.** The preceding considerations give rise to a need for political society. We stand in need of some sorts of settled expectations, without which we might find it impossible to be secure, in either our persons or in our property. Thus, I will assume that there is a need for states—by which I mean, institutions possessed of the right to coercively enforce certain collective norms. I take political society, in other words, to be a necessity for people as we know them to engage in the sorts of planning activities implicit in the concept of autonomy. I do not claim that these political societies must have taken the form we have developed; still less do I claim that the borders we currently have are in any sense obligatory or natural. I do claim, though, that some sort of political society is morally required, and that the states of the world now might be justifiable—were they to use their political powers in a justifiable manner.

(4) **Justification.** Because we have arrived at a world in which states are territorially based, we have a world in which states can do different things to different people; since I am not now in France, for instance, and have no claim to French citizenship, the legal machinery of France cannot directly coerce me. I am, in contrast, quite vulnerable to the decisions arrived at by the political and legal institutions of the United States. It can take my property, put me in jail, and—in the limit case—put me to death. These facts, though, mean that states may owe different things by way of justification to different persons. I have elsewhere argued that many norms of distributive justice are best understood as ways of justifying political coercion to those coerced; John Rawls's domestic principles of justice are not applicable to the global context, since there is no state there whose coercive decisions those principles might justify.[38] In the present context, I make no such claims; I simply want to assert the structural fact that states may have different obligations to those they coerce than to those they do not, and that this difference might derive from—rather than contradict—global respect for autonomy.

(5) **Human rights and civil rights.** I will, finally, assert a structural difference between kinds of moral right. Some rights exist as direct implications of autonomy. The right to be free from torture, I take it,

has this form; if one is tortured, one is no longer an autonomous agent, but someone for whom the body itself has been transformed into the tool of another.[39] There is therefore an obvious way in which the international human right to be free from torture reflects the cosmopolitan right to autonomous functioning. Other rights, though, exist as ways of justifying coercive political rule specifically to those autonomous creatures over whom that coercion is exercised. I take it that voting rights have this shape; if I am denied the right to vote in France, the fact that my lack of French citizenship is a mere accident of birth is irrelevant—I am not coerced by French law and so have no justificatory claim to a share of power in writing that law. We have reason, then, to distinguish those rights I have simply in virtue of my agency as a human, from those I have as a result of shared liability to the coercive machinery of a territorial state. The rights are not totally unrelated: in particular, we might have a human right to a society in which our civil rights are respected. This, however, does not mean that the two forms of right are not distinct, and I will proceed on the assumption that these two forms of rights work in different ways.

These ideas are, of course, brief and sketchy; but I think a sketch might be enough. What could these materials provide us, by way of a right to exclude? They might, I believe, provide us with a framework by which a liberal state might be shown to have some limited right to exclude the unwanted outsider. I will try, in this book, to defend the thought that—when people are already protected in their ability to create lives of value for themselves in their countries of origin—the liberal state has no particular obligation to allow those people entry for purposes of immigration. People are possessed of a great many moral rights, on the vision I defend here. They are entitled to the human rights, without which they cannot build lives of value, against a backdrop of choice and freedom. They are entitled, moreover, to political and civil rights, so that they can effectively work within their political societies to propose and defend particular visions of how political power ought to be deployed. These political and civil rights may include—as I think they should—rights to particular principles of distributive justice, without which political discourse may become deformed and political participation impossible. They are not, however, entitled to membership in that particular political society which most appeals to them—or so, at any rate, I will argue. Individuals may gain the right to migrate when migration is required for the exercise of their human rights; but those human rights do not include the right to migrate wherever they might choose.

This project, of course, might seem rather conservative; to defend the right to exclude might seem to defend all the ways in which states currently exclude. This is, however, mistaken. The purpose of my argument is not simply to justify exclusion, but to see what the limits of exclusion would be, even on what I take to be its best justification. If anything, I want what I write here to serve as a way of challenging the global realities of migration. The current reality is that we do have open borders—for certain people. Wealthy residents of developed countries—especially those possessed of financial or corporate power, or rare and valuable forms of human capital—can choose more or less any society in the world in which to live. Those who are the most marginal— who live under repressive regimes, who face severe poverty—are subjected to the most stringent and exclusionary forms of border control. If what I say here is correct, we have a reason to invert this picture. The people who have the strongest moral right to migrate are precisely those whose other rights are most poorly defended; those most excludable are precisely those least excluded today. One need not defend open borders, then, in order to offer a critical perspective on how those borders are now policed. I am, further, hoping that what I write here will have some purchase—both with my fellow philosophers, some of whom defend the right to exclude, and with my fellow citizens, very nearly all of whom do. I want, in short, to give, to those who do not defend a human right to migrate, some reasons on which we might think that the right to exclude is more limited than it at first seems—and that such a right is, at most, a beginning to our moral analysis, rather than its end.

Of course, another way of saying this is that I expect *no one* will much like what I have to say here. Those academics who defend a right to exclude will dislike the limits I place on that right. Those who defend a right to migrate will dislike the fact that I defend *any* exclusion. The current political discourse over migration, moreover, has become venomous, in a way that recalls earlier—and more frightening—debates about migration and membership. The current climate tends to reward radicalism and distrusts moderation. (Not that moderation has many friends, even at the best of times; as Jim Hightower notes, there's nothing in the middle of the road but yellow stripes and dead armadillos.)[40] Philosophy, finally, has a bit of a reputation for adversarial cruelty—a reputation that is, frankly, well earned. A book about the morality of migration, then, can expect—if the author is lucky enough not to be ignored—vigorous, not to say angry, criticism. As an entirely ineffective

way of heading off this criticism, I want to note that all the people I disagree with in this book have taught me a great deal, both about migration and
philosophy; I could not have developed my own view without engagement
with their own. Of course, none of that changes the fact that I disagree with
these other thinkers; and it is to the task of explaining this disagreement that
I now turn.

2

Justice and the Excluded, Part 1

Open Borders

Our public debates about migration are, above all else, debates about ethics. The thought that particular patterns of migration are unjust—that they are unfair—flows through recent public discourse about immigration. To take one prominent example: the 2016 election of Donald Trump began with his assertion that Mexican migrants included rapists, drug smugglers, and generally "bad hombres."[1] His signature campaign promise—to build a wall between Mexico and the United States, paid for by Mexico—was justified with reference to the ways in which Mexican migrants were unfairly stealing jobs from American workers. Trump's inaugural speech made this moral note clear:

> From this moment on, it's going to be America First. Every decision on trade, on taxes, on immigration, on foreign affairs, will be made to benefit American workers and American families. We must protect our borders from the ravages of other countries making our products, stealing our companies, and destroying our jobs. . . . We will bring back our jobs. We will bring back our borders. We will bring back our wealth.[2]

Trump's analysis is, at its heart, a moral one; the current global order is unfair. It is unfair that migrants are allowed to take the jobs and the wealth of current inhabitants of the United States. Trump's note of property is, I think, best interpreted as a particular sort of moral claim: those jobs and that wealth are *rightly* held by American citizens. Trump won the presidency, in part, because of his success at portraying Hillary Clinton as a "globalist," ready to countenance unfairness toward Americans because of her insufficient love for America itself. Whether one is attracted to this vision of populism—and, as will become clear, I am not—it represents a particular vision of how justice might be brought to bear upon migration: the United States must exclude the unwanted outsider, because the failure to do so is unfair.

Justice, Migration, and Mercy. Michael Blake, Oxford University Press (2020). © Oxford University Press.
DOI: 10.1093/oso/9780190879556.001.0001

If this vision of migration rests on a notion of justice, so too does it oppo-site. Much political resistance to the policies of the Trump administration rests upon the thought that particular patterns of migration enforcement can represent forms of unfairness. The rhetorical slogan *No human is il-legal* insists that the very language with which we describe the unauthor-ized can contain forms of unfair marginalization and dehumanization.[3] On a more practical level, the Left in the United States has resisted partic-ular methods and purposes of exclusion, citing morality as the rationale for doing so. Citizens and states alike have engaged in legal challenges against the Trump administration's so-called travel ban, which sought to prevent migration from a number of majority-Muslim countries; the brief opposing this ban made the case that it was discriminatory—and, hence, unfair.[4] A renewed sanctuary movement has made the case that cities, and individ-uals, should refuse to assist the Immigrations and Customs Enforcement (ICE) officers charged with deportation; to do otherwise, said one of the movement's founders, would be to be "complicit in injustice."[5] More broadly, some undocumented Americans have begun to make the case that status as undocumented can be the basis of a social marginalization as damaging as the historical marginalization of African Americans; Jim Crow has been transformed into Juan Crow—and this latter ought to be resisted, by un-documented Americans willing to take a stand for social equality.[6] These arguments, too, are grounded on an image of justice. They insist that some patterns of exclusion are unfair and therefore unjust. The United States must cease its current practices of exclusion because these practices constitute and condone unfairness.

Nothing in this, I should note, is unique to the political discourse of the United States. Much of European politics involves an argument between competing visions of justice in migration. In Germany, the issue of open-ness to Syrian refugees has emerged as the key point of conflict between Angela Merkel's Christian Democrats and such populist movements as the Alternative für Deutschland. In Italy, two populist parties—the Five Star Movement and the League—gained power largely as a result of hostility to migration; one of the coalition government's first acts was to turn away a ship that had rescued 629 asylum seekers from drowning.[7] Nor, indeed, is anything here unique to Europe; populist movements have emerged in soci-eties as diverse as Brazil, Zimbabwe, and Myanmar—and, in all these places, they have come to power in part by decrying current patterns of migration as unjust.[8]

Public arguments about migration, in short, often involve a particular pattern of moral argument: what one side or the other proposes to do is unjust, and it is unjust because it is unfair to some particular set of people. These arguments, of course, end up in wildly different places, despite these structural similarities. They endorse radically different sets of migratory rights and envision radically different futures for particular political communities. But these different conclusions rest upon conceptually similar foundations. It is therefore not surprising that these arguments often display, as David Miller has it, more heat than light.[9] The difference between the one who defends exclusion and the one who decries it as illiberal reflects not utterly distinct moral stating points, but more subtle differences in how similar moral values are deployed.

The public dialogue about migration, though, is often rather bad at subtlety. Immigration has emerged in the past decade as one of the most heated—indeed, explosive—parts of our shared public discourse. We are, to put it bluntly, good at arguing past one another; we can show how our own vision of fairness and justice can defend our chosen conclusions about who ought to have what rights to move where. We are equally good at demonizing and condemning those who would disagree with us. We are, however, quite poor indeed at engaging in open and careful discussion about what might be rightly said against our own vision of fairness—or what we might say to defend it against those whose interpretation of fairness is unlike our own.

What, in face of this, could political philosophy have to offer? Philosophy is unlikely to bring us to anything like consensus about how to understand the relationship between justice and migration. Disagreement is an inevitable consequence of freedom, and we should expect unanimity least of all on complex and heated areas such as migration. But philosophy might at the very least offer us the tools to understand how we disagree. It might offer us some clarity about the concepts and ideas that ground our shared discourse about justice in migration. And this, perhaps, will offer us a way forward, if not toward unanimity, then at least toward something like mutual respect. Being precise about how we use ideas like justice might make our debates about justice less vicious, if only by forcing us to be precise about how we—and those with whom we disagree—understand the nature of our claims.

How, then, can we understand the concept of justice? In the present volume, I am going to use the analysis offered by John Rawls, for whom justice represents the "first virtue" of social institutions such as the political state.[10] Justice, for Rawls, is a formal concept, which is susceptible of being interpreted in accordance with a multiplicity of possible conceptions—each of which fills in, as it were, the details about how this formal concept is to be used and understood. The formal concept of justice, though, is sufficient for us to begin to understand how the notion of justice in migration might be specified:

> [I]t seems natural to think of the concept of justice as distinct from the various conceptions of justice and as being specified by the role which these different sets of principles, these different conceptions, have in common. Those who hold different concepts of justice can, then, still agree that institutions are just when no arbitrary distinctions are made between persons in the assigning of basic rights and duties and when the rules determine a proper balance between competing claims to the advantages of social life.[11]

This concept is applied, in Rawls's own work, to the basic structure of society, by which Rawls means the "way in which the major social institutions distribute fundamental rights and duties and determine the division of advantages from social cooperation." Justice, understood in this way, is the most important moral aspect of political society, in that other virtues are not to be pursued prior to justice; an unjust set of institutions does not become legitimate in virtue of some other political virtue those institutions might instantiate.

All this is likely familiar to readers versed in modern political philosophy. There are, though, three aspects of this I would like to highlight. The first is that the concept of justice, as used here, entails *stringency*. When Rawls calls justice the first virtue of social institutions, he emphasizes the idea that justice creates powerful claims on the part of those who suffer what it identifies as injustice. Justice, in other words, creates a particular, and particularly strong, form of claim for rectification. The second aspect of justice I want to highlight is its relationship to some notion of *equality*. Injustice reflects inequality, in some particular space; indeed, it may be a conceptual fact about justice that it speaks of some particular aspect of persons in which they are entitled to be treated as morally equal to one another.[12] Rawls's use of the concept of arbitrariness reflects this vision of equality; when individuals are similarly situated before some set of social institutions, it is unjust to allow some arbitrary fact about them to issue in differential treatment by those institutions. The final aspect of justice I want to highlight here is its relationship to the *institutional.* The language of justice is capacious; we can refer to individuals as just or unjust and also use that language to evaluate personal commitments or personal relationships. The particular form of justice about which Rawls is speaking, though, reflects people bound together by social—and, generally, political—institutions.

How, though, can this broad concept of justice help us understand what forms of social institution are rightly condemned as unjust? Rawls, as mentioned, argued that we need to develop a particular conception of justice, which helps us understand how we are to interpret and apply the abstract guarantees of this abstract concept. We are, however, given some guidance in doing so. There are some provisional set-points that help us understand how the language of justice is best applied to the realm of the political. Rawls, in this, followed the logic of Abraham Lincoln, who noted that if slavery were not held to be unjust, then the language of injustice would cease to hold any meaning.[13] In our own more recent history, we might say similar things about patterns of marginalization and exclusion such as Jim Crow in the United States; in the segregated United States, those equally ruled by law were given radically unequal shares of political power, material resources, and public respect. As with slavery, we might want to say: if this is not unjust, then nothing could be. There is no rightful reason to think that this sort of inequality is compatible with justice, and a conception of justice that described Jim Crow as rightful would be rejected simply in virtue of that implication.

With this in mind: can we think that the abstract concept of justice can offer us any purchase on particular patterns and policies of migration? Can we find any conclusions that might be so clearly right, that future conceptions of justice in migration might be disciplined by their ability to confirm our convictions that certain migration practices are obviously unjust?

It is hard to think that there is anything in migration policy that would not be rejected by *someone*. I do, however, believe that there are some conclusions that would be hard to reject by anyone claiming to live up to the values of moral equality that undergird the concept of justice used here. There are, that is, some ways in which some particular migration policy might be regarded as unjust—and, indeed, obviously unjust—in a manner markedly similar to our reaction to Jim Crow. Any plausible conception of justice in migration, then, would have to either acknowledge these conclusions or come up with some rather heroic story about why it need not do so; and I cannot imagine what that story might even be.

The first of these set-points relates to the idea of equality of citizens before the state. Migration does not, after all, simply affect the outsider; how it is enforced and understood may make equality more or less achievable by those who are not migrants themselves. Think, in this, of how the racialization of migration law might affect the ability of Latinx and non-Latinx citizens to appear in public without fear. The particular patterns of migration enforcement employed by Sheriff Joe Arpaio, for instance, created a climate of fear and intimidation among Latinx citizens of Phoenix, regardless of their migration status; Arpaio regularly targeted and harassed Latinx drivers and indeed created a task force designed to seek out and punish non-citizens—in a manner that undermined the ability of Latinx citizens to simply go about their day.[14] The regular encounter with this sort of migration enforcement has the social function of disciplining and marginalizing all Latinx residents; Amy Reed-Sandoval rightly refers to the activities of Arpaio's officers as a sort of theater of inequality, in which those targeted were reminded of their subordinated and marginal status.[15] A theory of justice in migration, in short, will have to acknowledge that particular patterns of exclusion and enforcement can create inequalities *between citizens*, and those inequalities between citizens that tell against the justice of domestic legislation will tell similarly against the justice of migration policy.

The second set-point relates to the thought that there may be spaces in which the citizen and the non-citizen are entitled to equal treatment before the law. The extent of those spaces, of course, is the subject of controversy; the invocation of "illegality" is often intended to discount any particular right's being potentially invoked by a migrant. (The right-wing slogan, after all, seeks to rebut any possible moral status for the undocumented, with reference to their lack of legal residence: *What part of illegal don't you understand?*) But this invocation of illegality does not seem quite sufficient to deny the thought that there are some spaces in which even those who are outside the state—or who are present within that state without right—have the right to equal treatment. One simple example, of course, involves police protection; those who are unlawfully present in the United States are susceptible to deportation, but they do not lose their right to be protected against those who would kill and rob them.[16] Another example comes from the case of children, whose unlawful presence is rightly understood as the outcome of their parents' agency, rather than the agency of the child. The Supreme Court, in *Plyler v. Doe*, noted that this entailed a right to primary education, even for those present without right:

At the least, those who elect to enter our territory by stealth and in violation of our law should be prepared to bear the consequences, including, but not limited to, deportation. But the children of those illegal entrants are not comparably situated. Their parents have the ability to conform their conduct to societal norms, and presumably the ability to remove themselves from the State's jurisdiction; but the children who are plaintiffs in these cases can affect neither their parents' conduct nor their own status. Even if the State found it expedient to control the conduct of adults by acting against their children, legislation directing the onus of a parent's misconduct against his children does not comport with fundamental conceptions of justice.[17]

This means, in other words, that there are some clear cases of injustice in which those treated harshly are wronged despite having no particular legal right to remain in the country that seeks to provide them with harsh treatment. There are some things we cannot do, said the Court, even if doing them were an effective deterrent to preventing unauthorized migration. The recent efforts by the Trump administration to separate migrant children from their parents at the border, it seems, denies this moral point exactly; children, being not rightly held to account for the agency of their parents, are treated unfairly when they are denied the care of their parents—and it is unjust to those children, as well as to their parents, to subject them to this pain.

The final set-point I want to highlight here is perhaps the most important; there are some individuals, most of us believe, who have a right to migrate. The current legal notion of the refugee emerged from the horror of the Second World War, and the retroactive shame of many states at their refusal to admit those fleeing the genocidal intentions of the Nazi regime.[18] We can, and should, question the precise contours of those entitled to protection under the covenant setting up international refuge law; I will do so myself in chapter 7. But the revulsion at the decision of the United States to exclude the refugees of the *St. Louis*, I believe, should instruct us here. *Some* set of people, surely, have rights to be defended from particular forms of atrocity and evil, and a theory of justice in migration which refused to recognize that fact would be rejectable simply in virtue of this failure. The refugee has a *right* to refuge, we might say, and those who would deny her that right treat her unfairly; the language of justice allows us to assert this claim.

These set-points, then, provide us with some constraints on how we might argue about justice in migration. The problem, though, is that they don't provide us with much. We are still in need of more guidance about how we might apply the abstract notion of justice to the realm of migration. What I have said so far offers us some thoughts about what we cannot say; it offers us very little, though, to narrow down what it is that we *might* say.

Much of this book will attempt to provide a particular conception of justice in migration. I want to develop a particular conception of justice in migration which will give us a particular account of how much freedoms states rightly have to decide who may and may not join them as immigrants. I will lay out this conception over the next three chapters. My task in the present chapter, though, is to begin this task by examining—and, in the end, rejecting—those theories of justice in migration that argue against *any* right to exclude the unwanted outsider. For these theorists, who are often referred to as theorists of *open borders*, the attempt to develop a just system of exclusion is akin to the attempt to develop a just system of racial segregation. The task is not simply doomed to failure; it is, instead, something of a contradiction in terms.

Theorists of open borders represent an extreme version of one half of the dialectic mentioned above. Many people appalled by the Trump regime's treatment of migrants have sought to undermine that regime's perceived racist and nativist migration policy. Not all who have done so have thought that that borders should be open; many of them simply think that the Trump regime is closing those borders in the wrong way, and against the wrong people. The belief that there are limits in what a state can do with its borders is not the same as the thought that those borders should be open—although the Trump administration has often sought to tar anyone opposed to their exclusionary proposals as defenders of open borders. The defense of open borders is not, then, the only way in which one might resist the populist approach to migration. Indeed, in the present world one cannot find many political agents willing to defend the possibility of open borders. Nonetheless, the thought that states cannot justly exclude *anyone* is worth examining in more detail. If those who defend this idea are right, we have a reason to question the seeming inevitability of migration control. As Joseph Carens notes, we should not be dissuaded by the fact that open borders seem impossible in the present world; a world in which slavery might be eliminated once seemed similarly fantastic.

How, though, might we begin to defend the thought that borders should be open? We might, I think, take the very concept of justice to give us some ideas here. Justice, as Rawls discusses, is hostile to arbitrary differences, and hostile in particular to arbitrary differences that affect one's basic rights and one's material holdings. We might think that exclusion does both of these. When the United States refuses admission to someone coming from a relatively impoverished country, it condemns that individual to a life without the wealth that is often (although not always) a part of American life. When it refuses admission to an individual living in an unrepresentative regime, it condemns that individual to a life without political freedom. When it refuses to allow a would-be migrant to pursue a chosen project or relationship in the United States, it limits the ways in which that individual can create a life of value for herself and those she loves. It does all of this, moreover, on the basis of a border that is itself arbitrary from the moral point of view; no one deserves to be born on the "right" side of a particular line in the sand. The line, moreover, often reflects not simply an inequality of wealth, but a history of evil and colonial exploitation; much current exclusion involves wealthy former colonial powers excluding people from impoverished former colonies.[19] We can, simply with these materials, develop a conception of justice in migration in which all forms of exclusion are presumptively unjust. Chandran Kukathas provides a nice thumbnail sketch of the ways in which such arguments will go, as he condemns to irrelevance all attempts to justify the right to exclude:

> How, then, might restrictions on immigration, or free movement more generally, be justified? It is difficult to come up with a universal defense of restrictions on movement from the perspective of individuals or peoples. . . . An argument for limiting the free movement of persons will always be an argument offered to explain why particular (sometimes advantaged) groups should be protected in their enjoyment of the rents they have secured by having the relative good fortune to reside in one part of the world rather than another.[20]

This broad pattern of argument argues that the thought of a (potentially) justified system of exclusion is an illusion; the goal for liberal theorists is to break down all forms of unjustified hierarchy—and the patterns of residency rights that keep some people out of some places might simply be unjust. This would be, I think, to regard the project of opening borders as simply the extension of the broader pattern of civil rights. As Roger Nett argued a generation ago, the final civil right—one that may prove the most difficult to bring about—might be the right to move freely upon the surface of the world.[21]

I want to discuss four more precise visions of how this case might be made in this chapter. These visions are not so much arguments, as families of arguments; they are ways in which we might make the above argument against exclusion more precise and rigorous. As I have noted, I do not think any of these arguments succeed. My own disagreement with these arguments tends to begin with the ways in which they fail to understand what is distinctive about the relationship between the coercive political state and the individuals whose lives are organized with reference to the laws of that state. Put most simply, the arguments from open borders tend to ignore the ways in which states owe distinct things to those living within the coercive grasp of those states; they tend, instead, to think that anything that is a civil right ought also be a human right. In what follows, I will try to make clear both my disagreement with these theorists and my own tremendous debt to them. Too much of philosophy, I believe, is fault-finding, and the weakest parts of any theorist's view is the part in which she pokes holes in the theories of her competitors.[22] What I say here, then, should not be taken to provide a dispositive disproof of these arguments; these arguments are too good—and too complex—for that. What I say here represents, at most, an account of why I do not find myself able to accept these arguments, despite my debt to those who have provided them.

1. Justice and Exclusion

So: what might we say, to make more precise the thought that a state cannot justly exclude the unwanted? I should note, in passing, that the theorists I discuss here are often willing to accept that the state could justly exclude *some* people—such as, notably, those intent on doing harm to the state or its inhabitants. These theorists, though, argue that the right to cross international borders is much like the right to move about *within* a society, or the right to freely exercise one's religion; capable in the abstract of being suspended, but only in genuinely horrific (and, one hopes, atypical) circumstances. In the general case, in which a person simply wants to move across borders for the same reasons people move within them, the state wrongs that person— commits an injustice—if it prevents that person from so moving. What could we say, to defend the thought that the concept of justice ought to condemn that sort of exclusion?

I will discuss four versions of what might be said, which I will describe as the arguments from *arbitrariness*; from *distributive justice*; from *coherence with existing mobility rights*; and from *coercion*. The borders of these arguments, I should note, are rather porous; those who make one sort of argument might well also make the others. But, for the sake of analytic clarity, I will discuss them as separate arguments and try to explain each on the terms I think show these arguments in their best light. All these arguments are similar in structure: they use the broad outlines of the concept of justice, as discussed above, to demonstrate that the excluding state wrongs the one excluded, by treating her unfairly in an objectionable way. These arguments, moreover, often make use of a similar strategy; the norms and principles we already recognize as part of liberal justice, they argue, offer support for the thought that a moral right to cross international borders is rightly ascribed to liberalism. These arguments, then, are different versions of making one powerful point: that treating people with equal concern and respect means refraining from coercively preventing them from moving where they would choose to go.[23]

1.1. Arbitrariness

One way of making this argument is simply to rehearse what has been said above; borders are, in moral terms, arbitrary, in that they generally reflect a shared history of colonial violence rather than anything more morally significant; they are also arbitrary, of course, in that one cannot be thought to *deserve* in any strong sense one's birth on the favored side of a particular border. The quote from Chandran Kukathas, above, provides one way of spelling this out; if the current inhabitants of a place are allowed to exclude outsiders, they are using accidents of birthplace to determine who shall have what rights. This does, or should, make liberal theorists of justice uneasy. Joseph Carens's early work on this topic analogized citizenship in a wealthy, desirable state to feudal birthright privilege—"an inherited status that greatly enhances one's life chances."[24] The argument from arbitrariness, though, does not depend upon the presence of material inequalities, or one state being more favored than another. It is enough to say that the fact of arbitrary differences in rights—you are allowed to live in England because of your birthplace or parentage, while I am not—is enough, on this argument, to give us reason to think that exclusion is unjust.

Carens is not the only thinker to have thought the arbitrary nature of the border is a sufficient reason to think exclusion unjust. Philip Cole, in a similar vein, argues that liberals cannot think that the right to exclude the unwanted is compatible with the liberal concept of justice. Cole goes further than Carens, though, in thinking that the challenge from arbitrariness might force us to rethink the very notion of liberal justice itself:

> Many writers, we shall see, concede that, given its commitment to the moral equality of human beings as such, and therefore its abhorrence of arbitrary divisions between people, liberal theory should reject exclusive membership in principle and so oppose immigration restrictions in practice. But, having conceded this, they proceed to search for a justification for exclusion, often on the grounds that as it is such a widely accepted practice in liberal democratic states, a justification must be possible. But, as we shall see, this poses liberal theory with particular difficulties. The purpose of this book is to explore those difficulties.

On Cole's analysis, then, the arbitrary nature of borders provides us with sufficient reason to think that the practice of state exclusion is unjustified. The fact that we have not been willing to face up to this, argues Cole, is evidence that perhaps we need a rather new form of conversation—about borders, but about political justice more broadly.

1.2. Distributive Justice

The above argument, of course, gains power when it is acknowledged that the border divides not only the citizen from the alien, but very often the rich from the poor as well. The thought that exclusion is wrongful, not simply in itself, but because it undermines the distributive rights of the global poor, is a powerful and important argument against the right to exclude. The argument, though, comes in two distinct forms: the argument from *economic justice*, and the argument from *equality of opportunity*.

The argument from *economic justice*, to begin with, cites the simple fact of economic inequality—and the ways in which the exclusion of would-be migrants from the wealthier countries of North America and Europe tends to reinforce unequal distributions of wealth. This argument can be buttressed with arguments about the power of migration to create wealth. Michael Clemens has argued that the elimination of border exclusion might create a new economic gain equivalent to up to one-and-one-half times current global GDP.[25] Remittances from migrants who have moved from low-income countries to higher-income countries are a powerful force for development; the quantity of such remittances is estimated as greater than the sum total of all money currently devoted to international development.[26] The key, though, is not simply that exclusion makes the world more impoverished than it has to be. It is that the right to exclude the unwanted amounts to allowing the wealthy to preserve their wealth, in face of the legitimate claims of justice of the world's poor.[27] Hence, Kukathas's invocation of rent and Carens's talk of feudal birthright privilege; those who are wealthy, we think, should offer some justification for their wealth apart from lucky birth. Philip Cole, more than most philosophers, adds to this the thought that our shared global experience of inequality reflects a shared history of colonial violence and evil. It is not simply that we are perpetuating the poverty of those who had the bad luck to be born in a developing society; it is that we are continuing, in the present day, the ongoing legacy of colonial exploitation that determined which country shall be developed and which ones shall not.

The second aspect of distributive justice we might discuss is that of *equality of opportunity*. In the domestic case, we are convinced that equality of opportunity is a key value; as John Rawls discusses in his own theorizing about justice, a society that failed to provide robust guarantees of equality of opportunity would be an unjust society. The border, though, prevents people from going where they would want to go, and therefore creates a world of radically unequal opportunities. This version of the argument might be discussed under the heading of equal freedom, as Kieran Oberman does; or simply as another case of inequality of opportunity sets. The key, as Carens notes, is that we are using coercion every day to prevent people from achieving better lives for themselves and their families. Oberman is particularly emphatic on this point; what people are owed is not simply an adequate range of choices, but the maximal possible set of opportunities. People have essential interests in going where they want to go, to build lives that provide value for those that live them. Nothing more than global freedom of movement, argues Oberman, is compatible with the liberal vision of justice we claim to prize.

1.3. Coherence with Existing Mobility Rights

The argument against exclusion is helped by the fact that liberal theorists already tend to believe that certain forms of mobility rights are implied by liberal justice. There are at least two sorts of mobility right that have been discussed under this heading, and each has been taken as sufficient to ground a similar moral right to cross international borders. We can call these the arguments from *internal mobility* and from *emigration*.

The first argument begins with the simple fact that the right to move about within one's own society is generally taken to be a core human right; the right of internal mobility is defended by key international documents, including the Universal Declaration of Human Rights. The argument from internal mobility, though, notes simply that whatever can be said to ground the importance of *this* sort of mobility seems likely applicable to mobility more broadly. Carens, following David Miller, calls this the cantilever strategy; we start with what is already defended, whether in international law or in our best understanding of justice, and demonstrate that similar arguments could be made in favor of a broader conception of the right:

> If it is so important for people to have the right to move freely within a state, isn't it equally important for them to have the right to move across state borders? Every reason why one might want to move within a state may also be a reason for moving between states. One might want a job; one might fall in love with someone from another country; one might belong to a religion that has few adherents in one's native state and many in another; one might wish to pursue cultural opportunities that are only available in another land. The radical disjuncture that treats freedom of movement within the state as a human right while granting states discretionary control over freedom of movement across state borders makes no moral sense. We should extend the existing human right of free movement. We should recognize the freedom to migrate, to travel, and to reside wherever one chooses, as a human right.[28]

Similar thoughts are found in arguments from Oberman, as well as from Christopher Freiman and Javier Hidalgo.[29] Any justification we could find for guaranteeing the right to move about within the state, the argument runs, would provide us with reason to move about between them. If it is unjust to restrict internal mobility, then, it is similarly unjust to exclude the unwanted migrant.

The other international right we might use to ground these conclusions, though, is the right to *leave* one's country. Most liberal theorists—although not all—recognize the right to leave one's country as a morally significant right.[30] The countries that make it difficult for their own citizens to leave, certainly, provide us with some empirical reason to think that justice is incompatible with restrictions on emigration. The worry, though, is whether this right to leave is in any sense meaningful without a similar right to enter where one wishes to go. The thought that the right to leave, for it to be anything more than merely formal, must require the tools needed to make use of that right; and if there is no other society duty-bound to offer one admission, then the right is useless. Lea Ypi describes this well:

> [T]he asymmetry between emigration and immigration points to a serious moral deficiency in the theory and is incompatible with the general principle of justice in migration. Either freedom of movement matters or it does not.[31]

Ypi argues that resolving this tension might require us to rethink our approach to migration on a foundational level; I will ignore these complexities here and focus on the thought that there is something morally troubling about defending a right to leave without similarly defending a right to enter. Cole expresses similar ideas, echoing a version of this argument ascribed to Ann Dummett:

> [T]he liberal asymmetry position claims that there is a right to leave a state but no right to enter one, and this amounts to claiming that the right to leave the state does not actually include the right to cross the international border, because this would entail the right to enter another state. How coherent is a right to leave a state that does not include the right to cross the border?[32]

On this argument, then, the vision of justice in which people have a moral right to *leave* a place is incoherent if it does not guarantee a right to *enter* another; and the purported right to exclude is in tension, if not outright contradiction, with this latter right.

1.4. Coercion

The final argumentative pattern I will consider is the argument from *coercion*. Many liberal theorists believe that those who are coerced by an institution are entitled to particular rights against that institution. In particular, we tend to think that those coerced by an institution have particularly strong rights to have the policies and practices of those institutions justified to them; and this justification must treat those coerced as having equal moral status as compared with others similarly situated. I have written, elsewhere, a defense of these ideas.[33] Their relevance to migration derives from the simple fact that borders, as Carens has written, are generally guarded by people with guns.[34] The exclusion of which we speak here isn't simply an abstraction; it is, to be blunt, violent, both potentially and (all too often) in reality. The fact that borders frequently involve coercion, that is, ought to make us seek to understand what sorts of guarantees would have to be provided, to those coerced, in order for their coercion to be potentially legitimate.[35] Arash Abizadeh has argued that these facts are sufficient to mandate new international institutions, with power over migratory decisions; there is, he argues, no right to *unilaterally* exclude the unwanted outsider.[36] Carens echoes these thoughts, describing the powerful effects of exclusion upon the life of the one coercively excluded:

> [I]t is hard to imagine an exercise of the state's coercive power short of imprisonment that has a more pervasive effect on a person's life than refusal of admission. This is what we might call a gateway decision. It has enormous implications for all the subsequent life choices a person can make . . . for many people, even the ongoing exercise of state power in their daily existence does not have as pervasive an impact on their lives as this prior determination of where they belong and where they may (or may not) live.[37]

For Carens, the effects of the coercion upon the coerced here are so profound that we ought to think it unlikely that any adequate justification could be offered. Liberal justice, in short, must live up to what it claims to believe. It argues that we cannot coerce without adequate justification. No such justification seems available, in the case of a would-be migrant subjected to coercion at the border. The exclusion must therefore be regarded as unjust; and the state's supposed right to exclude the unwanted migrant must be recognized as an illusion.

2. The Political Justice of Exclusion

The above arguments, I believe, are powerful; as discussed, they are significant challenges to the ordinary political morality of our society, in which the right to exclude is generally regarded as beyond question. I believe, however, that these challenges can be met. I do not, that is, think that any of these arguments—powerful as they are—represent adequate reasons to think that exclusion is inherently unjust. I should be clear, again, that I do mean to imply that all forms of exclusion are justifiable; as I will discuss, in the chapters to come, this is emphatically not so. We stand in need of a theory of justice in migration—one that enables us to rightly determine what forms of exclusion are unjust. What I want to do in the present chapter is simply to discuss why I continue to think that those who regard *all* exclusion as unjust are in error.

Underneath my critiques of these arguments is my own belief that none of these arguments adequately deal with the fact of *jurisdiction*—by which I mean the fact that the state proposes to govern the individuals only within a particular part of the earth's surface. Those gathered together within that jurisdiction, I believe, have a particular relationship, both toward each other and toward the state that rules over that jurisdiction. This relationship is a *political* relationship, which involves the use of coercive legal rules imposed only within a particular territorial space; within that space, these rules build a social world 'for those particular individuals. This coercion, however, creates the need for justification to precisely those individuals over whom that coercive political relationship is exercised. This means, however, that these individuals have moral rights to have certain guarantees offered to them about *how* that coercion will be deployed. This, though, means that there are some rights that are best described as civil rights, rather than human rights—in that these rights are rightly deployed only within the context of a civic society, governed by a coercive political state. These rights are, to be clear, universal in their applicability; they do, or should, apply to all persons. All people, I have argued elsewhere, have a right to a state in which they are capable of having significant democratic voice.[38] We can thus have a human right *to* a society in which we are provided with civic rights. As I will discuss in chapter 4, once we have *that*, it is not clear that we ought to think we have a right to the *particular* society we would most like to inhabit. For the moment, I will note only that civic rights apply to people only as particular humans situated in particular forms of political community, rather than as abstract humans; and many of the arguments provided against exclusion seem to ignore the political context in which those rights gain their moral power.

2.1. Arbitrariness

The argument from arbitrariness notes that Rawls's concept of justice stands in opposition to arbitrary facts influencing the allocation of basic rights; it uses this thought to argue against the legitimacy of exclusion. The difficulty, though, is that the very concept of *arbitrary* tells us to avoid allowing inequality to rest upon what is not morally relevant to that inequality; it does not tell us that any inequality whose origin is ultimately based upon chance is therefore morally disreputable. We can see this by returning to an example from the previous chapter: it is not unjust for me to be denied voting rights in France, even though the borders between France and other countries are ultimately the product of either happenstance or moral evil—and even though it is a matter of random chance that I was born in Canada rather than in France. The fact that there is a great deal of chance in the system, that is, does not make the inequality in voting rights here arbitrary in any *pernicious* way. The French citizen has a relationship to her government that I do not have, given that I was not born in France and do not reside there. This relationship makes her distinct rights toward that government morally appropriate, even if it is a matter of blind luck that she was born French and I was born Canadian. The inequality between us is appropriate, even if it begins with a matter of random chance, because the *political relationship* between her and her state is distinct from my relationship with that state.

Why does all this matter, though? I think it matters because some of the arguments against exclusion that begin with the notion of arbitrariness seem to think that *any* admixture of randomness makes an inequality unjust. Carens's early work, for instance, argues that we ought to globalize John Rawls's conception of justice as fairness, so that the mobility rights Rawls defended are now applicable to the world as a whole. This, however, ignores the extent to which Rawls intended his view to discuss specifically how a political society might justify its coercive laws and practices specifically to those within its jurisdiction. When Rawls turned his own attention to international justice, he emphatically rejected those who read him as arguing that all forms of arbitrary difference ought to be eliminated—and, for that matter, rejected those who read him as requiring the elimination of exclusion. Cole, similarly, presents the idea of arbitrary borders as a theoretical embarrassment to liberalism. Those who—like Rawls himself—thought of liberalism as a distinctively *political* theory have no such reason to be embarrassed. We can continue the search for what liberalism would require of us, in the realm of immigration. But an arbitrary border is an embarrassment only for those who thought of liberalism as requiring the elimination of all random chance; and most liberals have no inclination to do anything of the sort.

It is worth noting, in a related context, that we may have a need to be more careful in general about the distinction between civil rights and human rights. Cristina Rodriguez, in her history of legal activism in the United States, notes that those who elide the two may make it more difficult to accurately describe the nature of the migrant's claim. Rodriguez notes that the temptation to regard migrant rights now as simply identical in nature to the rights of African Americans should be resisted:

> Immigration law developed in dialogue with the civil rights and civil liberties movements of the 1960s and 1970s, and meaningful similarities exist between the circumstances of many immigrants today and the subordinated groups whose struggle constituted the civil rights movement. Many poor, nonwhite immigrants perform essential but difficult labor, often at the mercy of the removal laws and without full capacity to defend their interests in the political process. But as important as these convergences might be, immigrant incorporation and the civil rights movement also implicate equities quite different in kind. *Whereas the protagonists of the civil rights movement sought recognition of the full citizenship guaranteed to them at birth by the Fourteenth Amendment, immigrants seek entrance into a new polity that has made no preexisting commitments to their inclusion.*[39]

As with activism, so too with philosophy. The claims made by the marginalized, governed by the state and seeking equality before it, cannot be easily equated by the claims of the outsider, not so governed—but seeking to *become* so governed. An adequate theory of justice in migration would have to attend to that difference. It would also have to acknowledge an account of arbitrariness that acknowledges that difference—and that does not regard distinct rights as morally suspect, when they reflect morally significant differences between persons.

2.2. Distributive Justice

We can continue these thoughts by discussing the argument from economic justice—and by noting, to begin with, my own inability to offer any pronouncements on the empirical effects of exclusion; the economics of migration are controversial, to say the least, and one should not look to a philosopher to determine empirical effects in the world.[40] As a matter of philosophical reasoning, though, I can say at least this: even if we were to determine migratory rights with reference to distributive justice, we would have to figure out what set of migration rights would tend to produce the most morally defensible set of results—and it is far from clear that open borders would be the policy prescription that would produce those results. Peter Higgins, for one, has argued that a pattern of open borders might tend to disadvantage those who—for reasons of disability, old age, or social marginalization—are less mobile than others.[41] A theory of migration devoted to distributive justice would thus insist upon a revolutionary alteration in migratory rights; but it is not clear that this alteration must be devoted to the elimination of the right to exclude.

Two more foundational challenges to the argument here are available. The first asks us, quite simply: why should we care about international inequality? This is not to say, of course, that we should not care; I have offered here no reason to think that international inequality does not matter—and, certainly, international *poverty* would seem to matter, whether or not the gap between the poor and the rich does. The challenge I want to offer is simply this: we have need for an account of *why* inequality matters—and it is not clear that the best accounts we have of this can easily be translated from the domestic realm to the international. Rawls, once again, was emphatic that he took his own stringent principle of distributive justice—the difference principle—to apply only within the state; it was not rightly applied across states, nor between them. I say this not to insist that distributive justice does not matter between states, again, but to insist that we are entitled to hear *why* it might matter. If we are told to ground a human right to move upon the right to a particular economic share, we are right to ask what it is that gives this latter entitlement its moral warrant.

The final foundational challenge to these arguments, though, asks us a slightly different question: if distributive justice were to matter, how would it relate to other norms of political justice—including self-determination? Distributive justice, to be clear, is not the only norm—in domestic politics, or in international. Other norms, including the right to govern one's own affairs, have a role to play. Even if it could be proven that open borders would make the world's allocation of goods more equitable, we could not therefore conclude that open borders were *mandatory*. To see this, imagine the following scenario, happening at the domestic level: a given country is governed with reasonable justice, but maintains a rather silly (but popular) fiscal policy in which a great many gold bars are stored in that country's central bank. Imagine further that Robin Hood appears, and liberates the gold, and gives that gold to the country's poor—with the result that the distribution of wealth after Robin Hood's act more closely resembles that mandated by our best accounts of liberal political justice. Is that country morally required to let the poor keep the gold? People's reactions, I suspect, will differ on this point— but, for me, the answer is no. Distributive justice is an important norm, but so too is political self-determination, and Robin Hood is not the right agent to determine what the country's fiscal policy ought to be. States—or, at least, democratic states—have the right, within certain limits set by human rights, to be stupid.

What this means, though, is that we cannot infer that a policy is *mandatory* simply because it leads to a more just distribution. The thought that open borders would make the world more closely approximate distributive justice, then, does not conclude the argument in favor of open borders; it will, instead, only begin that argument.

More, of course, could be said on this; I think the advocate of open borders might be able to provide some further defense, in favor of the greater importance of distributive justice over values such as self-determination—or, as in my own account of exclusion, the presumptive right to avoid taking on responsibility for the protection of another's human rights. In the present chapter, I want only to insist that some such argument *ought* to be made, for concerns of distributive justice to work. I do, however, want to begin looking at the argument from equality of opportunity, since this argument seems—to me, at least—more likely to succeed. Here, I will examine the argument of Oberman in more detail; these arguments are well developed and worthy of extended examination.

Oberman phrases his analysis of equality of opportunity as a response to David Miller's contention that we are entitled not to the maximal number of opportunities, but to an adequate range. Against this, Oberman defends the idea that all people are entitled to a maximal set of available options— what Oberman refers to as "the full range of existing life options."[42] Oberman argues, in response to Miller, that one is entitled to that full range in virtue of one's underlying *personal* and *political* interests. I might want to move to another country to pursue a plan of life, or to discover more about how politics is done elsewhere. And, argues Oberman, to refuse to give this person the right to do so, would be akin to removing options from the set open to people within the domestic political community:

> If the human right to freedom of movement only entitled people to an "adequate" range of options, then those living in a state with a larger than "adequate" range would lack a human right of freedom of movement across the whole territory of their state. If Belgium offers an "adequate" range of options and the US offers many times more options than Belgium, then the US offers many times larger than an "adequate" range. On the adequate range view, the US could divide its territory up into hundreds of Belgium-sized chunks, placing guards and razor wire at the borders of each one, without violating the human right to freedom of movement.[43]

This, says Oberman, is as foolish as the thought that one could ban Judaism without offending the right to freedom of religion, so long as an "adequate" range of religions was respected. In both cases, Oberman suggests, equality of opportunity is only truly adequate when everyone is entitled to the *full* range of available options—which means that *all* exclusion is presumptively unjust.

This, however, seems to misunderstand the moral structure of civil rights. To begin with: it seems simply wrong to think that any one person is entitled to the *maximal* set of options. Imagine, for instance, that a given country is facing the decision of whether to industrialize or to continue a primarily agrarian form of life. While I cannot say how that argument ought to be decided, I do think it unlikely that it ought to be decided simply with reference to *quantity.* The fact that industrialization creates more options, that is, does not in itself give us dispositive reason to think that the absence of industrialization is unjust.

What matters, instead, is not the size of the option sets, but why they *are* the size they are. Take, for instance, Belgium. If the United States were to carve itself up into smaller chunks, each guarded by people with guns, I would agree that something rather unjust has taken place. But the reason for that injustice has *nothing whatsoever* to do with whether or not Belgium (or Belgian options) are adequate. It is, instead, that a state cannot treat its people in the manner that the United States federal government treats people on American soil and then prevent them from moving around on that soil. If the justification for internal mobility rights looks more like a civil right than Oberman allows, then there is something wrong with both reducing my options to a Belgium-sized set *and* insisting upon ruling me from the federal capital. Adam Hosein has made a similar case; what's important about internal mobility is not that it's mobility, but the ways in which *restrictions* on internal mobility can be used to create inequality between citizens before the state.[44] To vary Oberman's example: if the United States were to break up into a series of sovereign Belgium-sized chunks, each guarded by razor wire and armed guards, I would regard that fact as regrettable. But my reaction to that case would be considerably different than my reaction to a United States that claimed the right to both coercively rule me *and* the right to keep me from moving about on American soil. The former is regrettable, but does not seem to me inherently unjust. The latter, in contrast, seems unjust indeed; if the federal government of the United States presumes the right to govern me, it cannot do so justly while preventing me from moving around within those United States.

I think similar considerations might apply to the issue of freedom of religion. Oberman and I agree, I think, that outlawing Judaism is morally impermissible. (Indeed, I think this might be one of the set-points discussed earlier.) The justification for the impermissibility, though, has a great deal less to do with the quantitative number of religions open to me than with the history of states seeking to treat some existing citizens as morally inferior to other existing citizens. One has a right, I think, to have one's religious convictions taken to be as morally significant as those of other citizens; this entails a right to freedom of conscience. We are wronged, then, when the state outlaws the practice of our religion—but we are wronged because of how this would treat us, and how it would treat our fellow citizens. Once again, it is not a question of how large the menu of religious options is; it's how, and why, coercive states are taking particular items off that menu.

One can condemn religious intolerance, in other words, without thinking there is a fundamental right to the largest possible set of religious options. The example, though, is instructive. The free exercise of religion, we often think, entails the right to be free from state coercion in the practice of my religion; it does not, in general, entail the right to the tools needed to exercise that religion—nor to the cooperation of those whose labor might prove necessary for that exercise. If, for instance, my religion requires me to make an expensive pilgrimage, it is not obvious that the free exercise of that religion requires the state to fund my travel.[45] If my worship requires a *minyan* of ten people, but only nine are available in my community, I cannot insist that the state provide me with a tenth person—either through migration or (perhaps) through incentivized conversion. The freedom to practice one's religion does not entail the use of other people's bodies or resources to do so.

These ideas are not unduly controversial, I think, in our analyses of freedom of religion. I think they ought to be at the forefront of our minds, though, in our discussions of migration. Oberman often speaks as if restrictions on migration were akin to coercively preventing someone from practicing a religion. I think exclusion is more complex than this; it can, I think, sometimes be compared more accurately to the refusal to provide a benefit, than anything else. When someone moves into a new place, she creates—as I will discuss in chapter 4—new forms of obligation and duty upon those already present within that jurisdiction. When someone seeks to enter into that jurisdiction, she is not simply walking across a line in the world; she is, instead, seeking to create new patterns of obligation on the part of existing citizens when she crosses. Preventing her from crossing that line might sometimes be best analogized not to the coercive prevention of religious practice, but to the refusal to provide the tools needed for that practice. While we are sometimes obligated to provide those tools, a showing must be made about why we are so obligated. This showing can be made; many of us think that—to take a case of recent controversy—those who make wedding cakes must make them for both straight and gay weddings.[46] But, once again, the story must make reference to something like equality before the state; gay relationships may become stigmatized when bakers are allowed to refuse to bake for those celebrating a gay relationship. Nothing in this, however, entails a human right to a wedding cake; if all bakers disappeared from the United States en masse, no one's rights would be offended. We can, in conclusion, defend religious liberty, without thereby thinking that anyone is entitled to the maximal set of options—or, for that matter, to a wedding cake.

One final point: Oberman describes "making important personal decisions and engaging in politics" to be the basis for his condemnation of exclusion. Even if I were willing to accept the former, I must admit I find the latter interest rather confusing. Politics, to put it simply, isn't for fun, or for one's own private sense of self; it necessarily involves the use of power over others. My political commitments, to echo Cheshire Calhoun, are different sorts of commitments than my personal ones; they are commitments about what *we* ought to be, rather than about what *I* shall be.[47] To take them as equally important in migration seems, to me, to mismatch problem and solution. Migration involves, as Kukathas says, "entering, remaining, and participating" in a new society. Why should we have the right to do all *that*, if the purpose of our doing so is the gaining of information about how politics ought to be done? Migration involves moving to a new place and making that place one's own. It seems odd to think that we must have this right because of the importance of doing politics. If the basis of the interest described here is fundamentally informational, then I think it isn't quite adequate to defend a right to migrate. We do not in general think that the right to enter into relationships with others ought to be grounded on *information*. I might have a great interest in how universities are run. I might therefore have a strong interest in seeing how the University of Miami runs its Department of Philosophy.[48] None of this, however, seems adequate to provide me with a right to a job at the University of Miami. From the fact that my presence in that community would provide me with good information, it does not follow that those already present within that community have an obligation to welcome me inside.

2.3. Coherence with Existing Mobility Rights

We can begin the discussion of this argumentative pattern by looking at Carens's analysis of internal migration. Whatever the rationale might be for the robust protection offered to internal migration, he says, the same rationale must apply to international mobility; the interests that make the first important must apply with equal force to the latter. Carens does not provide us with a particular vision of what these interests must be; indeed, he *deliberately* does not provide that rationale, noting only that any rationale one might choose to provide would seem to work both within and between states.[49] The key, for Carens, is that the interests that make the one vital seem to make the latter vital in precisely the same way.

The response to this argument, though, is to note that the *interests* we have in moving are only part of the story justifying the right to internal mobility. The other part is whether or not the entity claiming the right to prevent us from moving has the moral right to do so. We do not, in general, look only at the interests of one party, in figuring out moral rights. Your interest in going on public land might be quite the same as your interest in going onto private land; it does not follow that there are no morally salient differences between the two. Similarly, your interest in your dinner might be the same as *my* interest in your dinner. We do not therefore conclude that you and I have equal claims to the food in question.

So: how can these ideas help us speak back to the cantilever argument? To see why internal mobility is distinct from international mobility, we need only look at what it is that the state is proposing to do in the two cases. As noted above, the two cases seem distinct. One state is using coercion to prevent people from entering into the jurisdiction within which it is sovereign. The other state is simultaneously using coercion to rule over individual people *and* telling those people that they are not entitled to move freely within that jurisdiction. The two are not morally identical. Even if we have similar reasons in both cases for desiring to move—we want a new job, or to pursue a romantic relationship—we do not conclude that the two states are equally forbidden from preventing our movement. There is, we think, a civil right against the state, to be free from that sort of restraint over those people that state claims the right to govern. The right to internal mobility, in short, is a civil right. This civil right might be grounded upon a human right—a human right, perhaps, to be ruled by a government that refrains from coercively preventing internal mobility. But this does not stop the right from being rightly exercised only by those already present within that government's coercive grasp.

We can go further, though, by examining the more specific arguments Carens makes in pursuing the cantilever argument. He imagines five ways of distinguishing internal and international mobility—before arguing that none of them are up to the job. The distinction he discusses that is most similar to my rejoinder here is the idea that mobility is a membership-specific right, or a right to be free from discrimination in the administration of justice within the state. Carens argues that this won't work; and it is worth seeing more precisely how his arguments here might be rejected.

Carens notes, to begin with, that the interests grounding a right do not depend upon citizenship. "From the individual's perspective," he notes, "freedom of internal movement is important for many reasons unrelated to membership."[50] Thus, we should think that the non-citizen as well as the citizen has the right to move about within a particular country. The problem, though, is once again that the reason we might want to make use of a freedom does not provide us everything we need to know about why that freedom is an important one. I might like freedom of religion, for instance, because

I love church architecture and choral music and want them defended. (This is, I would note, actually rather true.) The point of guarantees of religious freedom, though, make no reference *at all* to my interests in such things. It is, instead, something more particular about the history of states demonizing and marginalizing members of disfavored religions; it is this history of attack on religious practice that makes religious freedom so important. We defend the freedom of religion not simply because the interest in religion is strong, but because of a history of denying the civil and human rights of particular adherents. And, once again, we might want to defend internal mobility for reasons that make reference specifically to the legitimation of political coercion—rather than simply upon the strength of the interests such a right might defend.

When Carens consider the relation between political equality and internal mobility, he rejects it with a few sentences; internal mobility, he notes, is "far too broad a right" for political justice to be its primary purpose.[51] I am not sure that this works. Rather strong—and broad—rights are often grounded in comparatively narrow purposes. Compare, for instance, a defense of freedom of speech that is grounded—as that of John Stuart Mill's is—in the search for truth in personal and political discourse. This defense of speech protects not only complex and insightful speech about political ethics; it also protects dime-store novels, blogs about cats, and the films of Michael Bay. Even a narrow justification, in other words, can ground a rather broad right, when we are worried about the natural tendency of states to overstep the bounds of their rightful rule.

I should note that, in this, Carens's view reflects a vision of mobility that is common among those who write in defense of open borders; they present mobility as a prepolitical right. It is as if we were rightly able to roam across the surface of the earth, until all these states sprang into being, each of them throwing up walls and barriers in our paths. This is, of course, one way of understanding the moral basis of mobility. I think it isn't the only way of understanding mobility—and I simply don't find it very attractive. The image of the state infringing upon our prepolitical right to roam doesn't seem to adequately describe the normative situation prior to the creation of the state. Prior to politics, our primary duty was to build a world in which politics was possible. The right to move about within the state, I think, is rightly held against any state, for reasons of political justification. But I do not think we have any reason to think of mobility itself as morally significant, in the manner supposed by Carens and others.

I think similar considerations might be used to reject the argument that coherence with the right to emigrate creates a presumptive right against exclusion. It is, I have said elsewhere, a bad thing for a state to have the right to coercively insist that an individual remain within its coercive grasp, when that individual is otherwise able to leave that grasp and join another political community.[52] The state should not be in the business of pointing guns at people, to make them stay in a relationship. It does not follow that it is never allowed to point guns at people, to prevent them from *joining* that relationship. The difference is the same as that between my locking the door to keep you in, and locking that door to keep you out. The latter is, often, morally permissible; the former is, in contrast, generally held to be a grave moral wrong.

David Miller uses these ideas to defend the coherence of a pattern of rights in which one is guaranteed the right to leave one's county, but provided no right to enter the particular country of one's choosing.[53] Christopher Heath Wellman analogizes this to the right to marry—which is to say, the right to marry someone who consents to marry *me*, without coercive interference. The right to marry does not guarantee the right to the spouse of one's choosing, since one cannot claim the right to the labor and bodies of others in the pursuit of one's plan of life.

Cole rejects this analogy, in defending the purported incompatibility between the right to exit and the right to exclude, by noting that one can live quite well without a spouse, but cannot live adequately without a state:

> One never needs to enter into marriage, or a golf club, or any of the other kinds of association that are often appealed to in the immigration debate. This is why it is plausible to suppose that here the right to exit does not entail a right of entry, because the right to exit does not depend on entry elsewhere. One can enact one's right of exit from these associations and never enter another one, and what is crucial to notice is the existence of this "space" outside of these associations that one can enter without restriction, and where one can develop one's life prospects perfectly well if one wishes. This is dramatically and importantly not the case when it comes to nation-states. . . . There is a "space" of statelessness, but it is not one anybody would wish to enter—it is deeply problematic and dangerous, and nobody can develop their life prospects in that space to any degree. While it is plausible to suppose that the right of exit does not entail a right of entry into the other kinds of associations, like marriages and golf clubs, because there is no need to enter another association in order to enact the right to leave, in

the case of the nation-state there is a need to enter another association in order to enact the right to leave, and so in this case it is plausible to suppose that the right of exit does imply the right of entry.[54]

For Cole, then, the *existence* of the right to exit requires the availability of an available option to leave. This, however, seems odd; I can have a liberty to do a thing, without having the concrete means necessary to make use of that right. Rawls himself distinguished between liberty and the worth of liberty, precisely to make this difference apparent; we want to distinguish between the freedom to do a thing, and the actual availability to me of resources to do that thing. It seems, in short, simply wrong to think that the right to exit only exists when one is actually able to make use of that right—any more that my right to religious freedom exists only once I can afford that expensive pilgrimage required by my religion. Carens himself acknowledges as much; the right to migrate, he notes, is worth defending for its own sake—even for those not possessed (yet) of the means needed to make use of that right.[55]

We can thus defend the moral importance of the right to emigrate, even in a world that may make it difficult for us to make use of that right. This is not an embarrassment for liberalism; it is, instead, simply another demonstration that liberal theorists ought to differentiate between rights and the means required for the exercise of those rights. I would reiterate, here, that rights are often understood not simply with reference to interests, but with reference to the agents proposed to act for or against those interests. The right to emigrate is the right to be free from being coerced by one's *own* state to remain in continued association with it. The state, to put it bluntly, shouldn't be in the business of forcibly preserving that relationship. But it does not follow that we are therefore entitled to those tools needed to actually effectuate a move between states.

2.4. Coercion

I would begin my response here by noting that the concept of coercion is not generally proposed as an independent reason to think that borders should be open. Rather, the recognition that we are engaged in coercion at the borders is intended to unsettle our thought that exclusion is morally unproblematic. We are using threats against individual people, and presumably need to offer them some justification for doing so. Abizadeh uses these facts to insist upon the impermissibility of unilaterally excluding those people. Carens, in his turn, uses these facts to say that the distinction I have drawn here—between the one present within the coercive grasp of the state, and the one seeking to become so present—is morally spurious. After all, the one at the border is being coerced too, and that coercion has "pervasive effects" that are likely equal in gravity to the effects of domestic coercion upon the domestic citizen.[56]

Once again, though, we might want to ask whether or not it is the strength of the interest in question that is all that is at issue in the determination of political right. I think it is not. States owe distinct things to distinct persons, in virtue of how and where they coerce them. This does not entail that all those affected by that coercion have the same rights against that coercion. We see this clearly in the domestic context. When my spouse is punished by the state, it doubtless affects me powerfully. I might, in some cases, be as damaged by my spouse's imprisonment as she is. This does not mean that we ought to think that the justification of my spouse's punishment shouldn't be made specifically to her; while we both have interests at stake, she is the one being coercively punished by the state, and that gives her rights that I do not have. It is not, in other words, the felt *importance* of what is done to me, but whether or not what is done to me is rightful, that ought to be the central part of our discussion.

We can apply these ideas to the case of coercion at the border. Imagine I wished to move to England, but was coercively excluded—in a manner that prevented me from attaining a number of things I want my life to contain. We might imagine that my exclusion from the United Kingdom was a "gateway decision," with "pervasive effects" upon the rest of my life. This does not mean, though, that I am entitled to the same rights under British politics as those already present within the United Kingdom. Those whose lives are already coercively organized by British law are entitled to distinct guarantees against the British political institutions—including, as I have argued, the right to mobility within the United Kingdom: My interests do not provide me with the same set of rights. One way to think of this is to imagine what would happen if, prior to the British government choosing to exclude me, a disaster were to cause the British state to fail, and the United Kingdom to slide into a permanent state of anarchy. This would be, of course, a bit of a problem for my future plans. But I would not, as an outsider to the United Kingdom, be *wronged* by the absence of British political institutions. I could stay here in the United States; I would be disappointed, but there cannot be a human right to be free from all forms of disappointment. My interest in British political institutions is simply my interest—strong as I may feel it to be—to *become* ruled by them. In contrast, the current residents of the United Kingdom—those ruled, until now, by British law—would be wronged profoundly by the absence of that law. Even if I feel, very deeply, that I want to become British, I am not wronged by the absence of Britain as a political society. The British people, though, would be wronged, and quite dramatically so. Those people have a right to a certain form of political community, and the newly lawless Britain violates that right. They, and I, might both plan for a future in Britain; but their relationship to what Britain *is* seems radically distinct. We cannot, in short, look simply to the ways in which exclusion from a political community will affect future plans, in figuring out what rights we have against particular institutions. How we relate to those institutions—what it is they propose to do to us—is part of the story; and it is a part of the story that those who defend open borders have generally ignored.

I will conclude this chapter, though, by acknowledging that the idea of *coercion* is an important one for theorizing about migration. Even if the border is not always defended by coercive means, potential migrants *often* face potential violence when they seek to cross a line demarcating jurisdictions. We stand in need, then, of a way of justifying this coercion. The present chapter has sought to provide reasons why we have no need to think that this justification is possible—why, that is, liberal justice does not entail the opening of all borders at all times. We stand in need, though, of some theory about how and when we might shut these borders—and why. It is to this task that we can now turn.

3

Justice and the Excluded, Part 2

Closed Borders

If the arguments of the previous chapter are correct, they have only established this much: there is nothing in the concept of justice that makes exclusion itself inherently unjust. We can, that is, look for a theoretical ground from which to figure out when and why states are allowed to exclude unwanted outsiders. The previous chapter has left open the question of just what that ground might be. Those who are excluded, presumably, are entitled to a reason that explains why their exclusion isn't wrongful. What could that reason be? What can be said to that person, to explain why she isn't entitled to cross the arbitrary line separating one state from another?

One response to these questions, of course, is to say that we have no need to do anything of the sort. Right-wing populists, as discussed in the previous chapter, have often argued that it is only the insiders whose rights and interests ought to be discussed when examining the ethics of migration. President Trump's inaugural speech noted quite explicitly that the interests of current Americans would be the sole basis on which policy decisions were made under his administration. On this view, there is no need to offer justification to the unwanted outsider; they are, as it were, *outside*, as a matter of both law and morality.

This, though, isn't quite enough. There are some things that seem unjustifiable, regardless of the citizenship of the people to whom they are done. As mentioned above, the Trump administration has admitted to separating families seeking asylum at the southern border of the United States—and then housing minor children in secure facilities that very much resemble jails. The parents have then been encouraged to abandon their claims for asylum, with reunification with their children used as a goad to ensure compliance. The injustice done to both parent and child by this seems profound; many observers have been horrified at the damage done to the children, in particular, given that they cannot be thought to bear any moral responsibility for the

Justice, Migration, and Mercy. Michael Blake, Oxford University Press (2020). © Oxford University Press.
DOI: 10.1093/oso/9780190879556.001.0001

situation in which they find themselves.[1] A host on Fox News responded to this by saying the following:

> Like it or not, these aren't our kids . . . [I]t's not like he's doing this to the people of Idaho or Texas. These are people from another country.[2]

The reaction to this was, rightly, swift and negative. There are some things you shouldn't do, to anyone, and figuring out what they are requires a theory of what people are entitled to at and across the border. We do not need much of a theory, I think, to condemn the policy of family separation at the border. But the fact that we want to condemn this policy entails a rejection of the populist view: the fact of someone's being an alien does not negate her right to a justification for what is being done to her.

We therefore need to see what a state can say, consistent with the liberal analysis of justice, to justify the ways in which it proposes to exclude some people who would like to cross the border. This justification has, we might think, two sides. The first would explain, to those who are excluded, why their exclusion is not morally wrongful—why the state that is excluding them is not acting unjustly, in their case, by excluding them. The second, though, guides the state itself, by noting the ways in which that sort of explanation is not always going to be available. This side of the story helps guide, and criticize, migration policy, by noting the ways in which what states propose to do is incompatible with our best understanding of why migration may sometimes be controlled. In chapters 5 and 6, I will discuss two ways in which migration policy might be restricted. The first will deal with that set of people who cannot be rightly excluded, because of the circumstances in their countries of origin. The latter will deal with the ways in which even those people who have no right to enter a country have a right to be treated fairly by that country, when it decides to give some (but not all) of those people the right to migrate.

In this chapter, though, I simply want to examine some ways in which other authors have tried to build a story about how and why exclusion might be justified. If we have such a story, then we can begin the task of figuring out who can be excluded, and who cannot—and what sorts of migration policy would be consistent with the liberal concept of justice. If we succeed, though, we have really only begun to figure out how to apply the concept of justice to the issue of migration. There are still going to be issues about those goods that are rightly pursued by a migration policy; even if a state can exclude a great many people, that is, we might want to ask whether this means that all social goods are rightly pursued by means of migration policy. There are still going to be a great many issues that are not about justice itself, but about how justice interacts with the particular histories of particular places; much of the debate about the separation of children at the border, I should note, involves a larger debate about American foreign policy in Mexico and Central America.[3] There are still going to be questions, further, about what sorts of means might be used in the pursuit of exclusion, even if exclusion itself is a legitimate state goal. We have already discussed the separation of children from parents; we might equally discuss the ways in which the physical walls already built on the southern border of the United States have pushed migrants to the most dangerous parts of the desert—with the result that many migrants have died during the journey.[4] We might want to question whether these means are permissible, even if we were to defend the exclusionary purpose to which they were devoted. All these questions, though, rest upon a first determination of why it is that exclusion can be justified in the first place. It is to that question that I now turn.

There are a great many stories that might be told, in order to explain why it is that the state is allowed to exclude the unwanted. I want to examine only four families of stories, each of which strikes me as being rather powerful. The first two of these families of stories deal with the sorts of goods that might be protected by an exclusionary border—and the rightful distribution of that good. The last two families deal with rights—with, in particular, the rights held by those people already present within a particular state.

The families of stories are, in the broadest terms, stories about *territory*; about *solidarity*; about *property*; and about *personal association*. Each of these offers the possibility of giving a reason, to a particular outsider, to explain why their exclusion is not unjust. (And each of these also offers a possible theory of who *cannot* be excluded—who it is for whom that justification is simply not going to work.) There are, I think, no sharp boundaries between these families of stories; they often overlap, and—just as in the previous chapter—theorists who make use of one sort of idea often invoke ideas from other families as well. But this grouping seems sufficient to get our discussion off the ground, and I will proceed as if the distinction between them were clear enough.

In what follows, I am going to explain how these sorts of stories might be thought to justify exclusion—and why it is that such stories ultimately don't succeed. All these approaches to exclusion, I will argue, understand exclusion from a political community with reference to something I take to be accidental about that sort of community. They are not adequately focused on the ways in which admission to a particular jurisdiction involves entry into a particular pattern of political and legal obligations; when I cross the border into Mexico, for instance, I create particular obligations to support my basic right that are incumbent upon both Mexican institutions and the existing Mexican people who support and run those institutions. It's this fact, I'll argue in the next chapter, that gives Mexico a right to exclude me. Those people who have written before have not, I believe, given the *political* nature of exclusion adequate attention. I want to say, though, that this is compatible with my being profoundly indebted to those people who have written in defense of exclusion. Once again, I want to present my ideas here not as definitive reasons to reject these views, but a simple explanation of why it is that I do not find myself entirely convinced.

I want to note, finally, that the stories discussed here are not the only ones that might be discussed. Other theorists have offered rationales for exclusion that are not reducible to the ones I discuss here. Philip Cafaro, for instance, argues in favor of migration restrictions with reference to environmental collapse; given the average American carbon footprint, he argues, the world should not have more Americans in it than need be.[5] Stephen Macedo, in contrast, notes that distributive justice within the state might provide us with resources with which to critique particular patterns of migration rights.[6] These are both important ideas, and deserve more space than I give them here. My only reply to these ideas is to note that, if there is no right to do a particular thing, then there is no right to do it even in the defense of good policy ends. Arguments such as those of Cafaro and Macedo, in other words, only work once we have established why and how states are entitled to exclude outsiders; if the state cannot exclude anyone, after all, it cannot obtain that right merely because their exclusion would make the economy more sustainable or just. We thus need an account of why it is that the state can exclude the unwanted outsider; and we can do this by looking first at the idea of land itself as a physical resource.

1. Territory

The one who is excluded is prevented from moving across a particular line on the surface of the earth. This line marks off many things: a political community, a legal jurisdiction, very often a linguistic or cultural community. But what it demarcates most directly is *territory*—the physical fact of land itself. When the would-be migrant is excluded, she is not permitted to make use of some particular chunk of land. Land, moreover, is the result of no one's particular agency. Bracketing cases such as seasteading, or the artificial islands being built by China in the South China Sea, the land we use is land that existed prior to any person's making a claim upon it. The land was, to use the language of earlier political philosophy, given to us in common by God, and it is a good to which all have some form of symmetrical claim. These facts have been thought by as great many philosophers—including Immanuel Kant and Hugo Grotius—to have important implications for political right.[7] More recent philosophers have expressed ideas; Henry Sidgwick took it as obvious that, while the state could exclude anyone it wished, that right came "with a certain reservation in the case of States that claim the ownership of large tracts of unoccupied land."[8] Michael Walzer, similarly, thought that the right to exclude might fail, when the land from which needy outsiders were excluded was sparsely inhabited:

> The right of white Australians to the great empty places of the subcontinent rested on nothing more than the claim they had staked, and enforced against the aboriginal population, before anyone else. That does not seem a right that one would readily defend in the face of necessitous men and women, clamoring for entry. . . . Assuming, then, that there actually is superfluous land, the claim of necessity would force a political community like that of White Australia to confront a radical choice. Its members could yield land for the sake of homogeneity, or they could give up homogeneity (agree to the creation of a multiracial society) for the sake of the land. And those would be their only choices. White Australia could survive only as Little Australia.[9]

Walzer's arguments here depend upon a prior theory of justice in territorial acquisition; many have wanted to question whether "White Australia" merited the right to survive at all, particularly upon land formerly inhabited by the Aboriginal Australians.[10] The point I want to examine here, though, is the broad thought that land's being "superfluous" makes exclusion morally impermissible. On this account, the fact of land's being underpopulated makes it presumptively unable to exclude outsiders; and, conversely, land that is overpopulated may ground a more robust right to exclude.

Ideas such as these have been best developed in recent years in the work of Mathias Risse, who has considered land over- and underuse as one of the grounds of justice in his *On Global Justice*. Risse's work here is complex and merits careful attention. I will focus here simply on the ways in which Risse defends the idea that *territory* itself should be viewed as an independent basis on which to adjudicate the moral rightness of migration regimes. Risse begins with a particular value of the land for human purposes—call this, for land S, the value Vs—and then compares this to the population of P, identified as P_s. For any state, then, we can compare V_s and P_s, and use that comparison to build pro tanto claims about the morality of migration:

> The territory of S is relatively underused (or, simply, underused) if $V_{s/}P_s$ is bigger than the average of these values across states (so that the average person uses a resource bundle of higher value than the average person in the average country). It is relatively overused (or, simply, overused) if this value is below the average. If V_s/P_s is above average, co-owners elsewhere have a pro tanto claim to immigration, in the sense that underusing countries cannot reasonably expect others to comply with immigration policies until such claims are satisfied. It is then a demand of reasonable conduct that the state permit immigration. . . . If a country is not underusing, others can be reasonably expected to accept its immigration policies (if nothing is independently problematic about them).[11]

Risse applies these ideas to the current migration debates in the United States. The United States has a population density of 80 people per square mile, in comparison to Japan's 830. This, says Risse, means that the United States "critically underuses resources"—such that it cannot justly expect undocumented migrants to stay away. Population density—which Risse acknowledges is a "very crude guide" to the value of land on which he focuses—is sufficient to reject the American claim that the Mexican citizen can be either excluded at the border or deported after unlawful entry.[12]

It is at this point that I want to speak back against the moral relevance of territory. This is, to some degree, awkward, since in arguing against Risse I am also arguing against an earlier version of myself;[13] some of Risse's ideas on migration were first expressed in a paper that he and I wrote together. I have become convinced, since that paper, that we ought to avoid thinking of land itself as morally central to the justification of exclusion. Land is, to put it simply, not morally important, except insofar as it is a precondition for the building of autonomous lives *upon that land*. It is these lives that ought to be the focus of our attention; are individuals provided with the circumstances and resources within which they are capable of building lives of value for themselves? Are they given the tools needed to live as autonomous agents? If the answer to these questions is yes, then however much or little land is required seems rather beside the point. We need some land in order to build lives of value; but the market price of that land—and the number of people resident on it—tells us very little.

One way of noting this is to look at the rise, in recent decades, of cities. More people now live in cities than in the countryside, for the first time in human history.[14] All this has been made possible by the invention, by Elisha Otis, of the safety elevator.[15] Prior to Otis's invention, housing was in practice limited to three stories. After Otis, however, multistory buildings—including skyscrapers, high-rise housing complexes, and so on—began to be genuine possibilities; with the result that the relationship between the physical *land* in a place, and the *surfaces* on which one might live and do one's business, has begun to diverge. In Manhattan, for instance, there are 550 million square feet of office space—very little of which actually involves standing on the original *land* given to us in common by God. We tend to stand on floors, which stand on other floors, which eventually stand on that original land. Two things are worth noting about this fact. The first is that Manhattan has, on the average weekday, nearly four million inhabitants, for a density of 170,000 people per square mile.[16] This is dense enough that, if the world were packed to a similar density, we could fit the entire human population into Texas. The second fact is that Manhattan *works*. Not perfectly, of course, and not for everyone. But well enough that the thought that population density, or the biophysical attributes of the land and its value, seem somewhat irrelevant to questions of migration. If Manhattan were a state, and Mongolia (population density: 1.4 people per square mile) continues to be a state, whatever principles of migration justice might be applied to them would be unlikely to rest easily upon their unequal population densities. If Manhattan works for the people who are in it, then they have what they are entitled to; the thought that Mongolia has a moral duty to admit residents of Manhattan seems to give the moral notion of *crowdedness* more moral power than it deserves.

The real basis for Risse's argument, of course, is that there ought to be something like distributive justice in the distribution of land—or, at least, the value of that land—in virtue of the common ownership by humans of the surface of the earth. It is at this point, I think, that he and I disagree most sharply. Risse thinks that principles of distributive justice apply to goods like the earth's surface. I think what matters most is that people are given the political communities within which their basic rights are protected; how we divide up things like *land* seems rather irrelevant. We can see this distinction most clearly in Risse's challenge to my own view of migration:

> [A] virus decimates the population of Syldavia that for unknown reasons affects only people within Syldavia. The virus strikes so fast that people die before they can leave. There are only 50 survivors. However, before the infection Syldavia built an electronic border surveillance system that includes machines that forcefully keep others out. Available robotics enables the survivors to maintain their high standard of living. They continue their proud institutional traditions by having weekly on-line council meetings, but live in small groups in far-flung parts of the country. Requests from Bordurians to take up residence and participate in the economy are denied. Bordurians unwilling to accept this decision are overpowered by border robots.[17]

Risse characterizes the behavior of the Syldavians as "unreasonable," and I agree. The question, though, is how this term is to be understood. One way of reading that word—which I favor—is to say that the Syldavians simply show themselves to be selfish and unpleasant, but that no Bordurian is *wronged* in a significant way by the decision to exclude. If Risse simply means that we should not expect the Bordurians to abide by the law excluding them, then he and I agree; as I will discuss later on, there can be cases in which we cannot regard disobedience with migration law as indicating a defect of moral character, even when that law is not itself unjust. But if we read Risse as arguing something sharper—that the exclusion of the Bordurians is a *wrong* done to those Bordurians—then I think my disagreement is sharper too. Imagine, for instance, that all states in the world—Borduria and Syldavia are the only ones, perhaps—are flourishing, and exceed whatever line of political adequacy you think makes states legitimate. Borduria and Syldavia, in short, are both doing fine. When Syldavia's population plummets, why should we think that that provides any Bordurian with anything that might begin to ground a claim to migrate? The only answer, I think, is if we think that the distribution of land itself, rather than the lives it makes possible, is morally important; and this seems more like fetishism than anything else. Land is a good; it is nothing more than that. Risse, of course, defends these distributive conclusions with reference to the idea of land being held in common by the population of the world. I don't, however, think that this ends the dispute. I have always understood the equal and reciprocal claim to land as embodying the equal and reciprocal claim to the sorts of lives made possible by land. Once that is achieved, though, equality in anything else—be it per capita population, value of land, or anything else—seems simply irrelevant.

Risse's analysis, in other words, might be read to place too much moral emphasis upon territory itself, rather than on the political communities that are built on that land; and this, for me, makes that version of his account unsatisfying. He and I accept that the Syldavians are terrible people. They are selfish, and mean, and striking in their lack of political virtue. But we must distinguish between this sort of judgment, and the stronger judgment that the Syldavians are wronging those they exclude. Justice in migration, I believe, must make reference to something distinct from territory, for it to be adequate.

2. Solidarity

Many of the most powerful defenses of exclusion begin with facts about what it is that is shared by the people already resident within a place. The defenses I examine here begin with what it is that these people share, not simply as regards their attributes, but as regards their self-description and identity. The people in a place, we often think, do not simply have things in common at the level of language or tradition; they *use* these commonalities, both in their daily lives and when engaging in reciprocal relations with one another. When asked to describe themselves—explain who they are—they will appeal to these commonalities, and will show distinctive moral attitudes toward those who share them. The relevance of these ideas for exclusion should be clear; if these commonalities are morally important in their own right—or if they make some other central category of human good possible—then excluding those who fail to show those commonalities seems morally defensible.

There are, of course, many different versions of what this sort of view might look like. Some theorists understood as academic nationalists provide particularly strong versions of this. For these theorists, the justification for exclusion stems from the moral importance of the particular relationship between current members of the group; this relationship is itself a source of value. David Miller's early work provides an exceptionally clear version of this nationalist vision; he argues that the national community represents a site of tremendous moral value, given the ways in which that community is a part of the moral framework within which particular individuals build their lives.[18] His later work argues that migration ethics ought to be developed with reference to the particular values that emerge from particular communities, whose members are concerned that these communities persist and thrive:

> These values are often collective, having to do with the general shape and character of the society that immigrants may be seeking to enter—for example, the overall size of its population, its age profile, the language or languages spoken by its inhabitants, or its inherited national culture. These are often matters of great significance to current citizens. . . . People want to feel that they are in control of the future shape of their society. They have an interest in political self-determination, which includes being able to decide how many immigrants should be allowed to enter, who should be selected if more than this number apply, and what can reasonably be expected of those who are allowed in.[19]

For Miller, it is enough that the character of the national community *matters* to those already resident within a place; from this premise, we ought to infer the moral rightness of that community's being able to determine the character of that place, through constraints on migration.

I use the broad category of *solidarity*, here, to refer to the ways in which the commonalities between particular people are taken as sources of value and motivation for those people. Miller's nationalism, then, might be understood as a particular view of solidarity; the bonds between the current members of a society are significant, and the people partly constituted by those bonds have a rightful role to play in determining the future identity and character of their society. Miller is not the only theorist to use this vision of national identity; in different ways, Michael Walzer and Will Kymlicka also ground the right to exclude on the needs of a national conversation and solidarity between those already present.[20] Solidarity, though, might also be used as part of the argument by those whose political philosophy is not itself nationalist in quite the same way. Sarah Song, for example, uses the notion of democratic self-determination at the heart of her justification for exclusion. Song's vision rests firmly upon democratic self-rule, rather than upon nationalism;

but, even here, the concept of solidarity is a central one that might be invoked in the justification of exclusion:

> As I will argue, political equality is a constitutive condition of democracy, and solidarity is an instrumental condition of democracy.... If we bring the normative condition of political equality to bear on the boundary problem in democratic theory, we see democratic reasons for why the demos ought to be bounded by the territorial state.[21]

For Song, the importance of solidarity is instrumental; it enables democratic legitimacy. But, emphasizes Song, the right to exclude will have to acknowledge and reflect the central importance of this solidarity. We have a need to preserve the sorts of commonalities that ground mutual identification, as a precondition for democratic self-government.

There is, of course, much more that can be said here about solidarity. I want to begin, though, by noting that there are traditional problems with the use of concepts like this—in, at least, the stronger sense in which they are used by nationalists such as Miller. Critics have noted the ways in which this sort of nationalism has the potential to alienate residents of a given society whose personal attributes are unlike those celebrated by the particular vision celebrated by that society's elite. Critics have also noted the right to one's own community must surely stand in tension with the right of outsiders to build lives of value—which requires an examination of just how strong these two rights are, in comparison to one another. Miller, I should note, acknowledges exactly this, giving some individuals refugee rights to enter particular communities. The broader question, though, has long been whether or not the national community is entitled to the presumptive power ascribed to it by the academic nationalists.

In this chapter, though, I want to make a slightly different argument about solidarity and migration—an argument that might undermine its use in both the stronger and weaker sense given above. Theorists like Miller and Song both make the case that solidarity is *useful* for a society; it is a good in itself or provides easier access to the rightful relations of democracy. But I do not think that something's being *useful*, even useful in the pursuit of a morally important goal, is enough to show that thing as being morally permitted. It seems, instead, as if some independent rationale is required, to show that this good is rightly pursued in this particular way.

To see this, we might imagine a society without any particular form of solidarity or group identity. This isn't actually all that far-fetched; many states, particularly after colonialism, were formed without reference to the felt solidarities within them. This fact is important in a variety of ways; as Paul Collier argues, it might explain why some African states have been slower to develop than economic theory might have expected.[22] But imagine that, for whatever reason, a particular society without much in the way of solidarity actually ends up working. It's efficient, it's fair, and it's no worse at democratic deliberation than anywhere else. The society is a ragtag group of individuals who share little and don't much like each other—but they do the job, because they think that job ought to be done. I am not interested in whether this example is possible; I'm more interested in what rights that society ought to have, were it to exist. I would argue that, if any society has the right to exclude, then that right ought to be ascribed with equal force to all rights-protecting societies, regardless of level to which they feel solidarity. If our imagined disunified society is capable of doing the job, then it would seem to have an equal claim to the right to exclude. Certainly, it would seem deeply perverse for it to lose that right simply because of the extent to which it is diverse. Why should a diverse society, without much in the way of commonalities among its members, find itself with fewer political rights than its more conventional counterparts? I cannot find an answer to this question that does not place the moral emphasis where it should not go. The markers of solidarity, I think, are useful for politics; but, if exclusion is to be justified, it's the politics that should do the justification—not the solidarity. Flags and songs, to be blunt, are useful for the doing of politics. But a society that lost those flags and songs would not lose the right to exclude.

I would note, in passing, that Song in particular has a complex vision of solidarity, which includes the thought that solidarity is compatible with deep diversity.[23] Indeed, for Song, solidarity can be grounded on our shared respect for the diversity within our borders. But, as before, this still makes the right to exclude depend upon the sharing of something within our shared attitudes—in this case, the sharing of an attitude toward precisely that which isn't shared. If we want to justify exclusion, though, we must go further, and figure out exactly why it is that a political community is right to use this particular method—and, I believe, that right would not be grounded upon solidarity, but upon politics. As I will discuss in the next chapter, I believe that solidarity can be very useful—but that this fact, however difficult or damaging it might prove to be, should not be used to justify the right to exclude itself.

I would end, once again, by noting my debt to theorists such as Song and Miller. The theories they have built are significant—and, as will become clear, I am greatly indebted to both. Song's jurisdictional view, in particular, bears close relationships to my own. If I disagree with them, it is only because I cannot think that solidarity—or, for that matter, any other good founded on shared facts in the head—can do the job of justifying exclusion.

3. Property

Both of the above ideas began with the importance of some good for those who hold good. Neither, I have argued, is entirely adequate. Justifications beginning with the good of land place too much importance on land, as opposed to the autonomous lives that exist on that land. Justifications beginning with solidarity place too much importance upon shared attitudes, as opposed to the political relationships such attitudes help foster. We might, then, proceed to look at those views that ground the right to exclude not on the production of particular goods, but on the particular pattern of rights held by individual people.

Arguments beginning from property rights are a particularly powerful way of doing just that. The idea of property rights, after all, entails the thought that some people have rights over particular things that others don't. If I own my house, that generally means that I can decide what to do with that house; sell it, repaint it, destroy it, and so on. And—more importantly—it often means that I can decide to keep you out of my house. Property rights, moreover, are often associated with labor. John Locke's theory of property right, notably, gives rights over land to those who have exerted their labor in the improvement of that land. It seems simple enough to combine these into a view about political institutions, and argue that the people already present within a place have property rights over the institutions that govern that place, simply in virtue of how they have worked to build and sustain those institutions. We can keep out the outsider, as it were, because we—and not they—have built up property claims over the institutions that govern our lives.

Ryan Pevnick has done more than anyone else to apply such ideas to the political morality of migration. His view entails the thought that there exists an intergenerational community, which has labored to build the institutions that govern a particular place; this community has a distinctive set of property claims that emerge from how that community has labored to build those institutions. The community in question, Pevnick is clear, must be understood in intergenerational terms; the institutions we enjoy were built by the past members of our community, and we pass them down to those who follow us in time. The institutions become ours, though, when we do our part to labor and maintain those institutions:

> Like the family farm, the construction of state institutions is a historical project that extends across generations and into which individual are born. Just as the value of a farm very largely comes from the improvements made on it, so too the value of membership in a state is very largely a result of the labor and investment of the community. The citizenry raises resources through taxation and invests those resources in valuable public goods: basic infrastructure, defense, the establishment and maintenance of an effective market, a system of education, and the like . . . [T]hese are goods that only exist as a result of the labor and investment of community members.[24]

This, then, allows us to distinguish insider from outsider, and to justify excluding the latter; the outsider, having not labored to maintain the institutions in question, has no right to exercise control over those institutions—and no right to complain, when excluded by those who do have property rights over those institutions. Since letting the outsider enter would be to give him proportionate control over those institutions, he can be excluded without injustice.

Pevnick's view is complex and provides a powerful way of justifying exclusion. I do not think it entirely works. There are two difficulties, I believe, with Pevnick's view. The first is that the labor theory of property seems to poorly describe how we ought to understand political society. The second is that the theory seems to license some results that are repugnant to moral equality in the present, by linking present rights to past labor. I will go through these worries in order.

Pevnick's view, then, involves two steps: if we build these institutions, we can be said to own them; once they are owned, we can exclude the unwanted outsider from using those institutions. Both steps, it seems, have some difficulties. The latter argues that the core of a property right is the right to exclude. This, however, is not necessarily so; property, as generations of law students have learned, involves a bundle of rights, and no single right is the conceptual core of property itself. More importantly, though, we have reason to question the first step in some detail. If we work together to build a thing, we can be said to have property over that thing. This may be true, for a great many things. It is not clear that it is true for *everything*. Susan Moller Okin, notably, highlighted the absurdity that follows from viewing women's reproductive labor through a Lockean lens; women do not own their children, despite the reproductive labor they expend in their creation.[25] What's true for children, though, might also be true for political communities. In these, the labor that went toward creating those institutions is not the only morally important factor. We might also compare the relationships of people within and to that political community. These relationships, we might think, should be morally basic; not the past story of how those relationships were set up.

To see this, examine the case of Pullman, Illinois. This town was set up by George Pullman, who understood himself to be the owner of that town. As Walzer describes it:

> Pullman (the owner) didn't just put up factories and dormitories, as had been done in Lowell, Massachusetts, some fifty years earlier. He built private homes, row houses, and tenements for some seven to eight thousand people, shops and offices (in an elaborate arcade), schools, stables, playgrounds, a market, a hotel, a library, a theater, even a church: in short, a model town, a planned community. And every bit of it belonged to him.[26]

Pullman, in short, viewed the town he had built as his property, and acted accordingly. His own view was dispositive in matters of religion, education, business, and even style. When residents chafed at his restrictions, he simply noted the fact that he had built this place, and still owned it outright; if his views were resented, the unhappy worker was free to leave.

Why does this matter, for Pevnick's view? It matters because it brings to light two distinct ways of looking at a set of social institutions. One of these begins with how those institutions were made, and argues that they are a sort of property; the history of who made them—whose labor brought them into the world—allows us to figure out who and how outsiders can be excluded. Another begins where I want to begin, with the relationships now between people and their institutions, and asks what could justify exclusion from those institutions—not as property built in the past, but as standing relationships in the present. What rights Pullman has depends upon one's view of this matter. In the real story, of course, Pullman was eventually ordered to sell off his model town. The Supreme Court of Illinois held that the holding of this sort of institutional set by Pullman as property as "opposed to good public policy and incompatible with the theory and spirit of our institutions."[27] What mattered for that court, in other words, wasn't the labor Pullman had exerted, but the present relationships that existed within the town of Pullman itself.

I think something similar might be said about the state itself, when it seems to exclude the unwanted outsider. The state isn't simply a thing, but the name we give to a complex pattern of human relationships. If we are trying to justify exclusion from those relationships, we have a reason to look at those relationships on their own terms. The history of how those relationships came into being might be relevant; but its relevance is necessarily complex. Our agency is temporal, and we experience agency through the plans we make; we have a reason, then, to acknowledge the past in understanding what is to be done now. But nothing here involves looking to an intergenerational community, or the labor done by that community in the past. Indeed, it seems a conceptual mistake to invoke that community in understanding the right to exclude. If the right to exclude is defensible, it seems as easily invoked by a new state as by an old one; if a state comes into being at midnight, it would seem to have the right to exclude the very moment it comes into being. Those resident within that state's borders need not wait until they have worked on that state's institutions, for them to have the right to use those borders to exclude.

This leads to the second worry with Pevnick's view: appeals to history—and to labor—have the potential to lead to moral perversity. In the first place, if the holder of the property right is the intergenerational community, then there is a persistent worry that those more closely related to that intergenerational community have more right to speak about that which has been built. Take, for instance, the social power in the United States of having been descended from someone who came over on the *Mayflower*; those who can trace their lineage to those pilgrims, notes the *Chicago Tribune*, "represent the top of the American establishment in finance, law, literature, entertainment and virtually every other field," including at least seven presidents.[28] If one's right to a society reflects one's place within an intergenerational process of building, then this might seem unexceptional; of course those whose families have been here longer are more entitled to have power around here. But most of us, I think, are likely to regard the power of *Mayflower* descent as more like illegitimate privilege than anything else. The migrant whose citizenship comes into effect at midnight might, on Pevnick's view, seem to have less of a right to speak about migration policy than the citizen born and bred within that community's borders than the descendants of the *Mayflower* pilgrims; and this, I think, has a deeply problematic aspect to it. One of the points of naturalization, after all, is precisely that the one naturalized is allowed to view herself as equal in right before the state to any other citizen. More broadly, to make the right to speak depend upon labor expended ignores the ways in which not everyone is equally able to exert labor. Children, the elderly, and the disabled all experience different constraints on how and how easily they are able to work on behalf of state institutions. Equal citizenship, though, would seem to demand that all of these citizens are treated as alike, in the extent to which they are entitled to speak out on behalf of policy.

Indeed, when Pevnick acknowledges that his account has the implication that unwanted children could be expelled from society, he has to invoke equality of citizenship as a secondary basis on which to adjudicate the claims of citizens.[29] For my part, the need to come up with ad hoc principles to prevent this tells us that there may be something problematic about the view itself. In beginning with labor, and with history, the view gives history the wrong sort of voice in present discourse—with results that might require appeal to equal citizenship to undo. It would be better, I believe, if we began with the state as it is now—as a relationship between particular people, regardless of the labor they have or have not expended in the past—and see what rights to exclude might emerge from this particular view.

4. Personal Association

I can conclude this chapter by examining a particularly powerful defense of exclusion. This defense, developed by Christopher Heath Wellman, grounds the right to exclude in the associative rights of its members. Wellman's view is admirably simple; it begins with three fairly uncontroversial premises. First: people, he argues, have a right to associate with particular others. Indeed, it is this right that is at the source of much of what is most important to us; we build lives with particular others, and in so doing create lives we have reason to value. Wellman's second point is that this right is important not simply in the right to associate, but also in the right to avoid unwanted associations. If a given club must be open to everyone—even to those hostile to the very aims of the club—then that club is not able to do the job that it might do, in the lives of those benefited by that club. The final premise demanded by Wellman is that this right is held not simply by natural persons, but by associations of people and other corporate bodies—including the state.

This argument, again, is simple in its presentation—but rather uncompromising in its implications. For Wellman, the right to avoid associating with the unwanted outsider is a strong right indeed; the state can keep out more or less anyone its inhabitants don't want to associate with. Wellman acknowledges the claims of refugees, but argues that even here the state can fulfill its duty to needy outsiders by means other than migration—including, perhaps, development assistance. The simple fact that people here don't want to see outsiders, in their streets or in their schools, is enough to motivate the right to exclude them. We need give no justification for the decision to exclude—any more than I need provide a justification to anyone with whom I choose to avoid friendship or marriage. Migration involves association, and association is the realm of freedom.

Wellman's view has been the subject of intense criticism.[30] For the moment, I want to highlight only a few of the reasons I do not entirely accept his methodology. The first is that I am not sure that the right to freedom of association is quite as strong as Wellman argues it is; certainly, in our domestic law, the courts have often found that other rights can trump my rights against unwanted association. The Jaycees, for instance, were compelled in the United States to offer membership to women—a fact that reflected, for the Court, the greater importance of equal citizenship than freedom of association.[31] Commentators have also argued that the methodology Wellman uses might have to acknowledge the different sorts of relationships in which we are enmeshed, with complex results. Matthew Lister, for instance, has argued that family bonds have generally been taken by the courts to be more important than other forms of association; so, if your desire to see your spouse comes into conflict with your desire to not see my spouse in the marketplace, perhaps your associative preference would have to bow to mine.[32]

I want to conclude, though, by noting one way in which I believe Wellman's view doesn't accurately describe what happens when a new person seeks to enter my society. Wellman argues that my choice to avoid association with that person should be respected. But I am not sure that association is the right term to describe what's going on. In any reasonably large state, I am unlikely to actually see a given migrant. I may, in fact, be so sheltered—or so distant from population centers—that I may never even know of their existence. The concept of freedom of association, though, seems to rely upon a notion of *association* that is more robust than this. For Wellman, the difference between my relationship with my spouse, and my relationship with this migrant, is simply one of scale; I associate with both, but I associate with my wife more often, for important purposes not found in my association with the migrant. I think the two might be different in *kind*. I *associate* with my wife; I see her face regularly, talk with her, and so on, and I get testy when I can't. What I do with the migrant, instead, is share something important—namely, liability to a particular state. This sharing is not morally irrelevant; indeed, as I will discuss in the next chapter, it is sufficiently important to ground a plausible view of exclusion. But to think of these as distinct only in scale seems to miss the fundamental difference between these forms of relationship. I think we ought to look at the relationship of shared subjection to law on its own terms, rather than as an example of the category of personal association. It is these shared legal bonds that I will examine in the next chapter, and not the felt emotional connection that undoubtedly binds me to my wife (and fails to do so as regards the migrant).

I believe, in short, that Wellman is right to look to the relationship found among those people already here, and to use that relationship to craft a reply to the unwanted outsider. I believe, though, that he isn't quite right in how he understands what that unwanted outsider proposes to do. We should look, I believe, to a specifically *political* notion of exclusion, which examines in particular what it is that is shared by those already here. It is this notion that will be taken up in the next chapter.

I have been brief in my criticism of Wellman, in part because much of it seems right to me; as will become clear, what I defend might well be rephrased as a rereading of Wellman's own view. On mine, of course, the relationship that allows us to exclude is not a personal one, but political; the structure of our views, though, are markedly similar. What I have had to say about Wellman, though, is much the same as what I have had to say about the other people I have discussed in this chapter. Many of these people have developed powerful theories of justice in migration—but have allowed these theories to rest upon the wrong bases: upon facts in the head, rather than relationships of law and politics; upon felt affinity, rather than the political community for which we feel that affinity; upon land, rather than upon the politics that are done with and on that land. We have reason, in short, to seek a new start in the justification of exclusion; and that fresh start will be the task of the next chapter.

4

Justice, Jurisdiction, and Migration

What has gone before has argued against those theorists who have claimed that all exclusion is inherently unjust. These theorists, I have argued, are insufficiently attentive to the ways in which civil rights are distinct from human rights; these theorists are, I believe, wrong in that they fail to see the moral difference made by political community. I have also argued against those theorists who have sought to defend the right to exclude, and done so on the basis of territory, solidarity, property rights, or associative rights. These theorists, I have argued, pay insufficient attention to the fact that the thing doing the excluding is best understood as a political community. It is the state, understood as a political entity, that is the excluding agent, and it is the political nature of that state that ought to ground its right to exclude.

It should be no surprise, then, that I want now to defend a particular vision of the right to exclude, on which this right is derived from the political nature of the state. I want to defend a vision of exclusion which rests upon the ways in which that right defends not upon facts in the head, or private association, but upon the specific form of political association in which individuals gathered together under the state find themselves. This is, I should note, a *thin* conception of the state. There is no thought, here, that the national character of the state is itself a source of value. The view of exclusion I defend is open in principle to the right to exclude being given to political communities without much in the way of character at all; it is enough that they manage to do the job of being political, rather than anything more substantive. I will also avoid making any essential reference to intergenerational community, or to territory, or to self-determination as understood to include a felt desire that one's state continue to be a particular character. I will, instead, try simply to derive the right to exclude from the political nature of the state.

On this argument, what is crucial in the right to exclude is the fact that the state is a territorial and a legal community, where that territory marks out a jurisdiction within which that state's laws are effective. This means that one who crosses into a jurisdiction places the inhabitants of that territory under an obligation to extend legal protection to that immigrant's basic rights. This

Justice, Migration, and Mercy. Michael Blake, Oxford University Press (2020). © Oxford University Press.
DOI: 10.1093/oso/9780190879556.001.0001

obligation, however, limits the freedom of the current inhabitants of that jurisdiction, and as such these current inhabitants are licensed in preventing
the entry into that territory of unwanted migrants. This right to exclude,
however, is not a trump against the rights of all would-be immigrants; these
immigrants have rights to the circumstances under which their human
rights are protected. As such, there will be many circumstances under which
the liberal state is not permitted to exclude unwanted would-be immigrants,
since liberalism obliges the inhabitants of that state to enter into a legal relationship with these prospective immigrants. The right to exclude, I suggest,
exists, but cannot justify anything like the exclusionary practices undertaken
by modern wealthy states.

I will try to make this argument in three steps. In the first, I will describe a
particular methodology, based upon which I will try to derive the right to exclude from the structure of human rights protection under international law.
In the second, I will seek to demonstrate how this methodology can defend
a presumptive right to exclude would-be immigrants, and the right to use
some forms of force in defense of this right. In the third, I will examine two
possible implications of this view. These implications do not give us a reason
to think that the view presented here is wrong—although they will demonstrate that the right to exclude this view defends cannot legitimate the sorts of
exclusionary practices undertaken by states today. In the final section, I will
discuss three patterns of objection intended to undermine the argumentative pattern I defend here. These objections—from *expulsion*, from *reproduction*, and from *liberty*—are powerful; but I hope the argument I present here
might survive an engagement with these objections.

1. Political Community and Human Rights

We should begin, then, by making clear what it is that I am claiming is shared
by those who are present within a society. What they share, I believe, is liability to the specifically jurisdictional powers of a territorial state. Whatever
else a state may be—a site for a culture, a particular sort of self-understanding,
a particular historical project—it is at its heart a *jurisdictional* project, in that
it is defined with reference to a particular sort of power held over a particular sort of place. If the state has a right to exclude, and has it in virtue of
being a state, it must have it in virtue of its jurisdictional aspect—the rights
it has simply in virtue of existing as a state. If a state has this right, of course,

it could always choose to exercise it in the defense of other goods—perhaps the promotion of a culture, say, or respect for the associative wishes of its member. The first question, though, is whether or not such a right exists.

I want, then, to start with states as they are, understood in their most foundational legal terms, and then to see what in these legal terms might be used to ground a right to exclude unwanted would-be immigrants. The idea here is to describe a state in its most basic aspect, those attributes without which we would not describe the thing in question as a state at all, and then see what in this image could be used to develop the right to exclude. I understand this method as something akin to that developed by Robert Nozick to justify the state; on Nozick's account, we ought to develop the most favored account of a nonpolitical situation, and see what in that situation would lead to the emergence of a legitimate political state. Nozick's idea is to justify the state through this process, by showing it as an emergent property of the most favored nonpolitical situation; if we would have reason to leave the state of nature, on this account, then we have reason to be reconciled to at least some forms of political organization in the here and now.[1] My own argument is not so ambitious. I take for granted that states exist, and that they have certain characteristics without which we would not describe them as states—but *not*, of course, any right to exclude. I want then to ask what, in these characteristics, might be invoked as the ground for a collective right to refuse would-be immigrants. If the right to exclude can be shown to emerge from the materials thus given, we may have some reason to think that a deontic right to exclude can be defended.

We have, in this, some advantages; international law, in particular, has given us some materials that can be used to define what it means to be a state. The Montevideo Convention of 1934 is most commonly cited, and describes a state as having four aspects: a permanent population, a defined territory, a government, and the capacity to enter into relations with other states.[2] The final test need not concern us at present; the first three, however, do. The idea is that a state cannot exist without the simultaneous existence of three things: a government capable of exerting its coercive control; a particular part of the world's surface over which that control is exerted; and a particular group of people over whom that control is exercised. This last is intended, of course, to eliminate from consideration the uninhabited or uninhabitable parts of the world's surface from consideration; Antarctica is not a state, and (barring rather extreme climate change) will never be one. For our purposes, what we ought to take seriously is the idea that a state is constituted by effective jurisdiction over a particular part of the world's territory. This jurisdictional principle seems to be foundational, even to the writers of the Montevideo Convention; this document specifies that all inhabitants within a territorial jurisdiction, foreigner and national alike, must be "under the same protection of the law."[3] A state, on this analysis, at its foundation comprises a set of institutions that are able to effectively rule over all individuals who happen to find themselves within a particular territorial jurisdiction.[4]

We can take this image as our starting point in our analysis of the right to exclude. On this analysis, states exist wherever there is an effective government able to exert political and legal control over a particular jurisdiction. This analysis does not include the right to exclude, since that is what we are trying to derive. It only includes the existence of the territorial state, and there seems to be nothing illegitimate about this assumption. Indeed, it seems to me that the very question of immigration itself makes sense only under where this assumption holds true; if the world contained only one government, ruling over all habitable land, the concept of the immigrant would seem to be inapplicable.

So: we assume that states have the indicia that make them states. We can also assume that humans have the rights they do in virtue of being human. Here, I want to be very careful about what I am not saying; I do not think we have yet any particular final answer about what human rights ought to be legally defended. Scholars and practitioners will continue to disagree about which rights are those we have reason to regard as universal.[5] All this is perhaps acceptable to gloss over, though, because what I want to explore more than the substance of human rights is its structure. Although human rights are defined as those rights that are held by humans in virtue of being human, this does not entail that all human rights are equally pressed against all human institutions at all times. Human rights, in a world split into distinct jurisdictions, impose distinct obligations on distinct political communities. In particular, we may invoke the standard tripartite distinction of obligations under human rights, to *respect*, to *protect*, and to *fulfill*.[6] These three sorts of obligations call upon states to act in different ways toward different persons. States are under an obligation to *respect* human rights, to begin with, in a global sense; the legitimate state cannot act so as to violate the human rights of others, whether those persons others are within its territorial jurisdiction or not. States are under a further obligation, though, to *protect* the human rights of those persons who are within its territorial jurisdiction. This means that the individuals within that jurisdiction have the right, against that particular state, to have their human rights defended and protected. This project of protection, of course, demands the creation of novel forms of political institution with the standing ability to offer concrete defenses of these rights, and act to vindicate them when they are violated. This demand is understood as the obligation to *fulfill* the human rights of those persons present within the jurisdiction of the state.

What I want to emphasize, in this context, is that, while the first demand is universal, the second two are emphatically local. The state is under a universal demand to avoid violating human rights, that is, whether the violation were to occur within its jurisdiction or not. But the state is under no correspondingly universal obligation to protect or fulfill the rights of humans qua humans. The state is, instead, obliged to protect and fulfill the rights of only some humans—namely, those who happen to be present within its territorial jurisdiction. This limitation does not seem to by itself run up against the liberal demand for the equality of persons; it is, instead, the means by which that equality is to be made operational in a world of territorial states. Thus, an assault in France upon a French citizen is undoubtedly a violation of human rights, and is undoubtedly to be regretted by all states, French and otherwise. But the United States is not obliged to devote its institutional capacity to the vindication of the rights of the French citizen to be free from assault. (Indeed, it would likely strike the French government as rather problematic if the Americans began to build institutions devoted to the punishment of French rights-violators.) The United States is able to devote its own institutional capacity to the protection and fulfillment of the rights of those present on American soil. It does this not because it values French lives less than American lives; after all, it would—if it were just—devote just as much time and effort to an assault upon a French tourist as to an assault upon an American citizen. It is able to devote its own institutional capacity in this way because of the jurisdictional limitation of the United States government, which is authorized and obligated to protect and fulfill human rights only within a particular part of the world's surface.[7] Those who participate in the American system, further, are authorized and obligated to help support this system's ability to protect and fulfill human rights in this way. If we believe—as I do—that we have as individuals a general duty to uphold just institutions, then those who live and work within the jurisdiction of the United States have an obligation that is both legal and moral to protect and fulfill the human rights of their (jurisdictional) neighbors.[8]

With this in mind, we can now proceed to examine just what happens when someone crosses the borders of a state. Assume, for the moment, that an individual from France simply swims to the United States. She arrives within the country and is now within its jurisdiction, as described above. If the United States would like to exclude her, I believe it will have to cite something relating to this jurisdictional picture. We might start by noting that the French citizen was, in France, possessed of institutions that are legally and morally bound to protect and fulfill her human rights, and a population that is legally and morally obligated to use these institutions in defense of these rights. (I should note, up front, that what is true of France is unlikely to be true of a great many other countries; this will be important, when we consider the limitations of the jurisdictional approach to the right to exclude.) In leaving the jurisdiction of France, she has to some degree abandoned the right to have French institutions act to protect and fulfill her human rights. The abandonment is not total, of course; she has every right to return to France, and she may have some recourse to French consular services if she is arrested in the United States. She is, however, no longer entitled to have French institutions act to directly protect and fulfill her basic human rights, so long as she is within the territorial jurisdiction of the United States. She has, however, acquired other rights now in virtue of her presence within the United States. In particular, she is entitled to have her basic rights protected and fulfilled by the legal institutions of the United States; the mere fact of her presence within the jurisdiction is sufficient to place these institutions under an obligation to act in defense of these rights. The individuals within the United States, moreover, have a moral and legal obligation to act in defense of these rights—an obligation they did not have prior to her entry into the territory of the United States. They are obligated to act in particular ways, so that her rights are effectively protected and fulfilled; they are obligated to help pay for the police that will defend her physical security, they are obligated to serve on juries that will serve to convict those who attack her—indeed, they are obligated to help create and sustain institutions sufficient to protect her basic human rights. This obligation, it should be noted, emerges from the simple fact of presence; no particular legal status within the jurisdiction is required. International law demands that states extend their institutional reach to protect and fulfill the rights of all those within their jurisdiction.[9] Domestic law has often echoed this jurisdictional concern; the United States, for instance, has held that the right to primary education is held by all those present within the jurisdiction of the United States, whether or not that presence is legal. This point is nicely made in the case of *Plyer v. Doe*, which we have already had occasion to examine in chapter 2:

> [T]he protection of the Fourteenth Amendment extends to anyone, citizen or stranger, who *is* subject to the laws of a State, and reaches into every corner of a State's territory. That a person's initial entry into a State, or into the United States, was unlawful, and that he may for that reason be expelled, cannot negate the simple fact of his presence within the State's territorial perimeter. Given such presence, he is subject to the full range of obligations imposed by the State's civil and criminal laws. And until he leaves the jurisdiction—either voluntarily, or involuntarily in accordance with the Constitution and laws of the United States—he is entitled to the equal protection of the laws that a State may choose to establish.[10]

All of this entails, I think, a strong set of obligations on the part of current residents within a jurisdiction to protect and fulfill the rights of all and only residents within that jurisdiction. These residents are not obliged to protect and fulfill the rights of others resident abroad—or, more accurately, they are not obliged to do that when those rights are adequately protected by the territorial institutions currently in place; American citizens may have obligations to the citizens of Somalia to help create political institutions in that country, or to allow Somali citizens to enter into the jurisdiction of the United States and to be protected by its institutions. But the residents of the United States are under no obligation to extend this protection to French citizens resident in France, and when such a French citizen enters into the United States, she imposes upon the current residents of the United States a new set of obligations. If there is a right to exclude unwanted would-be immigrants, on my view, it will have to emerge from these facts.

2. The Right to Exclude

So: how could a state, understood in these terms, argue that it has a right to exclude a would-be immigrant? The argument, I think, will have to begin with the fact that the one who enters into a jurisdiction imposes an obligation on those who are present within that jurisdiction: an obligation, most crucially, to create and support institutions capable of protecting and fulfilling the rights of the newcomer, and then to act within these institutions so as to ensure that they do in fact defend these rights. If we are legitimately able to exclude unwanted would-be immigrants, it will be because we have some right to refuse to take on this sort of new obligation. I should note, up front, that this argument is not one about the *costs* of that obligation, but about the fact that this obligation exists; I am concerned with whether or not we have a right to be free from an obligation to act in particular ways toward particular persons, not whether or not they impose financial costs on us by their presence. (We can stipulate that the unwanted French emigrant would actually be a financial blessing to the United States, since she will pay taxes and be unlikely to rely upon many social programs.) Is there a right to exclude a particular person, simply because her presence would impose upon us an obligation to act in a particular way?

I think it is plausible that there is, if one takes the idea of liberty seriously. Someone who imposes an obligation upon me is, in a very limited way, impinging upon my freedom. If it is a legal obligation, then my freedom to do a certain thing while not suffering a negative consequence is eliminated; the very nature of coercive law, after all, depends upon the law's being able to oblige particular actions, by eliminating certain options (such as the one in which I both steal your bicycle *and* don't have to go to jail). If it is a moral obligation, then my moral right to do a particular thing is limited by that obligation; if, for instance, I acquire an obligation to care for your puppy, then my moral right to spend my evening doing something other than walking your dog is eliminated. Philosophers who discuss obligations have tended to look at the morality of *being obliged*; that is, how we ought to understand the structure of a duty to act, and how the various sorts of obligations might interact. I do not think many of us have looked at the morality of *acting to oblige others*.[11] This is, of course, natural; most of the time, what we care about most is how to understand and follow the various obligations that comprise the normative backdrop to our lives. But we should care, also, about the morality of imposing duties on others. Indeed, I think the following principle might be defensible, although in the present context I cannot offer an adequate justification for it: we have a presumptive right to be free from others imposing obligations on us without our consent. This right is a presumptive one only, and it is possible that under many circumstances we have a standing obligation of sufficient force that we are duty-bound to acquire a new obligation. But the showing of that standing obligation must be made, or the new obligation is simply an unwarranted interference with freedom.

To illustrate this, we might repurpose a well-loved example from Judith Jarvis Thomson. Imagine that Thomson's libertarian objections fail, and we are in fact subject to an obligation—legal and moral—to share our bloodstream with needy violinists, when that support is required for the violinists to survive.[12] Violinists, further, can successfully place us under an obligation to offer them support, simply by touching us with the tips of their fingers. (Assume that this touching is otherwise permissible; a mere touch of fingertips, in this world, is not a battery.) Imagine, finally, that a violinist is now attached to one individual, and is being offered adequate support by that individual; the violinist, however, would like to be attached to you, instead. Does the violinist have a right to touch you, and place you under an obligation to provide him with those goods to which he is morally entitled? I cannot see why; whatever it is to which he is entitled, he is by hypothesis already receiving it from the individual to which he is attached. You are under no obligation to become the individual charged with the defense of the violinist's entitlements; indeed, you would be licensed in using some degree of coercive force in keeping your person free from violinists' fingers. This is not, of course, a blank check—there are many things you could not do, in the course of defending your liberty to be free from the obligation to support the violinist. But you would seem to have some right to defend your liberty to live your life free from the obligation to support any particular violinist, at least where that violinist's rights are already adequately protected by another. The violinist has a right to protection, but not to be protected by the individual of his choosing.

There are, of course, many distinctions to be drawn between the immigrant and the violinist. The violinist is burdensome; the immigrant may not be—the relationship she invokes is one that may or may not ever lead to a demand for a particular action from any particular individual. The immigrant's action is, often, done for good reasons—reasons of family, economic sufficiency, or mere survival; the violinist, in contrast, seems almost capricious in jumping from back to back. The violinist, further, offers no benefits to her host; the immigrant, in contrast, generally offers a very great deal to the countries in which they are situated—they offer, at the very least, their labor power, and the attendant taxation revenue that such labor power engenders. The violinist, in sum, is more easily condemned than the immigrant. Might we not, in view of this, simply abandon the metaphor?

I think, instead, we should treat these differences as going to the moral judgment of how we evaluate the *character* of the one who imposes obligations on others—rather than dispelling the idea that the imposition of obligation is itself morally problematic. The immigrant is often perfectly comprehensible to us; she does what she does for reasons we recognize. (Indeed, as I will discuss in chapter 8, we might have no moral right to condemn those who cross the border illegally as lacking in virtue; we may have the legal right to stop them, but we are not therefore entitled to regard them as morally monstrous.) The distinctions between the immigrant and the violinist, then, caution us to avoid transferring our moral condemnation of the violinist directly to the immigrant. Much of what bothers us about the violinist might be produced because of factors not shared with the immigrant.

We should, therefore, be careful before we condemn the immigrant with the same strength as our condemnation of the violinist. The source of our moral disquiet, however, seems to be the same. Even if the violinist's act is more burdensome and capricious than the immigrant's, they are both wrong for the same reason: they impose an obligation on those who have no independent obligation to accept being so obliged. The immigrant's burden is less significant, and more reciprocal, than the violinist's; but neither has a right to impose that relationship without consent upon an unwilling moral agent. I cannot justify an imposed relationship of obligation with reference to the lightness of its burdens, any more than I can justify my breaking into your house with reference to the fact that I am likely to make things tidier for you once I am in there. The one who breaks-and-steals, or who breaks-and-destroys-valuable-heirlooms, is more harshly judged than one who breaks-and-cleans; none, however, does what is morally right, because none has the permission of the owner.[13] So, I think, with the violinist and the immigrant; we may judge the former more harshly, but we are right to judge each as having done what is morally wrong.

At this juncture, I would like to introduce an objection derived from Michael Kates and Ryan Pevnick. Kates and Pevnick argue that the vision of obligation I present here faces a choice of how it cashes out the obligation to the newcomer. If the obligation is to the specific individual who has crossed the border, then the obligation is a new *token* of obligation, and Kates and Pevnick argue that this is morally problematic only if that token is actually costly. If, in contrast, the obligation is a standing one—help anyone within my jurisdiction—then the obligation to the newcomer isn't a new obligation at all, in which case the stated rationale for the exclusion seems to fail:

But if the inhabitants of a state incur no genuinely new types of obligations as a result of immigration, then it appears that immigration only changes their position by introducing new tokens of obligations from already existing types. The problem, however, is that the introduction of new tokens of existing obligations seems to alter the position of a state's current inhabitants only by altering the costs of fulfilling obligations that citizens must already fulfill for one another. Thus, if the new obligations in question are tokens of already existing types, it is unclear what is meant by Blake's claim that his argument is about new obligations rather than costs. For, once again, the "new" obligations change what is required of a state's current inhabitants only by altering the costs of supporting institutions they are already obligated to support.[14]

Kates and Pevnick thus introduce a fork: either these obligations are not really new, in which case nothing of great moral significance happens when a newcomer enters—or they are interesting only because they are costly, in which case considerations of cost might be sufficient to overcome any potential objection to the migrant's presence.

I think this fork misdescribes the moral landscape. Many moral duties are susceptible of being described at multiple levels of abstraction: I take care of the block on which my house is situated, which is a way of fulfilling the duty to help my neighbors, which in turn is an instantiation of the duty to leave the world slightly better than I found it, which in turn is perhaps an instantiation of my duty to God to obey His word. Even if it were true that my duties to the newcomer might be described under the heading of "take care of those around me," it does not follow that they do not *also* constitute individual— and novel—duties to those particular people. The two are compatible. Think, for instance, of adopting a child into your family. It would be very odd indeed to say that you did not have new duties toward that child—that you simply had the standing obligation to take care of the children who were vulnerable toward you. That standing duty is best spelled out with reference to the *particular* acts you owe toward that *particular* child. Nor, though, is it true that the duty here can only be cashed out with reference to the particular costs of raising that child. Imagine, for instance, that there is enough money in the family to easily accommodate that child—five, perhaps, can live as cheaply as four, without anyone really noticing a change in standards of living. It would be very odd indeed, though, to say that the child's entry into my household did not introduce a new set of duties into my life. They are new, indeed, simply because I now have to do things for that child I didn't have to do before; whether or not those things are costly seems somewhat beside the point. The point, instead, is that *I* am now the one that has to do them.

I persist, then, in thinking that the creation of a new set of obligations here is morally significant, quite apart from considerations of costs—and even if these new obligations can be described as derived from particular abstract duties. What matters, I think, is the fact that a relationship of obligation is created, in which I am obligated to do particular things—and to care about doing them well.

So: can we now defend the right to exclude? I think we can, in at least some cases. The would-be immigrant who wants to cross into a given jurisdiction acts to impose a set of obligations upon that jurisdiction's current residents. That obligation limits the freedom of those residents, by placing them under particular obligations to act in particular ways in defense of that migrant's rights. In response to this, legitimate states may refuse to allow immigrants to come in, because the residents of those states have the right to refuse to become obligated to those would-be immigrants. This general right imposes a duty on would-be immigrants to cite some particular reason why these residents have an obligation to become obligated to these immigrants. In the absence of such a reason, it appears that the state has the right to use some proportional forms of coercion to prevent the would-be immigrant from entering into the jurisdiction of the state—since it is the simple fact of presence within that jurisdiction that invokes the obligation to protect the migrant's basic rights. The state in question can decide on the purposes for which this right is to be invoked; it may choose to use this right to defend cultural unity, or solidarity, or any other particular good. The right itself, though, is derived from the general right to avoid unwanted obligations, where we have no obligation to become obliged. The right is therefore derivable from the rights of individuals; states that did not have this right could argue from these existing individual rights to the plausibility of a general right to exclude.

To illustrate this, I can discuss, once again, my own story: I moved from Canada to the United States at age twenty-two, to pursue graduate education in philosophy.[15] The United States became obliged to me in particular ways once I entered onto American soil. The United States might have chosen to exclude me, in virtue of these facts; it certainly had no obligation to become obliged to protect my rights, since these rights were already well protected in Canada. I am extremely glad that the United States chose policies that allowed me to enter and eventually to become an American citizen. I do not think, though, that I had any particular *right* to enter the United States; the decision to allow me to study at an American university was a discretionary act, and no injustice would have been done to an alternate version of me who was excluded.[16]

All this, of course, is only the first step in an argument. Even if legitimate states have a right to exclude unwanted would-be immigrants, much work needs to be done to figure out how the contours of that right. It is possible for us to have the right to exclude, after all, and still question whether or not that right is able to ground a particular exclusionary policy. We might ask, after all, whether the right to exclude allows the use of a particular program of enforcement; the militarization of the southern border of the United States, for example, might be morally problematic even if the United States is permitted to exclude migrants. [17] We might further ask whether all the goods cited in defense of a particular use of the right are, in fact, goods a liberal state is entitled to pursue.[18] We might, finally, ask whether or not a state, even if it had the right to exclude, would be likely to exercise this right fairly when it exercises it unilaterally.[19] For the moment, though, I want to ignore these issues and focus on two more worrying implications of the idea I propose here. I want to consider these ideas not only because they are plausible, but because I think they tell us something about the limits of the method I defend here.

3. Implications: Federalism and Refuge

We can deal with the first argument comparatively quickly. The argument notes that states are not the only entities defined jurisdictionally; federal subunits, including provinces, municipalities, and the like, all have a limited territorial space within which they are able to impose binding legal commands. The worry emerges when it appears that these subunits are, on the argument given here, equally able to exclude unwanted outsiders as sovereign states. Such a conclusion, needless to say, would impugn the validity of the argument; a theory of exclusion that gives the same right to exclude to the city of Seattle, the state of Washington, and the United States of America is one that is unlikely to provide us with much insight.

The proper response to this objection, I think, is to note that the structure of a federal state necessarily involves some particular constitutional project, which dictates how power shall be shared between the federal subunits and the central government. Under these circumstances, the federal subunits may be unable to exclude unwanted outsiders—not because it is in principle forbidden for them to do so, but because the particular purposes of the legal union between those subunits makes it impermissible for them to do so. This is, I think, the proper account of the United States' current understanding of the right to freedom of movement; this right is tied by the Supreme Court to the importance of the federal project of creating one political union:

> But this does not mean that there are no boundaries to the permissible area of State legislative activity. There are. And none is more certain than the prohibition against attempts on the part of any single State to isolate itself from difficulties common to all of them by restraining the transportation of persons and property across its borders. It is frequently the case that a State might gain a momentary respite from the pressure of events by the simple expedient of shutting its gates to the outside world. But, in the words of Mr. Justice Cardozo: "The constitution was framed under the dominion of a political philosophy less parochial in range. It was framed upon the theory that the peoples of the several States must sink or swim together, and that, in the long run, prosperity and salvation are in union, not division."[20]

This analysis means that the rights of particular federal subunits to exclude must be made subservient to the project of creating one political community under constitutional rule. The proper response to the objection, then, is that federal subunits do not have the right to exclude, when that right is anathema to the project of creating a single political community. There is nothing inherently wrong in imagining that the state of Washington, or even the city of Seattle, might have had the right to exclude outsiders, under a different set of institutions. (The novel *Snowcrash* describes exactly this sort of phenomenon.)[21] Under the institutions currently in place, however, these federal units have no right to exclude would-be residents journeying from elsewhere in the country—even when such residents might impose significant costs upon the current residents.[22] This is because the project of shared self-rule entered into at the federal level demands that only the federal government have the right to exclude. The federal subunits, in contrast, have no such right: in the terms I have used above, they are obliged to become obliged to those who want to enter.

This response, though, opens up one avenue by which we might criticize the jurisdictional theory—or, more accurately, criticize the ability of that theory to justify the sorts of exclusion states currently undertake. The response argues that some forms of political project require the jurisdictional units gathered together under that project to give up their rights to exclude. It is now possible for the critic to argue that some such project does, in fact exist. If this is right, though, then the supposed right to exclude would-be immigrants held by states might be as illusory as the same right when pressed by the city of Seattle.

There are two versions of this argument: a stronger version and a weaker one. The stronger one is global and argues that some sort of political community now exists at the global level that makes exclusion impermissible. The weaker one is particular and argues that some particular forms of political and legal integration between particular countries might make exclusion between those countries impermissible. The stronger version of the argument strikes me as extremely difficult to establish; the institutions that currently exist at the global level are sufficiently weak, and sufficiently dependent upon sovereign states for their legitimacy and for enforcement, that it seems implausible to suggest that they are at a sufficient level to make exclusion by states impermissible. I have not, of course, given anything like a full account of what it would take for global institutions to be sufficiently robust to preclude exclusion by their member states; I have simply asserted that the United States is sufficiently robust and the United Nations is not. It is therefore entirely possible for an argument to be developed that shows that my assertion is incorrect. I remain, of course, skeptical.

The weaker argument, however, seems more plausible. Again, without any more substantive theory of what sorts of political arrangement constrain the right to exclude, it is difficult to make any final conclusions. It seems plausible, though, to say that some forms of political integration create a political community of sufficient power and reach that the subunits of that community forfeit the right to exclude unwanted outsiders. The most advanced form of transnational community, on this vision, is probably found in Europe, which has an array of political institutions that create something like a single community for purposes of politics: a European Parliament, the European Court of Human Rights, and so forth.[23] This sort of integration might mean that the states comprising the European Union no longer have the right to exclude unwanted would-be migrants from other European Union states. If this is true, then the states of the European Union have created a set of political institutions whose needs include the creation of a common citizenship; the right to freedom of movement might emerge, as it did in the United States, from the needs of this conception of a common identity. It is possible, then, for states to lose the right to exclude, in virtue of their voluntary creation of robust political institutions within which they serve as component parts. On my own view, this has occurred within Europe to such a degree that freedom of movement within the European Union is a moral imperative and would be so even if the states of the European Union did not recognize it as such. I am not convinced that the European Union will survive the next century; that, of course, reflects not philosophy but pessimism (or honesty) about the challenges facing that organization. I am less concerned with defending the right to mobility within the European Union, though, than with acknowledging the force of the objection from which it emerges: it is true, I think, that we cannot rest entirely easy with the right to exclude in a world that contains robust transnational institutions. At the very least, we are right to ask whether such institutions are sufficient to impose limits on that right. An argumentative pattern is available to cosmopolitan critics of the right to exclude, on this view: the critic can argue that this right, even if defensible in the abstract, cannot be exercised in particular circumstances in the world we know. While I suspect the cosmopolitan critic and I would disagree about what would trigger this limitation, I am at least satisfied that we have now identified a common description of our argument: we are searching to discover whether or not the particular institutions we share are of the right character to make us obliged to become obliged to those migrants seeking entry into our jurisdiction.

The second objection is more simple, but also potentially more important. It notes, simply, that the structure of the argument is as follows: we can exclude unwanted would-be immigrants because these immigrants already have adequate rights-protection within their countries of origin and are seeking now to oblige us to act in defense of their rights. The argument only holds, that is, when there in fact *is* adequate rights-protection in the country from which the individual is seeking to emigrate. This was, of course, true for me in my emigration from Canada, and it is doubtless true of many would-be immigrants. It is unlikely to be true of most immigrants, however, many of whom are fleeing circumstances that could be described (rather bloodlessly) as insufficiently rights-protecting. This means, of course, that the justificatory story now fails to hold. We are unable to exclude the unwanted migrant, because the story we would have to tell—namely, that we have no obligation to become obligated to protect that migrant's rights—is inaccurate. The migrant would, upon entry into our territory, simply acquire that set of rights protections to which she is entitled. If we propose to use force to prevent that individual from entering into our territory, we are simply using force to keep her in a morally indefensible situation. There is no possibility of that use of force being legitimate. Accordingly, we might think that the story I tell here—despite its general defense of the right to exclude—is, in fact, considerably more radical than it would at first appear. It would mandate something like a radically revised account of refugee and asylum law, on which we cannot use force to exclude outsiders from entry when those outsiders are coming from countries that are insufficiently attentive to basic human rights.

This is, again, an objection to the view if interpreted as a blanket defense of our current practices; it is not, however, an objection I want to reject in its entirety. I will suggest two means by which the objection's force is potentially subject to some limitations, but on the whole I believe the objection to be accurate. Indeed, if we focus on the justification for the use of force, I believe we are likely to arrive at an account of refugee and asylum law on which we are unable to refuse admission to a great many would-be migrants. This view of immigration will be, I think, considerably more robust than the related view given by Wellman, who allows the legitimate state to purchase the right to exclude, by devoting an adequate share of its resources and efforts to development in foreign countries.[24] On my view, this is not even in principle permissible. We cannot justify the use of force against one party by citing benefits to others; the justification must be in terms that the coerced party can accept, without requiring that party to unduly identify with the interests of others. This is, after all, the lesson John Rawls taught about the separateness of persons; it is wrong to demand that an individual who is treated badly by a coercive institution be mollified by the comparatively greater benefits received by others.[25] The idea that we can justify using force against someone whose rights are unprotected, by citing the fact that we have helped other people elsewhere, seems to fly in the face of this idea. We can only justify the coercive force of the border if we use it against people whose rights are adequately protected in their current homes. To use it elsewhere seems simply to use force to defend an illegitimate status quo; this is morally impermissible, regardless of how just our foreign policy might otherwise be.

If we are going to limit the rights of immigrants from oppressed countries, then, we will have to do so in a manner that defends their right to be treated as a moral equal. Is there any way of doing this? I believe there are, in principle, two ways of doing so—although neither will offer much consolation to those who want to defend the international status quo. The first way begins with the simple fact that the obligation to become obliged is held, not simply by an individual state, but by all legitimate states collectively. To return to the modified violinist case: a dying violinist might have a right to have someone offer him the necessary support needed for a decent life—but he does not have the right to pick his favorite agent as provider. Nothing in the picture of basic rights we are imagining here mandates that we are allowed to insist that the *general* obligation to protect the rights of persons can be made into a *particular* obligation—that is, an obligation to be pressed against one particular agent—simply through the wishes of the one to whom we are obliged. This means, I think, that the story we can tell about exclusion might have to be more complex. We are not entitled to use force to exclude individuals who want to enter our jurisdiction, when they come from jurisdictions that do not adequately protect their rights. But nothing in this says that we are obligated to be the jurisdiction in which those individuals ultimately make their lives. If the burden of refugee flows is one that ought to be borne by the wealthy states of the world collectively, then it is entirely open to a particular state to argue that some other state is refusing its share of the bill. This opens up the possibility that we can develop a secondary moral analysis of what fairness would demand in the allocation of the burdens of doing justice through immigration. It also opens up the possibility of legitimate international covenants excluding individuals when they have passed through rights-protecting countries on their way to their chosen country of refuge. The Dublin Regulation, for example, insists that an individual's asylum claim must be heard by the first European Union state into which that individual first enters.[26] This regulation may be unfair toward border states, which tend to bear a higher proportional cost from refugee flows; but it cannot be said to be unfair toward refugees themselves.

The second sort of restriction we can imagine is more complex—and, potentially, more dangerous. It goes to the idea that we can, under some circumstances, demand that people pay some costs to maintain just institutions. This is, of course, hardly a controversial idea, stated this generally; we accept that individuals have the duty to pay taxes to support just states, for example. But we might similarly think that individuals have the obligation to bear some costs involved in setting up just institutions, too. We might, for example, demand that individuals from a particular state bear some of the costs involved in transitioning that state toward democratic legitimacy. These costs, moreover, might include things other than financial burdens; we do, under some circumstances, insist that individuals bear some personal risk in the name of justice. (Most accounts of just war, after all, include the idea that justice is a sufficient ideal to warrant the imposition of a risk of violent death.) So: if individuals want to emigrate to a given country from a non-rights-respecting country, we might want to have the right to insist that they stay there to help make that country better.[27] Is this a sufficient reason for us to think that we can insist that people fleeing from a non-rights-respecting country return to that country and improve it from within?

I do not want to reject these ideas entirely; I do believe, however, that they are insufficient to generate anything like a right to exclude would-be migrants from oppressed states. The reason is, I think, the fairly simple one that it is unfair to insist that someone fleeing an oppressive state has more duties to that state than someone outside of it.[28] The relationship between that state and the emigrant is hardly that of someone who is a party to an ongoing, valuable relationship, who thereby acquires some duties to the other parties in that relationship. If we did not accept this simply in virtue of the fact that the state is engaging in unjustified coercion, we might accept it in virtue of the fact that the emigrant is actively trying to sever that relationship. To insist that this relationship generates duties, then, is something very much like insisting that an ascriptive fact—a mere fact of birth—is sufficient to generate an obligation. This, however, seems to be morally impermissible. Why, the migrant might ask, should she be asked to bear a higher burden of the shared task of democratizing her country of origin? She was born there, but that hardly seems sufficient to justify a greater obligation to help that place than those lucky enough to be born in more wealthy jurisdictions. (She may have greater knowledge, and therefore ability, to help, but those seem to be separate issues; and, besides which, it seems unjust for us to insist that obligation increases with ability.) The only way, I think, in which we might use the idea of a burden to work for democratization is if the argument treats all parties—current residents and would-be immigrants—as moral equals, with each having an equivalent duty to build the democratic capacity of the state in question. This might legitimate asking would-be immigrants to bear some costs in rebuilding the state from which they come; but it would equally ask those who currently reside within the rights-respecting jurisdiction to give of themselves to help the shared task of building a rights-protecting world. The idea of a special duty to one's home country, I said, was dangerous because it tempts us to see those who come from a place as specially obligated to sacrifice themselves to improve that place. The shared sacrifice, I think, must be actually shared—justly, among all the citizens of the world; it seems hard to imagine that we could actually use these ideas to exclude would-be immigrants, at least unless we are ourselves bearing costs equivalent to those we expect these migrants to pay. This is a test, of course, I do not think any current state is likely to meet.

The result of all this is that the right of a state to exclude people from underdeveloped and oppressive nations is likely to prove rather weak. I do not think this is a defect; it strikes me as true that a state that proposes to use force to keep people out of its jurisdiction has to account for the rights of the people against whom that force is directed. I have ignored, here, many relevant questions. We have reason to ask what human rights are those that ought to be defended by international law and by immigration law. We have reason to ask what sorts of considerations other than the protection of basic human rights ought to affect the right to exclude.[29] I will consider these questions more fully in the following chapter. What I have said here, though, might already give us some reason to think that the right to exclude exists—and that this right is far from able to justify the sorts of policies all wealthy societies currently undertake. We have, collectively, the right to exclude some unwanted would-be immigrants. We should not, however, take any comfort from this fact; much of what we are doing now is profoundly unjust and should be recognized as such. This defense of a right to exclude should therefore be taken as a plea for reform, not for quietism; we can indeed seek to exclude some unwanted immigrants, but we should not therefore conclude that we are allowed to exclude as we currently do.

4. Objections: Expulsion, Reproduction, and Liberty

I want to conclude this chapter by examining some particularly important worries about the view I defend here. Critics have responded to my analysis of migration with some important worries. I want to discuss three of these in the space that remains: we can think of them as the argument from *expulsion*, from *reproduction*, and from *liberty*.

Kates and Pevnick provide the argument from expulsion. Since, on my view, there is no essential appeal made to this state as an intergenerational community, it seems as if my view is open in principle to allowing unpopular individuals to be expelled. After all, on my view, the migrant who is coming from a society in which her human rights are protected has no particular claim to the society of her choice; she has what she is entitled to. Why should we not say the same about the non-migrant, whom we are simply choosing to kick out?

> [I]magine that you are born in a country that finds your accent or taste in music distasteful. While they reliably and effectively protect your rights out of a sense of jurisdictional responsibility, they would prefer to get rid of you. Now imagine that some other country comes along and insists that it would be happy to protect your rights and could even do so quite reliably. Suddenly, it seems, you would be in the same position as the immigrant since you now have a reserve option that is perfectly adequate (at least in the sense that another country is able and willing to protect your rights). And so, secure in the knowledge that this new country will both reliably protect your rights and not face any unwanted obligations (since they are welcoming you with open arms), your home country decides to deport you. We certainly do not typically think that such a deportation is acceptable. But is there anything in Blake's framework that would allow him to resist such a policy?[30]

The answer, I believe, is yes. The very notion of human rights, I believe, requires us to see humans as agents who move in time; we make plans and take the success of those plans as indicative of the success of our lives. To borrow the language of Kieran Oberman: possibilities and attachments are different things.[31] We can say, I think, that the right to be free from deportation rests upon the importance of the individual's ability to build upon the plans and relationships already made in this particular place. I will discuss, in chapter 7, how deportation might—under some circumstances—be made morally rightful, in response to particular forms of lawbreaking. But that deportation would have to be shown to be compatible with respect for the human rights of the one deported—and that is a high bar indeed; the one deported, after all, is facing the destruction of her attachments, and this sort of damage requires an extraordinarily powerful form of justification. What Kates and Pevnick propose to ascribe to me, instead, is a blanket state right to deny *everyone's* attachments—and I think my theory can easily reply that there is no permission to do *that*. But these conclusions can be grounded, I would note, without having to do what Kates and Pevnick recommend— which is to make the right to exclude relative to the particular history of the community itself. There is nothing here that requires us to inquire about the vexed question of what a given community's history really is, or how to understand the nature of intergenerational community. All we need to assert is this: that the future, for creatures like us, is unlike the past.

Kates and Pevnick and I are thus all in agreement that the unwanted citizen should not be deported. Their justification, though, makes reference to something beyond her own agency. For Kates and Pevnick, we need to imagine a self-determining community, which exists apart from the individual people within that community, as an intergenerational entity that bears responsibility for that state's institutions. I think we need not assert the existence of that thing for us to explain why this deportation is wrong. We can explain it with reference to the *individual's* history—not with reference to the community's. This seems to me to have two advantages. First, it is metaphysically rather simpler; we can agree that the individual exists, even while disagreeing about the nation. Second, it avoids the problems of marginalization discussed in the previous chapter. To ground the right to be free from deportation on something historical and intergenerational is to put in jeopardy those who do not easily identify with that something. Our imagined citizen's right against deportation would seem as important if he is clearly a part of that intergenerational community, or if he has become a citizen this morning.

The issue of *reproduction* has also been presented as a possible objection to this view. Many commentators have felt that the right to exclude the outsider, if it is present, must also involve the right to prevent reproduction on the part of my compatriots; this, surely, would count as a reductio ad absurdum of the view in question. Jan Brezger and Andreas Cassee intend this to be a fatal objection to any view that provides a state with the right to exclude outsiders:

> If access to the benefits of membership in a state is to be regulated exclusively by reference to freedom of association, freedom from imposed obligations, or property rights, it follows that the current citizenry may deny access not only to would-be immigrants, but also to resident citizens' offspring.[32]

I think it is worth emphasizing, then, that the principle I defend entails the right to be free from having obligations imposed upon me—*except* when I have an obligation to become so obligated. There can be, and likely are, many cases in which I am not free to refuse to become so obligated. Refugee law is one case, of course; those who are not defended in their human rights may impose upon us, and insist that we enter into political relationships with them. But reproduction seems similarly a case in which others may rightly expect the freedom to impose upon us.

I think we can say more, though, about this case. It is taken as being obviously true that your reproduction cannot—by means of my obligations to you—harm me. But it is worth figuring out why this should be so. It does *not* seem implausible—to me, at least—that the presence of new people in my social world can affect me in morally significant ways. Is it actually wrong to think that new arrivals—whether as migrants, or as newborns—might make demands on us? People are, quite frankly, demanding, morally speaking, and their moral rights place demands upon us. I think our revulsion at the thought that we could prevent our compatriots from reproducing cannot rest on a view that their reproduction does not affect us. Of *course* it affects us. The only question is whether or not that could be the basis of a right to prevent reproduction.

It cannot, of course; but that isn't because babies aren't demanding, but because the means we would have to use to *stop* people from reproducing would be obviously and horrendously unjust. If we were to use coercive medical intervention to prevent reproduction, we would be engaging in a grossly unjust act. But it would be unjust because it is an unconsented-to bodily invasion—not because the child that is at issue does not affect me or my freedom. We admit, elsewhere, that the presence of people can make things harder for us. We might as well do the same here. The real basis for the freedom to reproduce isn't the fact of the new person, but the bodily invasion the prevention of that new person would demand.[33]

I think we might, then, think that there is something like a three-stage defense of the impermissibility of preventing reproduction. The first stage is to acknowledge that the particular relationship between the woman and her own body makes the proposed bodily invasion presumptively wrong. The woman has the right to use her body without being political invasion—for reasons both of gender and of basic human rights. The second stage is to acknowledge that the child that is produced is a creature of profound vulnerability. Newborns, to put it rather blandly, are terrible at taking care of themselves. They are, as it were, automatic refugees, entitled to a place and a community in which their rights are protected. The child can be protected in a number of ways; but it seems that the right of the parent to *be* that protector might be defended as one particularly important method of helping ensure that child's long-term development. The final stage, though, would be to look away from the human right to one's own body, or to one's parents, and toward the social meaning of parenthood. The rights of queer couples, and adoptive parents, to be seen as equal parents would mean that we would have to build a society in which all forms of parenting are provided with equal rights to guard and guide the child as it grows.[34] Thus, I think, we end up with something very much like where we are: a world in which the rights of parents are defended, and in which my own right to not be obligated cannot hope to overcome your rights to reproduce. We need not think, however, that anything here necessarily troubles the right to exclude adult migrants. The precise story that tells us why we cannot stop pregnancies tells us nothing at all about why we can or cannot close the border.

The final issue to be dealt with is that of *liberty*. Andy Lamey has suggested that, if freedom is what grounds the right to exclude, then we might lose that right to exclude if our freedom is either left alone or if the costs of exercising that freedom are minimal:

> There is a threshold of severity that automatically generates a duty to admit the immigrant; but there is no reverse equivalent threshold of burdenlessness on the other side that can automatically permit entry. A receiving society can always turn away an immigrant from a liberal state, even if the cost of admitting them is miniscule, or even if they gain from the immigrant's arrival. . . . It is hard to see this asymmetry as justified. In one case the cost is borne by the subject of a potential obligation, in the other case the bearer. It seems more consistent with the moral equality underlying jurisdiction to say that costs to both parties matter when determining whether an obligation obtains. On such a view, we would make room for the thought that an obligation can be so minimal that we have no grounds to reject it.[35]

In one sense, I believe Lamey is right; where the costs of admission are minimal—and where the benefits to the migrant are significant—we have good moral reason to admit that migrant. But this seems to me to reflect the ideas of mercy I will discuss later—not justice. Justice looks, instead, toward whether the one who is excluded is wronged; and, as before, it seems simply incorrect to say that we are *obligated* to enter into particular relationships with you, when those relationships are costless. (I don't have to go to the movies with you tonight—even if you can prove to me, empirically, that I'll enjoy it more than staying home.) Why should I be thought to wrong you, when I refrain from entering into a particular relationship with you? One way of reading Lamey, of course, is to think that the loss of freedom here is *compensated* for by the lack of costs I experience due to that migrant's presence. This vision of freedom, though, seems simply wrong. We do not in general think that I can justify overturning your moral expectations, based upon my later ability to offer you money. If I have the freedom to not enter into a relationship with you, it is a freedom that I have quite apart from whether or not I would be well advised to abandon that freedom. Rights, in short, do not await considerations of costs; if I have a right to not do a thing, the fact that it is costless does not make that right evaporate.

Lamey's final consideration involves the thought that one who chooses to sign a waiver of her rights thereby becomes immune from exclusion. After all, it is her effects upon my freedom that grant me the right to exclude her; and if she avows that she will never take advantage of any bit of my agency, it would seem impermissible for her to be excluded:

> But on what grounds, exactly, would it be wrong for her to waive her rights? There are cases in which we do permit individuals to occupy territory where their access to a government able to fulfill their rights is effectively non-existent. . . . Individuals who make round the world sea voyages similarly travel beyond the effective reach of states and thus occupy positions in which for all practical purposes there is no law available to protect them. It seems as best conditionally rather than inherently immoral for individuals to voluntarily place themselves beyond the reach of human rights law. If that is the case, why not permit well-informed individuals to place themselves beyond the reach of the law inside existing states?[36]

This objection is ingenious; but I think it fails, if only because I share with Kant the thought that the first duty of anyone in the state of nature is to do whatever is necessary to *exit* that state of nature.[37] As to whether or not it would be permissible for an individual to voluntarily sacrifice the most basic protections of her human rights, I cannot say; I am convinced, though, that it would be deeply immoral for any state to offer to an outsider the right to live within its borders, on condition that she live outside the protection of the law. In premodern legal systems, the harshest punishment was often outlawry— the status in which one was unable to draw upon the political community in seeking to defend one's life and one's rights. The concept of *homo sacer*—the man who can be sacrificed—emerges from the terrible nature of this punishment. I rather doubt that we could, consistent with the moral imperative of human rights, offer anyone a life as *homo sacer*. As regards sea voyages and other forms of life outside the protection of the state: I think it is worth emphasizing that those who explored the oceans nonetheless had rather rigid—indeed, rather brutal—systems of governance on board those ships.[38] Take, for instance, the code of Captain Bartholomew Roberts, pirate captain of the *Royal Fortune*. Captain Robert's pirate code looked like nothing less than a small vision of a constitution, used to govern the relationships between the men on the voyage. Take the first two clauses of this code as representative of the (lengthy) document:

I. Every man has a vote in affairs of moment; has equal title to the fresh provision, or strong liquors, and may use them at pleasure, unless a scarcity (not an uncommon thing among them) makes it necessary, for the good of all, to vote a retrenchment.

II. Every man to be called fairly in turn, by list, on board of prizes because, (over and above their proper share) they were on these occasions allowed a shift of clothes: but if they defrauded the company to the value of a dollar in plate, jewels, or money, marooning was their punishment. If the robbery was only betwixt one another, they contented themselves with slitting the ears and nose of the him that was guilty, and set him on shore, not in an uninhabited place, but somewhere, where he was sure to encounter hardships.[39]

I take these ideas to suggest that there are comparatively fewer places in the world in which we have been comfortable with people living outside of some coercive governing structure. One who is genuinely outside the realm of coercive law is unable to defend his rights, except by his own hand; and to have only this method for the defense of rights is a bad thing indeed, and, while I cannot prove it here, I rather think it's impermissible for a state to offer to anyone something quite this bad as a form of life. (Certainly, no one would accept that deal, except someone whose rights are already in serious danger, and those individuals are entitled to much more than this bargain suggests.) I am, at any rate, unconvinced that it provides us with a reason to rethink how we ought to approach the rights of the migrant, very few of whom are— we might imagine—eager to abandon their rights and enter into the state of outlawry.

I would conclude this chapter by noting the modesty of what I have sought to defend. The vision of exclusion I defend here does not rest upon nationality, or territory, or intergenerational community, or anything more metaphysically demanding than the fact of political community. I believe that this vision of exclusion is the most likely one to succeed at the task of making sense of how and why the liberal state might rightly exclude. I have not, however, given any clues about how it is that these ideas might be used to make sense of the more precise dilemmas that often form the backdrop of debates over migration policy. It is to that task that I now turn.

5

Coercion and Refuge

The previous chapter offered a particular vision of how we might justify restrictions on immigration. On this vision, we have no need to ask about national identity, or social solidarity, or any other particular good that might be defended by means of exclusion at the border. We look, instead, to whether or not the human rights of the prospective migrants are already well protected in their countries of origin. When those rights are protected in the state of origin, other states have a presumptive right to exclude. People have a right to a political community in which their rights are protected; but they do not have a right to a membership in the particular community they might choose. Those already resident in a particular country have a right to refuse to enter into a particular relationship with newcomers—and, were those newcomers to cross the border, they would necessarily create that relationship, simply in virtue of the territorial jurisdiction of the state. Where, in short, a prospective migrant's rights are adequately protected in her country of origin, the other countries of the world have a presumptive right to exclude her.

The issue that must be faced, though, is that for a great many people, the antecedent clause of this principle is not satisfied. The world is full of profound injustice. People throughout the world face a variety of forms of evil; they are persecuted, of course, but they are also impoverished, marginalized, starved, imprisoned without right, and ignored. They are subjected to human evils, but also to natural disasters and any number of unexpected catastrophes. The world, then, is full of people who might seem to be immune from the justification for exclusion I defend here. What can the analysis of migration I defend say, in light of these facts?

The most obvious conclusion we might draw is this: those people whose antecedent circumstances involve grave injustice have a right to cross borders—or, more precisely, the states of the world that might want to exclude those individuals will be morally unable to coercively exclude them. This obvious conclusion seems simple; the view I defend here would entail, if not open borders, then at least open borders for a great many of the impoverished and marginalized residents of the planet. There is some truth

Justice, Migration, and Mercy. Michael Blake, Oxford University Press (2020). © Oxford University Press.
DOI: 10.1093/oso/9780190879556.001.0001

to this—certainly, the jurisdictional view I defend will be unable to justify anything like the exclusionary practices we see in the world today. I believe, however, that the implications of the jurisdictional methods might be slightly more complex than they at first appear to be. Exactly how this view constrains state actions at the borders—and how it might also constrain state actions beyond the borders—will be the focus of the present chapter.

The thought that there are some people who are immune from the ordinary rules of exclusion has a long pedigree, in both theory and in practice. The medieval practice of sanctuary, notably, had elements of both ecclesiastical and political power and provided a means by which some individuals could use ecclesiastical resources to argue against the legitimacy of the temporal punishments they were facing.[1] While the granting of sanctuary was originally a religious act, it was easy enough for this form of relief to be granted by the institutions of one nation to the persecuted of another—and, during the wars that emerged after the Reformation, both Catholics and Protestants began to regard foreign states as places in which sanctuary might be sought. Philosophers, of course, began to argue about how to understand the moral basis of a state's act in granting sanctuary. As early as the seventeenth century, philosophers such as Hugo Grotius, Samuel von Pufendorf, and Christian Wolff developed complex views about how and when states ought to refuse to extradite those who claimed that they would be subject to injustice in their countries of origin. Grotius's view is particularly relevant to our present concerns; his argument was that asylum was to be granted to those who "suffer from undeserved enmity" (*immerito odio laborant*)—which is to say, those who faced an injustice in the punishments that awaited them in their countries of origin.[2] Grotius argued that a state could rightly refuse to use its coercive force to return a stranger to a place in which injustice awaited him. This vision of asylum persisted throughout the early modern period. Thomas Jefferson, for instance, refused to extradite fugitives to Spain, reflecting that those who fought for reform of unjust governments were often accused of treason; those who fled Spain for the United States after working for justice in Spain deserved protection, not extradition. "We should not wish," he argued, "to give up to the executioner the patriot who fails and flees to us."[3] This vision, though, reflected the idea that the patriot here is worthy of protection only when she is subject to unjust punishment in her country of origin. As before, the idea that the rightful state should not use its own coercive force to deliver an individual into injustice forms a core part of the moral story.

The concept of asylum has always been complex, both in morality and in law—and it became more complex during the course of the twentieth century; the First and the Second World Wars left both scars on the world and a legacy of refugees made vulnerable by that century's global conflicts. I cannot hope to adequately discuss that history here. I will, instead, simply turn to the documents that were intended to serve as an international response to the horrors of this century: the 1951 Convention Relating to the Status of Refugees, along with its 1967 Protocol. These documents outline the modern legal conception of the refugee—and a particular vision of what it is that cannot be rightly done to those seeking refuge. The Convention is a statement intended to guide state law; but it is also a statement of international morality, and as such it is strikingly simple.[4] It commits its signatories to a recognition that they are unable to exclude those who are facing a particular kind of evil in their countries of origin. The refugee is identified as one who,

> owing to well-founded fear of being persecuted for reasons of race, religion, nationality, membership of a particular social group or political opinion, is outside the country of his nationality and is unable or, owing to such fear, is unwilling to avail himself of the protection of that country; or who, not having a nationality and being outside the country of his former habitual residence as a result of such events, is unable or, owing to such fear, is unwilling to return to it.

Those who fall within this status have a number of distinct rights—including, most importantly, the right of *non-refoulement*, on which they are immune from being coercively returned to the circumstances under which they are facing persecution.[5] Those states who are signatories to the Convention and its Protocol agree to provide a number of other legal rights to those claiming refuge, including access to a hearing in which the validity of their claim to asylum might be fairly adjudicated.

It is hard to provide any accurate thumbnail vision of the legal regime initiated by the Convention; understanding that regime requires both an understanding of international law, a sensitivity to how that law is lived by individuals and by states, and an awareness of how international law both shapes and is shaped by domestic politics. In the present chapter, I will abstract away from much of this and focus on one aspect of this regime. I want to notice in particular the fact that *persecution* is given a privileged role, in the international morality defended by the Convention. In order to claim the right to cross borders, and to insist that other states have a moral obligation to let me do so, I must claim that I am being persecuted; it is not enough that I am—for example—simply facing starvation, randomized violence, or the breakdown of political society. This particular focus on persecution has faced sustained attack, both in philosophy and in legal practice. Documents such as the 1984 Cartagena Declaration on Refugees have expanded the notion of the refugee, to include those threatened by "generalized violence, foreign aggression, internal conflicts, massive violation of human rights or other circumstances which have seriously disturbed public order." In philosophy, too, the centrality of the concept of persecution has been criticized.[6] The concept of the refugee is now so associated with the Convention that some, such as Alexander Betts, have proposed doing away with the concept; we ought to focus, he argues, on "survival migrants," whose lives depend upon being rescued by a foreign society.[7] Others—including Matthew Price and Matthew Lister—have argued that the Convention includes some significant moral wisdom; only persecution, they argue, adequately captures the distinctive moral wrong that is only rightly ameliorated by the granting of residency rights elsewhere.[8]

I will not, at present, directly address the question of whether or not the Convention reflects morally defensible ideals—or whether, as its critics would have it, it is merely a product of a particular time and place. I want, instead, to back into this question, by asking what sorts of restrictions on exclusion might be implied by the jurisdictional view I defend. I will begin this by outlining two distinct ways in which the view I defend here might offer guidance to the state. I will then offer a more particular analysis of how it is that the jurisdictional view might constrain what the state can do at its territorial borders. I will then offer a provisional account of what a view like mine might demand, which might serve as a critical posture from which to criticize or defend more particular legal institutions.

I will therefore do three things in the present chapter. I will start by discussing distinct ways in which one might understand the notion of a right to cross borders. We might, in understanding the constraints placed on the right to exclude, differentiate a *positive* and a *negative* right to mobility, based upon what it is that the right demands of the state against which that right is claimed. I will then proceed to examine what the jurisdictional approach would demand when pressed against a state proposing to use coercion in defense of its borders. The concept of persecution, I will argue, is inadequate when it is used to describe that set of people who ought to be regarded as immune from coercive exclusion at the borders of the state. The final section of this chapter, though, will go beyond coercion at the border, and will ask what principles ought to determine how a state might provide resources for those seeking refuge from a state—but who seek those resources while not yet present at the borders of the state. There are some individuals, I will argue, who have a right not simply to immunity from exclusion, but to positive assistance in their journey to refuge—including, I think, some claim on proportional use of coercive force in their defense. I will argue, in this section, that the concept of *persecution* might have a role to play in determining who can call upon such resources. This might make the Convention's focus on persecution legitimate—but only if that Convention is made to operate within a broader set of principles demanding coercive sanctions against those states that engage in persecution. We might, in short, defend the Convention, but only if we are willing to live up to some more stringent demands placed upon us by later legal materials.

1. Positive and Negative Rights of Migration

We might start by examining two sorts of things we might mean by the right to cross the border.[9] One thing we might mean is that we are morally entitled to be free from coercive interference in our efforts to cross that border. We can think of this as a *negative* right of migration. It prevents others from using coercion to stop me, as I seek to move in physical space across the lines that demarcate the jurisdiction of the state. Many morally important rights are best expressed in similar terms. The right to a free press ensures that the state cannot rightly shut down a newspaper and arrest its editors. It does not guarantee me, as an author, the right to be published by that newspaper, and if I can find no press willing to publish my words, my freedom is not offended. Similarly, my right to an attorney in a civil case involves an immunity from state coercion when I hire an attorney to plead my case. My right is not disrespected when I cannot afford an attorney, nor when my case is so weak that no attorney chooses to represent me.

Often, of course, we mean something stronger than this. A *positive* right to migration would involve not simply the absence of coercive interference with my plan, but some particular acts done by an agent to make that plan attainable. It would involve, that is, that the state do something to make my migration possible—which might involve the use of coercion *against* those who would seek to make that migration impossible. The right to an attorney in a criminal trial, in the United States, is like this. I am not simply entitled to immunity from interference in my hiring of an attorney; if I cannot afford an attorney, I am entitled to have the services of that attorney provided to me.[10]

All this, of course, isn't new. The distinction between positive and negative rights has been familiar, if controversial, for a long time. The reason for being careful to distinguish these, though, is because we tend to think that there is a moral difference between a positive and a negative right. What it is they demand of us is distinct, and how wrongful we ought to understand a violation of that right to be is likely distinct as well. Thomas Pogge's work relies upon these moral reactions. Pogge argues that we should not understand global poverty as a failure to abide by the demands of a positive duty to assist the global poor—which, of course, would be simply the logical correlative of the poor's positive right to assistance. We are, instead, subject to a negative duty to avoid *causing* the poverty of the global poor—and, Pogge argues, that is a negative duty we are collectively failing to fulfill. The basis of Pogge's work is the common moral thought that there is a stronger moral prohibition on harming than on failing to prevent harm; a greater moral wrong in failing to respect a negative right than in failing to respect a positive one.[11]

I believe a similar moral reaction might make sense of how we react to particular ways of understanding the right to cross the border. The right to cross the border might be understood in a positive way, such that the right entails a claim on the assistance of others agents—including states—to cross international borders in search of refuge. But it might also be understood in a negative way, such that the state is called upon simply to avoid coercively interfering with a prospective migrant's journey across state borders. There seems to be, intuitively, something worse about threatening someone who tries to cross the border, than failing to provide someone with the tools needed to cross that border. Kieran Oberman acknowledges this; his view commits him to a right to cross borders, but it does not entail that everyone be provided with a plane ticket to whichever society she might find most congenial. We can defend the right to migrate, that is, without defending the thought that one must be provided with the means required to exercise that right.

We can, in short, differentiate between an immunity from coercive interference with our plans, and the moral entitlement to positive assistance with the project of making those plans come into being. The former may appear rather thin and inconsequential—although it is worth noting that Joseph

Carens, for one, defends the thought that the right to migrate might be valuable even if one does not have the means to take use of that right.[12] The stringency of his negative right to cross a border would persist, even when particular people cannot acquire the transportation needed to arrive at that border. A negative duty, in short, may be less onerous than a positive duty; we are not called upon to help migrants move, but to cease preventing that movement. What the negative duty *does* require, though, seems required with a particular stringency. The state that fails in its negative duties harms particular people, and those particular people have particularly strong claims against that state for rectification.

We can see this, I think, by examining how we react to particular cases of migration policy. Not all forms of policy designed to reduce migration achieve their purposes by coercively preventing migrants from moving across borders. Carrier sanctions, in particular, work by assigning financial penalties to airlines and boats that carry migrants without the legal documents required for entry into particular countries.[13] These financial instruments work by giving carriers a financial incentive to refrain from carrying individuals who have not been given permission to arrive at the borders of the state in question. The result of these instruments, of course, have been an increase in the number of human smugglers, given the desperation of many people to escape from violence and atrocity in their countries of origin. The consequence is, then, a thriving secondary market in migration services, which involve greater sums—and much greater risk, both of . accidents and of violence, during the journey. To travel from the Bodrum peninsula to Kos, in Greece, for instance, costs either $19 if one has a visa or $1,000 if one does not. Similarly, a boat from Libya to the Italian island of Lampedusa costs either $200 or $2,000, depending upon whether one has the "correct" documents.[14]

These policies have been put into place, of course, to reduce the number of people who arrive at the borders of the wealthy European states. Arriving at the border entitles one to an adjudication of one's claim to asylum; the European states are therefore keen to reduce the number of people whose claims will be heard, given that many of these claimants may succeed in showing themselves to have rights to asylum under the Convention.[15] Carrier sanctions, consequently, bother a great many people; they seem to make it more difficult for vulnerable people, including people with valid claims under the Convention, to obtain the relief to which they are entitled. But do carrier sanctions actually violate the right of such individuals to move across borders? How we answer that question, I think, may depend upon how we understand what it is that the sanctions are actually doing to those migrants, as they seek to move across borders.

On one view, these sanctions are coercive, and they are coercive against the migrants themselves. The migrants, after all, are the ultimate target of the coercion, and even if the coercion is aimed in the first instance at the carrier, the ultimate purpose of the sanction is to make travel to Europe difficult or impossible. We can thus understand these sanctions as being structurally akin to coercive exclusion at the border. Teresa Bloom and Verena Risse analyze carrier sanctions in terms such as these; these coercive sanctions ought to be understood as morally equivalent to the coercive exclusion of a migrant at the border. The coercion is, as they have it, "hidden," but that is a matter of concealment, rather than a moral distinction:

> In 1990, four major airlines (Lufthansa, Swissair, Iberia and Alitalia) refused to pay the fines levied against them by the UK government, on the grounds that they were being asked to "act as immigration officers." The British Home Office responded that if the airlines did not pay, they may lose their landing rights. *This is clearly an attempt to coerce in some form, as described earlier in this article, irrespective of the wider nature of the relationship, and the coercion is related to the border.* However, the coercion is not explicitly directed by the state towards the potential migrants, but hidden through other coercee/coercer relationships.[16]

If this analysis is correct, then there is no morally significant difference between the coercive exclusion of a migrant at the border, and the coercive exclusion of a migrant by an airline crew in consequence of a threatened sanction against the airline. Both of these are coercive acts directed, ultimately, against the migrant herself; and, if there is a negative right to move across borders, these sanctions violate that right as surely as a gun pointed at that migrant when she approaches the border.

This is not, however, the only view of carrier sanctions. Another view might describe these sanctions not as coercive toward the migrant herself at all; they are coercive against the airline, of course, but they are coercing that airline into withdrawing a necessary means for successful travel—and, as such, they only violate the right to migrate when that right is understood in a positive way. A failure to provide a necessary means, after all, is not in itself coercive. If the ferry between the Bodrum peninsula and Kos ceased to run, because it was no longer profitable for that ferry to be run, it would be hard to imagine that this would be viewed as coercive against the inhabitants of the Bodrum peninsula. The carrier had no obligation to provide ferry service, at least in the usual case; when it ceased to provide that service, or failed to introduce it, no one was subjected to anything that seems rightly understood as coercion. It is not clear, though, that anything here is changed when a state *makes* this ferry unprofitable, at least as regards a great many potential passengers, by financially penalizing the carrier that proposes to transport those passengers. The regulations, of course, coercively constrain the carriers; the fines imposed are not mere suggestions. But this coercion does not seem transitive. Its imposition against the carrier does not seem to entail that it is coercive against the travelers themselves.

I want to be clear, at this juncture, that I am not defending the carrier sanctions themselves. As will become clear, I think these sanctions are frequently unjust. My point, instead, is to say that the injustice of these sanctions might require us to think of the right to mobility as sometimes involving a positive right, which involves a positive obligation on the part of some other people—whether carriers or states—to provide the means through which one might arrive at a state of refuge. We feel—rightly—a great deal of empathy for the Syrian migrants who are seeking passage from Bodrum to Kos. This sympathy, though, does not entail that we must describe the sanction against the carrier as a sanction against the migrant. The sanction, instead, might be understood as merely the removal of the means by which the migrant might make use of her right to migrate. Our aversion to these sanctions, I think, might be explained with reference to a positive right to migration, on which that migrant is entitled not only to the absence of coercion at the border, but to help in the process of arriving at the border.

I should note, at this juncture, that the question of whether or not all means of preventing migration are equally coercive has been discussed before. An important debate between Arash Abizadeh and David Miller has similarly sought to illuminate the question of whether all impediments to mobility are rightly understood as coercive.[17] Miller's argument, put most simply, is that much of what we do to prevent migration is not coercion, but prevention; we do not take away all options, but merely one, through our efforts at preventing migration– and not all ways of taking away that option are genuinely coercive; an enormous and impassible wall, for instance, would seem to effectively prevent mobility across the border, while still not being rightly described as coercive. What I say here agrees, in part, with Miller; we have a reason to make sure that we are not illegitimately assuming that all ways of making movement more difficult are morally akin to threats.[18] Not all impediments to movement, then, are necessarily described as coercive; the removal of a pathway to the border might not be morally reducible to the use of coercive threats at the border itself.

I will return to the case of carrier sanctions at the end. The reason I have raised this case is because it is useful, because it shows us that we must be careful in distinguishing coercive interference with mobility, versus the failure to provide the tools needed for mobility. Coercion, I have argued, is morally significant, and those who use coercion must justify that coercion to specifically those against whom the coercion is directed. If there are some people who have a negative right to migrate, then those individuals would be immune from that sort of coercion; it could not be justified to them, and they are thus entitled to be free from interference when they try to move across the border. If some individuals have a positive right to migration, though, these individuals might stand in need of more than mere forbearance; they might stand in need of our help. We might make some progress on understanding how the jurisdictional approach might understand the morality of refuge, by examining how it would approach these two distinct sorts of right.

2. Coercion at the Border: The Negative Right to Refuge

Thus: we might begin by imagining that there are a group of people at the border to a territorial state. These people are fleeing a country in which their rights are inadequately protected. Whatever it is that constitutes an adequate degree of protection of human rights, that from which these people are fleeing falls below it. We could let these people in without ceasing to be able, ourselves, to administer a just political society, in which human rights are protected, respected, and fulfilled. Do we have any right to exclude these individuals? The answer would seem to be no; certainly, these people are not covered by the principle described in the previous chapter, which sought to explain how exclusion might be made legitimate. If we were to use guns to threaten these people when they tried to cross our borders, we would be using force to insist that they continue in a morally inadequate form of life. We would not be failing to provide them with a means; we would, instead, be actively bringing it about—through our threatened coercion—that they continue in a morally unrightful form of relationship. We would be, in other words, using force to bring about a world in which some people's most basic rights would be violated; and that seems to be a morally illegitimate use of force. In the previous chapter, I noted two possible restrictions to this conclusion: we might want people to bear some rightful share of the burden of reforming unjust states, and we might not think that individuals are always entitled to be rescued by the state they find most congenial. These restrictions, however, do not seem sufficient to rebut the basic conclusion that a state cannot rightly exclude the one at its border fleeing a state in which her human rights are inadequately protected.

The legal notion of non-refoulement reflects ideas such as this. States are wrongful when they use their distinctive coercive agency to push people back into the states from which they are seeking refuge, when those states are failing to provide a morally adequate political society. How we ought to understand the nature of "moral adequacy" here is quite complex—both as philosophy and as law. In law, the notion of non-refoulement was originally intended by the drafters of the Convention to apply only to the set of refugees themselves; signatories to the Convention were precluded from pushing refugees back to the countries from which they were escaping. The set of people entitled to non-refoulement, though, has grown larger, and now includes a number of people whose vulnerabilities do not reflect persecution but a number of distinct evils—including randomized violence, social breakdown, and other forms of inadequate rights-protection.[19]

This vision of refuge, of course, does not require us to provide everyone similarly vulnerable to injustice with the means to travel to the borders of our state. Why not? It would seem, after all, as if everyone facing an equivalent evil might have an equally strong claim upon rescue from that evil—such that all individuals, whether at our border, within their countries of oppression, or elsewhere, ought to be provided with what is needed to make use of the rescue our country represents. Why, in short, should we not think of the right to refuge as always and necessarily a positive right to help? Why should the United States, for instance, not be using its considerable military power to be airlifting people out of objectional circumstances around the world, and providing them with rights to reside within the United States itself?

There are, I think, a number of possible answers to this question. One is that the refugee at our borders stands in something like a one-to-one relationship with the particular agent from whom refuge is sought; she is seeking *our* help, not the help that might be offered by any state capable of rescuing her, and she will receive that refuge unless *we* choose to deploy coercion against her person. In other cases of refuge, the individual is offering a petition to the states of the world as a collective; when she is at our border, her speech is addressed particularly to *us*. A second answer to the question follows on from this one; she is seeking a particular *form* of relief—the right to entry into our political community—rather than relief more broadly. The one marginalized or brutalized in her own country might, in principle, be helped in any number of ways; her life might be improved by means of development assistance, humanitarian intervention, or some other form of intervention. The one seeking refuge at the border, however, is asking for one particular form of help—that which is involved in letting her cross the border, to begin her life within the political jurisdiction marked out by that border. The most important answer to the question, though, is the most basic: there is, or seems to be, a moral asymmetry between threatening to shoot at someone and refraining from offering that person some positive form of assistance. The former, to most of us, seems more difficult to justify. If this is right, then we may be right to ascribe different rights to those at our borders than to those who are similarly needy abroad. We might find it morally impermissible to threaten someone with bodily violence, as a means of preventing her from crossing the line that marks out our country's border—even if people just as needy as that person, who have not arrived at that border, cannot rightly demand that we provide them with the means to make the trip.

There are, of course, enormous issues still remaining to be dealt with. Even if someone has the right to cross the border, we might still want to examine what she will acquire after having made the crossing.[20] The distinction between permanent resettlement and more temporary forms of protection seems both important and poorly theorized. We might also inquire about the *location* of the border—in particular, when people are at sea and are prevented by a state's military from arriving on its soil. The governments of both the United States and Australia have used this form of migration control—and both have faced criticism for having done so.[21] We might, finally, ask whether or not the refuge that is demanded must be provided on the territory of the state into which access is sought. Australia, again, has begun to contract out refuge seekers to Vanuatu; the Australian government has insisted that its only obligations are to ensure that refuge is provided, rather than refuge within the borders of Australia. We might question, as many have, whether this is morally adequate, either in principle or in this particular case. At present, though, I want to ignore these issues and ask a fairly basic question: if there are people who have a right to be free from being coercively prevented from crossing a border, how might that set be understood? Who, exactly, are those people who cannot be refused entry when they present themselves at the jurisdiction's edge?

However this set might be understood, I think it could not be done with reference to the 1951 Convention. That Convention identified a particular set of people as having particular claims—and, as I will discuss, there is a certain moral wisdom in the thought that there is something held in common by the members of that set. The set of people who cannot be rightly prevented from crossing the border, though, seems to be wider than this. There are any number of ways of being treated unjustly. One can be persecuted in virtue of one's group membership, of course, but one can be brutalized for idiosyncratic reasons, subjected to arbitrary violence, victimized by official corruption, or simply starved. It would seem plausible that all of these involve people being placed into relationships that are best characterized as unjust. Certainly, these relationships involve people being deprived of those moral rights that seem rightly ascribed to them. We could, I have argued, defend the use of coercive force to prevent people from crossing the line that marks our border, given that the crossing of that line involves forcing the people already present in a country into a particular form of relationship. But we cannot similarly justify using force to ensure that someone *stays* in a morally malignant relationship. Even if I have no particularly strong obligation to provide you with positive assistance in escaping your circumstances, I cannot be held to have acted rightly in using force to ensure that you remain in those circumstances. When we use coercive force to exclude someone at the border, though, this is precisely what we do—when those circumstances involve injustice in that someone's country of origin. These moral facts are often ignored, in the modern rush to secure borders. The Trump administration, for instance, has recently announced that it will no longer regard those seeking refuge from gang violence in Central America as legitimate targets for refuge.[22] This decision, though, necessarily involves the use of American political might, to coercively return people to circumstances in which their most basic rights—including the right to life—are made vulnerable. This is precisely what I am insisting the state cannot rightly do; in using coercive force to maintain an illegitimate set of circumstances, it is not merely failing to rescue, but actively preserving a relationship of violence and injustice.

Having mentioned the Trump administration, it might be worth asking briefly about the proposed border wall that was the cornerstone of Donald

Trump's Presidential campaign. The wall might be thought to make the above analysis more complex; a wall, after all, does not propose to use violence; to use Miller's terms, it is a program of prevention, rather than coercion. If I am right, and the United States cannot use coercive force against a wider set of applicants than is anticipated by the 1951 Convention, does it follow that the United States cannot exclude that set by erecting a barrier to their movement?

I think the answer to this might be solved, in part, by noting that the wall is not simply a wall; it is, instead, a particular tool used in the course of coercive enforcement of the border. As David Bier trenchantly put it: a barrier wall or fence cannot stop illegal immigration "because a wall or fence cannot apprehend anyone."[23] Trump's wall might make it easier for guards to threaten border crossers; it is not a substitute for those guards—as is evidenced by the fact that the Trump administration's plan for the wall involves spending $8.5 billion on new border agents and inspectors.[24] (It is also worth noting that the same administration has authorized the use of "lethal force" at the border, in response to a caravan of migrants approaching that border.)[25] At a more philosophical level, we might ask what would happen were we able to effectively close a particular state's jurisdiction without having to rely upon coercive means. If the United States as we see it cannot exclude a person fleeing Central American violence, would a United States surrounded by an impassible wall be able to do so? The means by which she would be excluded, after all, would no longer involve the use of coercion. I suspect our answer to this case would depend upon the degree to which we choose to emphasize the importance of physical presence, as opposed to coercion. The one applying at our hypothetical perfect wall, after all, is still applying to *us*, and that fact might be enough to place us under a particular burden of justification as regards that person. In the world we inhabit, though, we do not need to answer this hypothetical. In this world, borders come with guns, regardless of whether or not they also come with walls.

It might be thought, though, that this is an impossible large set. The world, of course, is full of injustice; there is no society on earth that exemplifies perfect justice, and a great many that do not even come close. Do all these people have the right to enter into (say) the United States or Greece, were they to find the resources needed to make the trip? Would this not involve the vast majority of the world having strong rights to seek refuge, in the few countries in which refuge might be sought?

This impression is, I think, mistaken; the set is large, but not quite as large as it might appear. There are two reasons for this. The first is, as discussed in the previous chapter, that we are rightly held accountable, to some degree, for injustice in our own country. The burden of building justice out of injustice is incumbent upon all people, and if it ought to burden the wealthy and privileged more than it currently seems to do, it will nonetheless continue to burden those present within unjust societies as well. It is at least potentially possible for a state to insist that someone ought to work in favor of justice within her own country, when she has the resources and power needed to do so. That principle is, of course, capable of being misused; but this impugns the selfish and hypocritical appeal to that principle, rather than the principle itself.

The second reason, though, is more philosophically interesting. There is a relationship, I think, between the notion of tolerance and the notion of refuge. In foreign policy, philosophers have argued that we might have to match our own moral convictions with a certain form of principled respect for the wrong convictions of others. John Rawls gives an analysis of this sort in his analysis of the decent hierarchical society—whose laws, although not democratically legitimate, reflect a common-good conception of justice and impose genuine moral duties upon the populace.[26] I have argued elsewhere that we are right to maintain a certain degree of modesty about the degree to which we believe we have arrived at truth about what justice demands.[27] This modesty is not the same as relativism; we are not called upon to think that (for example) democratic and totalitarian forms of government are equally valid, so long as they somehow "fit" the history of a particular community. We can—and, I believe, should—insist that democracy is morally better than tyranny. What we are called upon to do, instead, is to recognize that we are very likely biased and wrong in our convictions about what democracy *requires.* We tend to examine these ideas only in the context of foreign policy; but we might also take them to have implications for who can rightly claim refuge, as well.

To see this, examine the ways in which the United States and Canada disagree. Canada takes public provision of healthcare as a morally necessary part of legitimate governance; the United States disagrees. The United States believes that the death penalty is morally legitimate; Canada disagrees. In face of these sort of disagreements, states generally accept something like a notion of toleration. The United States does not presume the right to pressure Canada to abandon its public healthcare system, and Canada rarely pressures the United States to abandon its use of the death penalty.[28] Rawls's analysis here entails the thought that both Canada and the United States—and, for that matter, some non-democratic countries as well—are reasonable ways of organizing society and ought to be treated with principled respect in international society. My own vision of this, as noted, would reflect the idea that we ought to differentiate the existence of a right answer about healthcare (or, perhaps, the death penalty) from our own confidence that we have arrived at that right answer. But Rawls and I—and many others—would agree that there is something like a notion of principled tolerance for the wrong answers arrived at by other countries. We can believe we are right, but we cannot insist upon that in justifying our foreign policy.

What I would argue, though, is that similar ideas might also affect our migration policy. Imagine that a Canadian citizen walks to the border of the United States and claims refuge on the basis that Canadian healthcare policy is an unjust infringement of freedom of contract. The US government, we might think, believes something very much like that last statement; certainly, American law reflects the thought that market freedom trumps the right to medical assistance. But the United States would wrong Canada if it were to intervene into Canadian society so as to make Canadian law reflect the American vision of freedom. The United States is bound to regard Canadian law as reflecting a mistaken view that nonetheless deserves American respect. This respect, though, entails the thought that the Canadian people should not be "rescued" from their mistaken laws—whether by means of intervention or through asylum. The principle that animates Canadian healthcare is, at worst, tolerable; and that means both that Canada is entitled to tolerance and that the one fleeing Canada is not fleeing something intolerable.

We might defend these conclusion by means of Rawls's own analysis of international justice. Rawls borrows from Philip Soper the thought that a legal system need not be fully just for it to impose duties of obedience upon those governed by that law.[29] A legal system that is capable of imposing duties, though, is one that does not wrong those within that system—they have no right to be rescued from it. Certainly, it would be odd indeed if the people had a duty to obey the commands of a legal system, and outsiders had a right to undermine that very same system. The same might be thought true for migration policy. We might think that another society's legal system reflects a false vision of justice, while still thinking that vision reflects a conception of justice that merits principled respect. My own view makes a similar point: if a state is governed with reference to a principle of public morality that can

be understood as a principle of justice, without requiring systematic decep-
tion or the abandonment of self-respect, then it is presumptively entitled to
our principled toleration. If so, then the set of people who have the right to
cross borders may not be quite so large as we would at first think. If Canada is
entitled to continue to govern in accordance with its mistaken conception of
justice, then those who are so governed are not wronged by the continuation
of that pattern of governance.

I think something similar might be said about many of the countries Rawls
would refer to as decent hierarchical societies—although I cannot hope to
make that case here. My point in the present context is simply to make the
structural point that the set of people given the right to cross borders on my
view is large, but not quite as large as it might at first appear. That view would
have to be supplemented with an account of toleration, which I have not provided here. I would also note that I have not discussed the possibility of particular vulnerabilities, as opposed to systemic ones. It is possible, after all,
that individual people might have valid claims to refuge, even when their
countries of origin are entitled to toleration, simply because of how those
countries have treated *them*, as particular people. For the moment, though,
I will return to the primary thought that the set of people entitled to immunity from coercive exclusion at the border is likely larger than the set given
rights under the 1951 Convention. There are a great many people fleeing a
great many forms of evil in this world, and however we draw the line between
the tolerable and the intolerable, it is unlikely to reflect the particular ideas
animating that Convention.

3. Coercion beyond Borders

At this point, though, I would like to return to that convention and see if it
reflects any moral ideals worth defending. The Convention begins with the
thought that persecution is a distinct category of moral wrong. There are at
least two possible responses to this idea. The first is to say that the Convention
is, simply, wrong—or, perhaps more gently, that it is a product of its origins.
It reflects the particular evil that had wracked the world in the decade before
its writing—but cannot be thought to express a timeless form of moral truth
for those of us reacting to it now. The second response is to say that there
is, indeed, something special about persecution, such that it merits particular forms of protection. Being persecuted is, morally speaking, unlike the

various other forms of moral evils we might cite in seeking refuge—and it is a form of evil to which the states of the world ought to be particularly attuned.

I want to defend a particular version of the second response. I believe there is something particular about persecution—but that the Convention reflects an adequate moral response only when what the Convention guarantees is considerably stronger than what it is generally taken to demand. To see this, we would have to go beyond the question of when we are allowed to use coercion at the border, and the related notions of toleration and justice. We would have, instead, to understand when states are morally permitted to use coercion against other states, by means of positive assistance in overcoming state oppression. The Convention, on my view, is right to focus on persecution—but it ought to be read as one of a set of legal and moral guarantees offered to those facing persecution, which collectively provide the authorization for coercive force to be directed against their persecutors.

I will, in other words, be reading the Convention as reflecting the values that later came to be codified under the heading of the Responsibility to Protect (R2P).[30] The documents defining R2P were drafted between 2001 and 2005 and argued that each state had a primary responsibility to protect its citizens from the four mass atrocity crimes: genocide, war crimes, ethnic cleansing, and crimes against humanity. Most importantly, for our purposes, R2P entails a "residual responsibility" on all states to act in defense of rights "when a particular state is clearly either unwilling or unable to fulfil its responsibility to protect itself or is the actual perpetrator or crimes or atrocities." On my reading of the Convention, that document might become morally coherent—fifty years after its drafting—by being understood as the shape taken by R2P as directed toward a particular population. However, even this form of coherence can only be defended when the Convention is understood to operate within a broader pattern of responses to state wrongdoing.

We might begin to make this case by noting what is distinct about persecution by the state. When the state becomes predatory, the normative world is inverted; that entity which is supposed to protect one's rights has become, instead, the source of the threat. Matthew Lister notices this distinct aspect of persecution and argues that the Convention reflects the thought that those who are persecuted cannot be helped where they are; we cannot offer assistance to the local authority when it is that authority that is the source of the evil.[31] This seems correct; but I would emphasize, more than the prudential worries, the fact that the evil in question seems unique precisely in how it reshapes the social world of the persecuted. The wrong seems unique, in at least three ways. The first is the simple fact already noted: the state is not simply inadequate or failing to do its job, but actively using its coercive power to wrong the individual in question. The second aspect of the wrong is more empirical and reflects the thought that persecution often ends in atrocity. If the goal of the Convention might be to pick out a distinct category of wrong, it might be relevant to note that those who begin with persecution often end with genocide. This is, of course, a matter for empirical study; but it seems, at the very least, plausible that persecution in the present is morally distinct because of what it indicates about the future. The final way in which persecution might be distinct is with reference to how it lets us associate people and communities. I have stated that the burden of making the world just falls on all, and that it might be fair under some circumstances to demand that people begin by working for fairness in their own societies. When the political organs of those societies become the origins of persecution, though, it seems unfair—to put things rather mildly—to demand that the persecuted continue to work with their persecutors in the task of building justice. One can become, as it were, *alienated* through persecution. Jean Améry describes this phenomenon nicely, as he recalls hearing the voice of someone from his native Vienna while fleeing Nazi persecution:

> I had not heard this accent for a long time, and for this reason there stirred within me the mad desire to answer him in his own dialect. I was in a paradoxical, almost perverse emotional state of trembling fear and, at the same time, surging intimate cordiality; for the fellow, who at this moment, to be sure, was not exactly after my life, but whose joyfully fulfilled task it was to take people like me in as large numbers as possible to a death camp, appeared as a potential friend. . . . At that moment I understood *completely* and forever that my home was enemy country and that the good comrade was sent here from the hostile motherland to wipe me out.[32]

This paradoxical mixture of reactions—my homeland has become my enemy—might explain what is potentially distinct about persecution. When one is persecuted, one is made an alien, while remaining jurisdictionally at home. The state that is charged with protecting one has instead chosen to make an enemy, and to treat that one accordingly.

These ideas, I think, might be used to explain what is morally distinct about the category of the *persecuted*. How, though, can we use these ideas? Not, I think, in developing an account of who it is that is immune from coercive exclusion. Instead, we might think that the set of people who are persecuted is precisely those who are *entitled* to coercion—not, here, used against their movements, but against those entities and agents that would restrain their movements. The Convention, in short, does pick out something morally significant about a particular population; but what that population shares is not best understood as a right to move, but a right to *protection*—where that protection entails both distinct rights to migrate and also some title to coercive intervention by the other states of the world. This is, perhaps, anachronistic; the Convention, after all, predates R2P by half a century. But it is perhaps not an accident that the Convention emerges from warfare and in particular from a war fought partly in defense of the proposition that humans have certain rights even against their own states. The Convention does not limit its application to times of warfare and violence. But it might be true nonetheless that the question of violence—or, at any rate, coercion—is one that should not be ignored in interpreting how this Convention should be read.

To see this, we might examine the internal moral logic of the Convention itself. That Convention gives migratory rights to those who are persecuted, when they are outside the jurisdiction of their countries of origin. That Convention seems morally incoherent, though, if it does not come along with a substantive guarantee that other countries will work on behalf of the rights of those persecuted—whether or not they have escaped the jurisdiction that has persecuted them. If there is a responsibility to protect, then this responsibility must be to *protect the persecuted*; only some members of this group, though, can protected simply by means of a granting of migratory rights. R2P, after all, demands that states bear some costs in order to assist those who are unable to escape from countries that are engaging in atrocity. The Convention must come with some obligation to engage in coercive actions against the state that is engaging in persecution. Without this obligation, there would be a difference in rights that is inadequately justified by difference between persons.

What, though, would a coherent vision of protection for the persecuted look like? It would have to entail, I think, some form of positive assistance for those who are not able to escape from the countries in which they are persecuted—whether because they do not have the means needed to move between countries or because the persecuting country is too effective in the control it has over the persecuted. We might therefore imagine that the Convention would only be morally coherent were it to be supplemented with some possible defense for coercive intervention in the governance of the persecuting society. We might, further, imagine that there might be a legitimate demand for some positive form of assistance in mobility for those unable to leave a place using their own resources. The refusal to do either, though, would seem to reflect a preference to avoid taking positive actions to assist those people most in need of being rescued from atrocity and persecution; and that, in turn, seems to reflect self-interest, at best, instead of justice.

We can, in short, defend a focus in international law upon persecution—so long as we take persecution to ground a pattern of international actions involving not only the absence of border exclusion but the taking of positive actions to assist those persecuted. The modern legal conception of the refugee might be taken to reflect valid moral considerations—but only when that conception is taken to demand more from the states of the world than they are currently willing to provide. The Convention, then, might simply reflect one way in which R2P might make demands upon the states of the world; it tells us what cannot be done to the persecuted who have made their escape. We should not read it as defining the limits of what we owe to the persecuted who have not. They are owed much more—by means of active assistance, and in the limit case military coercion—than either the Convention or conventional practice allows.

I would want to conclude this chapter with a note of modesty about even these conclusions. I have offered a partial defense of the morality undergirding the Convention; but I would not be read as insisting too strongly upon the uniqueness of persecution. It might be the case that forms of evil other than persecution similarly demand coordinated international effort. Climate change, for instance, seems potentially as capable of destroying a political community as atrocity; a society that is literally under water is, after all, unlikely to have a flourishing future.[33] I would also note that the world might arrive at circumstances in which it cannot do anything—at least, anything both morally permissible and effective—for the persecuted who remain within the country persecuting them. Moral tragedy is an unavoidable fact of life, and there may be times at which the best we can do is offer help to the few people who have managed to escape. There may well be times, in other words, in which one might be unable to both help the persecuted and to work against the persecutor. But I would insist upon the fact that we ought—sometimes—to *try*. Even if those outside their country of origin are more easily helped, it does not mean that they are morally more *deserving* of our help.

There is, I would note, something unsatisfying in the account of refuge I have offered here. I have offered a two-tiered account of refuge. One principle applies to those who arrive at the borders of the state of rescue; quite another will govern what can be expected by those who have not done so. The concept of persecution might be useful for the latter group; I cannot think it will be terribly helpful for the former. There is, however, a deeper logic in this vision. The former analysis governs what the state cannot do, by means of the coercive tools at its disposal, to prevent people from crossing the line that marks its borders. We cannot, on this account, use coercive force to force people to continue a morally malignant relationship. But the latter analysis speaks to what the state is obligated to do, by means of positive help—and, in the limit, coercive violence—to help those who are persecuted abroad. There are some people who are entitled not simply to immunity to coercion, but to coercion being done on their behalf; and the Convention is best read as part of the broad task of figuring out who those people are.

This analysis, naturally, leaves us with a great many issues unanswered. I have not discussed how we ought to share the burdens of compliance with justice; I have not offered anything close to an account of what would make a state tolerable, nor what sorts of rights those provided with rescue might rightly demand. My main point, instead, has been to argue that even the question of who has a right to move is rather more complex than it seems; it demands a focus on what that right actually requires—and may, as a result, have more than one answer. I would end this chapter by returning to the issue of carrier sanctions, as discussed above. The initial response given by many of us is that the carrier sanction is coercive and hence a violation of non-refoulement. I think this isn't quite right. The carrier sanction isn't coercion against the one seeking to migrate, but against the carrier providing him with the means needed to migrate. The real problem with the regime of carrier sanctions, instead, is that they are removing means from people who have a right not simply to purchase the means to escape from atrocity in Syria, but a right to have the other countries of the world do what they can to *rescue* Syrians from that atrocity. If the states of the world were to respond adequately to the horrors emerging from Syria, they would have to not simply refrain from using carrier sanctions, but *to start providing carriers themselves*—and, more controversially, seeking to coercively interfere with any attempt by the Syrian state to prevent access to those carriers. Most states, of course, have not and will not choose to do so. It is worth, however, ending on a note of optimism; the government of Canada, in 2016, used military aircraft to help Syrian refugees leave the Middle East for new lives in Canada. This operation—dubbed Operation Provision—was, perhaps, inadequate; it provided homes for only twenty-five thousand Syrians and focused only on those Syrians who had already fled Syria itself.[34] The government of Bashar al-Assad, moreover, continues its campaign of atrocity, with the support of the Russian government. Operation Provision, though, at least reflected the fact that those facing persecution are entitled not only to cross borders, but to our help in doing so. We have reason to prize these small bits of moral adequacy in a world that all too often makes them impossible.

6

Choosing and Refusing

On Migration, Exclusion, and the Bigot's Veto

In the previous chapter, I defended a particular vision of what states cannot do. They cannot exclude, when that exclusion causes people to remain in circumstances in which their basic rights are not respected. They cannot use coercion to exclude the people who face inadequate rights-protection in their countries of origin. While there is some need for our understanding of this set to be informed by a concept of toleration, this is still a significant constraint. And, as I have emphasized, this is merely one part of how we the basic rights of outsiders might constrain what a state can do abroad. A broader vision of refuge—one in which states not only avoided coercive exclusion, but sought to use their coercive power to defend the rights of those facing persecution abroad—might be a necessary part of our moral toolkit as well.

Not all cases of migration, though, are motivated by the denial of human rights. People move for any number of reasons: for love, for money, for professional advancement, or simply because of a desire to end up somewhere other than where we begin. I assume, for the moment, that none of these people have an antecedent general moral right to be admitted into the place they seek to resettle. Some individuals among that set might have particular claims; I will consider that question in the next chapter. But, for the moment, we can assume that no such moral claim can be made. A group of people simply want to move into a particular country—more people, in fact, than that country wants to admit. That state, moreover, has the power to admit some particular people from that set. How can it choose, while continuing to abide by the moral egalitarianism that makes liberal political theory attractive? What sorts of principles of discrimination are morally permissible, when no individual candidate for migration has a right to entry?

This chapter will consider this question—and a related one, which begins when the answers to the first one place strain upon the liberal

Justice, Migration, and Mercy. Michael Blake, Oxford University Press (2020). © Oxford University Press.
DOI: 10.1093/oso/9780190879556.001.0001

political community. The first question, then, begin with the subject of what sorts of principles of differentiation might be acceptable. States have long acknowledged that they prefer some migrants to others. Some of the reasons they have cited—such as the simple racism of the Chinese Exclusion Act, in the United States, seem profoundly unethical. Others— such as the extra points given in Canada and in Australia for youth or for education—seem potentially more permissible.[1] To see whether they are, however, we need some theoretical framework that helps us figure out what sorts of claims of justice might be made by those not selected from a set of prospective migrants. I will argue that there are significant constraints on what can be used to differentiate between migrants, even when no particular migrant has a right to admission.

The related question, though, begins with the recognition that this con-clusion will likely be unpopular, regardless of whether or not it is correct. A question rarely asked by political philosophers is what happens when the gap between what is just and what is politically possible becomes too great. We may arrive, I think, at a set of circumstances in which we can expect even tentative moves away from injustice in migration to be met with resistance from a great many current residents of a democratic community—including resistance that might place the future of that polity at risk. These circumstances, I believe, push on the limits of what political philosophy can be expected to do, precisely because they entail that we cannot move away from injustice without risking the institutions that guarantee what justice we currently have. The world, I believe, might be not only unjust, but tragic—in that we cannot find just ways to arrive at a just world, and must therefore try to figure out what sorts of injustice are the most tolerable.

Before I can arrive at these questions, though, I must defend the thought that there are significant constraints on criteria by which migrants are selected. I will discuss how we might begin to understand justice in selection in the first part of this chapter. The second part will discuss four distinct prin-ciples of exclusion that might be attractive to a state, and will examine how these might be understood from the standpoint of justice. The final section of the chapter will return to the worries about the attainability of justice, and will defend the thought that we might face in migration policy a tragic choice between doing justice and preserving the institutions through which justice might be done.

1. Immigration and Equality

I have stated that we are considering a group of prospective migrants, none of whom possess any antecedent claim to entry. None of them, in other words, are in the situation discussed in the previous chapter; their rights are adequately protected in their states of origin, and they do not make a particular claim that they are entitled to rescue by the state to which they seek admission. They would not be wronged by exclusion, as the one facing the abuse of her human rights would be wronged. That might be thought to end the ethical question; if they are not wronged by exclusion, why can the state excluding not simply exclude as it sees fit?

The reason, I think, is that particular *patterns* of granting benefits can be wrong, even when no person involved has an antecedent right to that benefit. If the United States initiated a program in which it gave free cars to all and only white male citizens, that program would seem unfair; indeed, it would seem profoundly unjust, and its injustice would be best explained with reference to the facts of its unfairness. The example is unlike that of migration, of course, in that it begins with a particular political relationship; the citizens of the country who do not receive the cars are right to feel that they have been treated as moral inferiors, in a particular political relationship—that of fellow citizen—in which they have a right to be treated as equals. But similar thoughts might extend even outside the relationship of fellow citizen. It is possible for a particular pattern of decision-making to demonstrate objectionable unfairness, even when the people involved do not share the sorts of political relationship that form the backdrop to most of our theorizing about politics.

In this chapter, then, I will conceive of the set of people who have submitted themselves for migration as having a distinct form of political relationship—both to each other, and to the state in which they seek admission. I begin by insisting that the ideal of moral equality must hold place within this relationship, as well as within the relationship of fellow citizen. To be liberal, a liberal state must acknowledge the moral importance of all persons—not simply citizens, but persons generally. To do otherwise is to place an illegitimate range restriction on the applicability of liberalism's moral guarantees, which would indeed place a notion of feudal birthright privilege back into the heart of liberal equality. The notion of moral equality, however, does not determine a unique set of political entitlements. Moral equality will demand different packages of rights and obligations in different institutional contexts.

Moral egalitarianism, in other words, is in fact compatible with distinct patterns of rights; when people live under different institutional relationships, it is only appropriate for us to infer different duties and rights as particular visions of what equality would demand. A valid analysis of the morality of immigration will have to take account of these facts. Prospective immigrants ought to be regarded as having a certain highly specific institutional relation- ship to the state to which they seek immigration. Their relationship is distinct from that held by current citizens. For example, prospective immigrants are not yet enmeshed in the set of civil and criminal laws maintained by the state; they are under no obligation to pay taxes to that state, nor can they invoke the machinery of that state in the settlement of private disputes. Accordingly, it would be a mistake to insist that their mobility rights must be identical to those of current members.

But if the relationship of prospective immigrants to the state is not that of current citizens, neither is it the relationship of foreign nationals more gen- erally. Even if the world is sufficiently interconnected that no one is without some ties to some foreign state, prospective immigrants have one highly spe- cific tie to a state that is not their own. Through their voluntary action, they have placed themselves within the coercive grasp of a foreign state for at least one act of adjudication. Prospective immigrants have voluntarily come to a border, whether literally or through the legal act of application, and have agreed to have the legal machinery of the state determine their application for membership.

This fact might be the beginning of our understanding of the rights of pro- spective immigrants. The mere fact that they are seeking a benefit to which they are not already entitled, and so have voluntarily placed themselves within a political and coercive relationship in the pursuit of this benefit, does not mean that the state in question has a right to use that coercive power in any manner it might choose. Instead, if we take the relationship of prospec- tive immigrants as a *sui generis* form of political relationship, we arrive at the conclusion that a just state has an obligation to treat such prospective immigrants as equal to one another, in virtue of the more general obligation such states, in their exercises of coercive power, have to treat individuals as moral equals. The state does not have the obligation to treat such prospective immigrants as political equals to current citizens; for instance, it is not ille- gitimate to refuse prospective immigrant the right to vote or to invoke the civil law prior to their admission to the status of immigrant. The distinct institutional circumstances of citizens and prospective immigrants mean that nothing in that treatment will violate moral equality. But the state surely does violate its duties when it treats prospective immigrants as morally unequal to one another. The reasons it gives for distinguishing among such immigrants, that is, must be reasons that could not be reasonably refused even by those whose claim to admission is denied. On this model, the state has a general right to keep out prospective immigrants; egalitarianism does not demand open borders. But when the state selects only some prospective immigrants for admission, it must rely upon reasons that reflect the moral equality of all prospective immigrants—reasons that might be accepted in the end even by those excluded. This is all that political equality among prospective immigrants ought to demand.

What would this mean in practice? It is helpful to examine here more closely the idea of having reasons that we could not reasonably reject.[2] If they are to meet this test, the reasons we give to persons must take their interests seriously as separate and inviolable moral persons. What this would mean is always difficult to determine with any degree of specificity. It will always depend upon the specific institutional context in which the guarantee of equality is to be applied. The justification of state actions to current citizens, for example, may require quite a thick package of rights and duties, including some guarantees of material equality. What is required in the context of prospective immigrants, by contrast, will be more simple, given that what is to be justified to equal persons is not an entire set of coercive political institutions, but a single coercive decision regarding admission. What we seek here are not the political guarantees of equal citizenship but the more thin forms of equal treatment appropriate to this context. Thus, the justification must be of a character that takes seriously the moral equality of persons and that could be accepted by those to whom it is addressed without requiring them to agree to their own moral inequality.

Much more could be said; but I propose to go forward with this broad vision of how to evaluate a state's proposed principle of discrimination between prospective migrants. The principle will have to treat those migrants as alike in moral dignity—and the principle will fail to do that, I believe, if one could not accept the principle's validity without also accepting one's own moral inferiority. If we could not agree with the reasoning offered in defense of the exclusion except by means of agreeing with our own moral inferiority, then we have arrived at a principle that fails the most basic test of fairness.

I do not claim that this is the only way in which a principle of discrimination might fail to accord with the demands of justice; but I believe a great many wrongful principles can be shown to be wrongful by means of appeal to this thought.

Take, for instance, the justifications offered by the Trump administration for increasing security at the southern border of the United States. Donald Trump, as candidate, began with the assertion that Mexico was "sending" criminals, including drug dealers and rapists. As president, he followed up this rhetoric with the statement that Mexican gang members (and, potentially, all Mexicans) were "animals."[3] The Trump administration claimed that such language is fair, given the crimes committed by gangs such as MS-13.[4] The problem, however, is that the justification for the increased border security has very little to do with the actual facts surrounding crime. What social science there is tends to tell us that migrants, including undocumented migrants, commit fewer crimes than non-migrants. The real justification for the increase in border security is the emotional appeal—to a world in which migrants are presumptively frightening, and Mexican migrants, presumably, more frightening than migrants from Norway. The Trump administration, similarly, has taken to hosting events with Angel Families—families who have had a loved one murdered by an undocumented migrant. The use of the Angel Families does not rest upon an impartial belief that the presence of undocumented migrants leads to murder. In discussing the Angel Families, President Trump simply insisted that undocumented people had to be more likely to commit crimes:

> I always hear that. I hear, "Oh, no, the population is safer than the people
> that live in the country." You've heard that, fellas. Right? You've heard that.
> I hear it so much. And I say, "Is that possible?" The answer is it's not true.
> You hear it's like they're better people than what we have—than our citizens. It's not true.[5]

Instead, the justification for the exclusion seems to begin with the thought that certain people are inherently worse than others, inherently more likely to commit murder—regardless of what the evidence tells. One who is excluded on the basis of this sort of emotional appeal is, I think, not capable of accepting the reasoning behind that appeal, except at the cost of accepting something very much like her own moral inferiority.

Of course, the history of immigration law is largely a history of this sort of demonization. In an earlier period, the United States sought to exclude people of Chinese descent from migration; in the election of 1888, both political parties made the continued exclusion of Chinese people a part of their respective platforms. The Republican Party platform was emphatic about this:

> We declare our hostility to the introduction into this country of foreign contract labor and of Chinese labor, alien to our civilization and constitution; and we demand the rigid enforcement of the existing laws against it, and favor such immediate legislation as will exclude such labor from our shores.[6]

The thought that the Chinese laborer was "alien" to both democracy and to the civilization of the United States was a widespread one—and, as before, it did not depend upon any showing of fact, but simply upon the assertion that the Chinese migrant ought to be excluded because he was Chinese. What is remarkable about this sort of principle of exclusion is the extent to which it is impervious to fact. What we can predict about a person's choices is a matter of empirical science, if anything; but the principles of exclusion used here barely pretend to reflect such empirics. They reflect, instead, the belief that some people are simply less suited than others to be a part of a given country's future. Those excluded because of this sort of belief, though, can rightly argue that this principle is one that does not treat them with adequate moral consideration. They could not endorse that principle without endorsing their own moral inadequacy; and those who rely upon this principle treat them unfairly in doing so.

We can say more about this sort of principle; but this might be enough to begin our discussion. So let's examine four potential principles of discrimination, that might be used by a state to differentiate between prospective migrants.

2. Principles of Exclusion

There are, of course, any number of possible principles by which states might seek to differentiate between prospective migrants. I will not try to address all possible principles here. Many states, for instance, offer migration status on the basis of wealth; one can buy the right to citizenship in Dominica for a $100,000 "donation" to its National Transformation Fund, for instance, and can acquire permanent residency in the United States by investing one million dollars into an American business.[7] A great many states, too, have principles of migration that reflect the concerns of political power; the United States, for much of the past forty years, has offered migration rights to Cubans, so as to "mark the stamp of failure" upon the Cuban regime.[8] The number of principles of discrimination is as high as human ingenuity can make it; but I believe that the moral legitimacy of any given principle might be usefully illuminated by comparison to one of the three principles discussed below.

2.1. Randomness and Idiosyncrasy

We can begin by examining those principles of exclusion which seem to involve the use of chance. There are elements of randomness found in migration law; the United States, for one, holds a Diversity Lottery, in which applicants from countries that don't send many migrants to the United States are given a chance to acquire the right to migrate. This is not, of course, the same as allocating migration places by means of a lottery, full stop; the Diversity Lottery begins with a particular vision of what sorts of diversity matter, and so reflects political philosophy as much as probability. But we could imagine a world in which the use of randomness could be extended. Alexander Guerrero has argued in favor of the use of randomness in the administration of politics.[9] Might we apply similar ideas to the governance of migration?

These uses of randomness might, or might not, be good policy—in the ordinary sense in which good policy is the best way of achieving a particular valid public objective. It's hard, though, to see how they could be judged as *unfair*. The lottery, if it obeys the standard tests of fairness in the distribution of chances, seems not to be wronging any particular person who chooses to play. The fact that some of us will react poorly to this use of randomness in migration likely reflects the thought that some of the people playing this lottery have a *right* to win—that this lottery, for instance, might exclude some people who have valid claims to asylum. Sometimes, we dislike the random distribution of a good, because we think there are particular people who can make claims to that good. (The same thing, I should note, might be true of bad things as well; David Lewis's provisional defense of randomized forms of punishment bothered many people who thought that a criminal had a *right* to that punishment.)[10] But if we're dealing with a case in which those people who have rights have been dealt with adequately, and all that remains are those people without those sorts of claims, then it seems hard to see what our complaint could be. Randomness, in short, seems fair, at least in this particular context.

A more interesting case, though, begins with the thought that randomness sometimes results not from a decision to randomize, but from the idiosyncratic desires of the person put in charge. If I am a red-headed man, and Ezekiah Hopkins founds the league of red-headed men to help people such as myself, then from my point of view it is as if a random event has placed an opportunity in my pocket. If there is no particular message of superiority for the red-headed, though, it is hard to think that those without red hair would experience their exclusion as a sort of marginalization. Similar things might seem true of migration. Between 1992 and 1994, forty-eight thousand Irish citizens were granted the right to move to the United States, under a program set up by Representative Bruce Morrison.[11] Morrison inserted language setting up his program in the 1990 Immigration and Nationality Act and seems to have been moved to do so primarily out of affection for his ancestral homeland. (It is worth noting that the United Kingdom received only six thousand visa waivers under his program.) Might this sort of proposal be defensible, as reflecting something very much like randomness?

The response here, I think, is to acknowledge the possibility that arbitrary inequality is not inherently unjust—when that arbitrariness fails to track some objectionable form of hierarchy. But there are at least three things to worry about here. The first is that many idiosyncrasies will, in fact, track objectionable things. Ezekiah Hopkins's love of red-headed men is, perhaps, unproblematic. I do not want to say that it is; we might construct a case in which Hopkins's supposed love of the red-headed is experienced by the non-red-headed as a form of social marginalization. I am more worried about the Morrison visa program, precisely because it was created out of the particular desires and affections of a member of the US Congress—which is to say, someone with an extraordinary power. It is not, therefore, surprising that Morrison chose to help Ireland, rather than (say) Gambia; there have been a great many more Irish-descended politicians in the United States than Gambian ones. That, however, might be the problem. Something that looks like a harmless decision to promote one's idiosyncratic interests can, in the aggregate, look entirely too much like a blanket policy of defending and promoting the particular interests of the powerful. The potential legitimacy of randomness as a decision-rule, then, cannot simply be assumed to defend the rule that lets powerful people rely upon their own idiosyncratic interests in giving out goods. What begins with idiosyncrasy might end up with something much more like objectionable inequality.

The second thing to note about the difference between idiosyncrasy and randomness begins from this fact; idiosyncrasy places a lot of power within a very few hands. Even if all the problems discussed above were avoided—even if, for instance, there were no misallocations of power, so that we would not worry about idiosyncratic preferences reflecting racist preferences—we might still be concerned that it is not good to have so much power here in so few hands. Explaining why this might be so could, I think, require us to go beyond liberal political philosophy and enter into the literature on domination found in the republican literature.[12] I do not have time, or the skill, needed to do this. But I think it might be true that there could be something morally objectionable about this sort of concentration of power in one particular person's hands. I am not sure that this is so; it is entirely possible that the one person doing the choosing can do so for reasons that do not marginalize or demonize anyone in particular—and, if so, then perhaps we are right to insist that the decision made by that person, since not unfair, does not constitute injustice. I think, however, that I ought to be open at least to this much: that we might want to think further about the extent to which idiosyncrasy is inherently wrong, not because of how it divides goods between prospective claimants, but because of how it divides power between the chooser and those affected by choice.

The final thing to note, though, reflects something I have mentioned above—that some of our reaction against idiosyncrasy might actually be a reaction against the use of idiosyncrasy in contexts in which some people have a right to the good in question. If I have a claim in justice to a thing—whether it be the right to migrate, the right to vote, or something else—then I am wronged when institutions work to keep that thing from me. The wrong is the same, I think, whether the decision to treat me unjustly emerges from a particular decision that I ought to be treated poorly, or from an idiosyncratic process in which a particular agent gives that good to some people (and not to me). In both cases, my primary complaint is that I have not been given that to which I am due. It does, to me, seem more galling to be denied one's rights because of idiosyncrasy; it seems, to echo the language of Avishai Margalit, both unjust and somehow humiliating.[13] But this reaction is about the use of randomness, or idiosyncrasy, in the wrong context; it does not impugn the potential usefulness of the principle itself.

2.2. Identity

When I speak of identity, I mean to refer to the aspects of the self that are used to locate one's self in the social world: one's gender, one's racial identification, one's religion, and so on. The category itself includes any number of aspects of the self that would be useful—but I want, here, to discuss two aspects that have become relevant in recent political controversies: racial identification and religious identification.

We can start with race, not because it is simple—it isn't—but because racial discrimination and oppression are widely (and rightly) taken to be the canonical forms of illiberality. If, in domestic politics, a principle can be shown to be racist, that generally suffices for us to regard that principle as having failed the test of political morality. Joseph Carens argues that we can simply say the same, in the context of migration: a racist principle of exclusion is wrongful, and wrongful in precisely the same way as a racist domestic law is wrongful.[14]

I will agree with Carens's conclusion, but I think we can do more to get there. The first thing we can note is that a racist principle of exclusion might be wrongful for a particular reason—one that is worth highlighting. Even if we were to ignore the migrant himself and simply look to the rights of the citizens of a given state, we might think that there are restrictions on how a state can rightly use its power of exclusion. What a state says at the borders, after all, is heard by people within those borders; and a given pattern of migration might prove wrongful, not because of how it treats migrants, but because of how it treats those who are socially related to those excluded.

President Trump's demonization of Mexican migrants, in other words, has effects not simply upon Mexican migrants, but upon a wide variety of people who are *perceived* as Mexican, or for that matter perceived as migrants. Quite apart from the rights of the migrants themselves, the rights of Latinx people to be treated as moral equals in the development and administration of policy—like their right to be treated as equals in policing—may be placed at risk by the Trump administration's pronouncements of how the border ought to be policed. Amy Reed-Sandoval develops the concept of the "socially undocumented" to get at this problem; one can have all the documents needed to make use of one's rights, but still be made substantively unequal by the administration's migration policy.[15] President Trump's pardoning of Sherriff Joe Arpaio, to take one example, brought home the fact that the Trump administration was quite willing to undermine the rights of Latinx citizens, so long as in so doing it showed itself to be tough on the undocumented.[16]

The structure of argument here is one that begins with the equality of citizens. A given policy of exclusion is wrongful when it sends a message to one group of citizens that they are not worthy of equal concern and respect in political life—that we look forward, in short, to a society in which they and people like them are absent. This message, of course, is not one a legitimate state can rightly send.

We can extend this argument and examine what sorts of things we can say when we look at the rights of the migrants themselves. Racist principles are wrongful, we might think, because of how they would be received by the disfavored members of that racial group—quite apart from their effects upon citizens holding to that racial identification. Race, for some philosophers, is a category that cannot be found in isolation from considerations of power and marginalization; the use of race in exclusion, then, necessarily involves the sending of an impermissible message. Take, as above, the Chinese Exclusion Act and its description of the Chinese national as "alien to [the United States'] civilization and constitution." It is hard to know how the one excluded here could interpret this, *except* to view it as a statement of moral infirmity. No Chinese person would be obliged to accept this as a potentially motivating statement; indeed, one who endorsed the sentiment it contains seems almost objectionably lacking in self-respect.

The problem, though, is that not all principles of discrimination are quite as overt about their racism as the Chinese Exclusion Act. One key thought, here, is the legal concept of a pretext. Even if a given piece of law could be justified with reference to a neutral principle, capable of being endorsed without endorsing one's own moral inferiority, we are not always obliged to understand it that way—when it is clear that the purpose for the law is one that is best understood as stigmatizing or demonizing a particular group. The history of Chinese exclusion itself offers us help here; the Supreme Court in the case of *Yick Wo v. Hopkins,* from 1886, decided that a law could be a violation of equal protection even if facially neutral, because of how that law was written and used to marginalize a particular group. The law in question was a San Francisco ordinance banning commercial laundry services from operating in a wooden structure without a permit; at the time, a great many Chinese laundries operated in wooden structures, and the law was used by the city police as a tool with which to harass Chinese laborers. The law claimed to be about safety—but how it was used demonstrated that safety was a mere pretext; racial hostility was the real ground for the law and for that law's administration:

> [While the supervisors have refrained from granting permits to] two hundred others who have also petitioned, all of whom happen to be Chinese subjects, eighty others, not Chinese subjects, are permitted to carry on the same business under similar conditions. The fact of this discrimination is admitted. No reason for it is shown, and the conclusion cannot be resisted that no reason for it exists except hostility to the race and nationality to which the petitioners belong, and which, in the eye of the law, is not justified. The discrimination is, therefore, illegal, and the public administration which enforces it is a denial of the equal protection of the laws and a violation of the Fourteenth Amendment of the Constitution. [17]

The promise of *Yick Wo* was not adequately lived up to in the years after the decision; but, at the level of morality, it demonstrated that even a facially neutral principle might not be enough to justify a particular legal act. We are often aware of the real purposes behind a law and can see clearly enough the ways in which it injures and marginalizes those people against whom it operates. As Oliver Wendell Holmes had it: even a dog distinguishes between being stumbled over and being kicked.[18]

What all this tells us, though, is that it is at least possible for a given principle of exclusion to fail the test of political morality, even if a facially neutral rationale might be provided for that principle. The interaction between race and migration is a complex and powerful one—and I can only acknowledge, here, the work that must be done to deal with that intersection. Much more can be said, in other words, about how to understand the ways in which a given principle of exclusion might be shown to violate the tests I have proposed here, in which one can rightly reject a principle that would require its recipient to assent to her own moral inadequacy. At the moment, I want to rest with the broadest possible conclusion: namely, that the use of racial animus in migration policy is morally impermissible, even when that animus is disguised by means of a fig leaf of pretext.

This, though, brings us to the issue of religion. I want, in particular, to focus on the use of religion—and the use of pretexts—in the analysis of the so-called travel ban defended by the Trump administration, which sought to bar entry from people from certain majority-Muslim countries. There are—and were—a number of problems with the ban, of which one of the most important is the fact that the ban was drafted poorly and failed to distinguish between permanent residents of the United States and those who had never even visited to the United States.[19] This is a legal failure, but it has some moral significance; a law that can't be understood is, after all, a law that can't be followed. But the most important moral question about the travel ban is simple: is there any way in which this particular sort of policy might be defensible?

We might begin by ignoring for a moment the later version of the travel ban, which sought to present the ban as being a statement about global security. While on the campaign trail, Trump called for a "complete and total shutdown" of Muslim migration to the United States. The reasons to think that this version of the ban is wrongful mirror the reasons given above. First: this ban would be experienced by Muslim citizens as a statement about their unfitness for American citizenship. In arguing that Muslims are inherently to be suspected, the ban would articulate a vision of American citizenship that could be rightly rejected by Muslim Americans. Second: the ban would likely be experienced by Muslim migrants themselves as containing a statement of their own moral infirmity. The ban asserts that the Muslim migrant is presumptively more likely to be a criminal than others; at least, Donald Trump's campaign argued in favor of a ban on Muslim migration, "until our country's representatives can figure out what the hell is going on." This presentation of the ban certainly seem to imply a shifted presumption for Muslim migrants, in which they are suspects until proven innocent—an implication that was only bolstered by Donald Trump's proposal of a Muslim registry. All these together seem to create a message in which people of a particular faith tradition are held up as uniquely unsuitable to the United States.

This, however, leads us to the travel ban itself, as eventually put into effect by the Trump administration. This ban does not begin with religion, as Trump's campaign proposals did. Rather, it articulated a national security basis, on which certain countries were described as hostile to the interests of the United States. There were at least two ways of reading this ban. The first is on the terms offered by the ban itself, which makes no reference to religion of any kind. The Supreme Court, in *Trump v. Hawaii*, chose this method of reading the ban:

> The Proclamation is expressly premised on legitimate purposes: preventing entry of nationals who cannot be adequately vetted and inducing other nations to improve their practices. The text says nothing about religion. Plaintiffs and the dissent nonetheless emphasize that five of the seven nations currently included in the Proclamation have Muslim-majority populations. Yet that fact alone does not support an inference of religious hostility, given that the policy covers just 8% of the world's Muslim population and is limited to countries that were previously designated by Congress or prior administrations as posing national security risks.[20]

Justice Sotomayor, in dissent, argued in favor of reading the ban in terms more closely related to the ones I have defended here:

> Based on the evidence in the record, a reasonable observer would conclude that the Proclamation was motivated by anti-Muslim animus. That alone suffices to show that plaintiffs are likely to succeed on the merits of their Establishment Clause claim. The majority holds otherwise by ignoring the facts, misconstruing our legal precedent, and turning a blind eye to the pain and suffering the Proclamation inflicts upon countless families and individuals, many of whom are United States citizens. Because that troubling result runs contrary to the Constitution and our precedent, I dissent.[21]

There are, of course, matters of constitutional interpretation I am ignoring here; Justice Roberts's decision argues, in particular, that the Court ought to be mindful not to try to replace the judgment of the executive with the judgment of the Court—and that the Court should therefore defer to the executive in determining what motive can be ascribed to the ban itself. Deference aside, though, the Supreme Court's decision here refuses to read the ban in precisely those terms that are most appropriate to understanding how it will be lived by Muslim Americans. The presence of a pretext of national security should not be enough for us to ignore the fairly obvious conclusion that the ban is motivated by antipathy, rather than security; and, if what I have said here is right, this sort of ban cannot be taken as morally legitimate.

All this, of course, tracks what was discussed above under the heading of race. But there are some added complexities, in this context, that are worth exploring. The first is that we might, under some circumstances, arrive at a world in which concerns such as security are highly correlated with religion. (For a possible example, we might look at Aum Shinrikyo, the religion responsible for the Tokyo sarin attack, and whose stated goals included bringing about the end of time.)[22] Religion, in contrast with race, brings with it canonical statements of belief, as well as rules of conduct; it is not outside the realm of possibility that a religion could emerge whose adherents are highly likely to engage in certain forms of wrongdoing. I do not think we are at that place; I also believe that it is highly likely that those claiming that we *are* at such a place are doing so for bad reasons—they are likely asserting that we are in that emergency situation for reasons of political demonization, rather than security. Nevertheless, it is worth asking what our response ought to be were we to arrive at these circumstances. From the fact that religious identity would provide, here, good information about criminal proclivities, it does not follow that we could use that information. Randall Kennedy's analysis of racial profiling seems appropriate here: even if we could use race well in policing, we should not use it, because the long-run effects on equal citizenship might be worse than the short-term effects on policing. A society in which African Americans are regularly stopped by police, Kennedy argues, is one in which the fabric of unity between citizens and policy begins to fray—and that is a fate worse, Kennedy argues, than the failure to maximize number of criminal prosecutions.[23] We might say something similar about migration. Even if we could use this information to exclude the violent, we might do some damage to the ability of the marginalized citizen to see herself as a member of society—and that, in the end, might be morally more significant than even the maximization of security. The argument of the previous chapter was, in part, that there are moral reasons apart from self-interest for states to act; states must bear some costs, in the name of protecting rights. The same holds true here; we cannot think that the most efficient means of providing security is necessarily a permissible one.

The final bit of complexity is that, if we are looking at the ways in which religious preferences in migration are going to be understood, we have to acknowledge that not all forms of religious preference are going to be the same. At a time in which there is a significant global bias against a particular religion, say, a preference *for* members of that religion might reflect justice rather than bias. Thus, the United States in the 1970s put pressure on the Soviet Union to allow the migration of Jews to Israel—a decision justified because of the antecedent Soviet *hostility* to its Jewish citizens.[24] A decision to prefer adherents of one religion, in other words, might reflect something other than animus, when the world in which that decision is made is treating the members of that religion poorly. Even here, there is some room for worry; it is one thing to use this sort of method and quite another to use it well. Ted Cruz, for instance, argued that the United States ought to focus on Christian migrants, given the extent to which they were persecuted throughout the world.[25] Even if the structure of his argument is right, the content of that argument seems wrong; Christians are indeed persecuted, but so too are Muslims, Buddhists, and any number of other people—and we could only evidence a preference for Christians were we able to make the case that they are uniquely persecuted, and we are uniquely positioned to help them. These are matters of empirical fact; but I think it unlikely that either case could be made.

2.3. Skills

Countries tend to look for newcomers who provide what is in short supply among those already present; those who have scarce and valuable skills often find doors open to them that would be closed to their less-skilled compatriots. The degree to which skills are valued differs for each particular country. Canada, for instance, prioritizes scarce skills more than the United States—which tends to prioritize family unification. What counts as a valuable skill, moreover, tends to be somewhat distinct in different societies. All countries, however, provide some means by which to hold open a pathway to migration for particular people who have scarce and valuable skills. The United States, despite its emphasis upon family unity, also makes migration easier for those with such skills—including a particular visa classification for what are called "aliens of exceptional ability."[26]

All this is quite interesting from the standpoint of policy; but what can be said about these facts, from the standpoint of justice? If something is unjust, after all, it must be unjust toward someone. If we want to advance a claim that the preference for the skilled is unjust, we must understand who it is that could make that claim. Who, here, might have be able to make the case that they are being treated unfairly?

There are at least three possibilities, I think: unfairness might be felt by the prospective migrants not selected; by those who are already present in the country to which migration is sought; or by those who have been left behind in the country from which migration is sought. The latter possibility is often discussed under the heading of the "brain drain," and I have argued previously that brain drain does indeed represent a potential form of injustice. I have also argued against the right of a developing society to keep its own human capital by making exit from that society more difficult.[27] Here, I would want only to note that we might impugn the decision to allow the migration of the skilled, because of the effects of the migration upon the impoverished citizens left behind—but that we should be very careful indeed, before doing so, for two reasons. The first is that the empirical effects of migration are exceptionally complex, and the decision to close the borders to the skilled might end up damaging the skilled and the unskilled alike. The second is that we ought to be quite careful before thinking that the burden of bringing the world into compliance with justice is one that ought to be borne by the skilled citizens of the developing world.

We might, instead, look to the thought that the preference for the skilled is unjust because it is unfair to the local citizenry. This is the thought behind Donald Trump's claim, discussed in the first chapter of this book, that the United States has inadequately protected its own citizens. The contours of this justification, though, need to be made clearer. Imagine, for instance, that it is true that the importation of a given group of skilled workers—say, skilled computer engineers brought to the United States under an H1-B visa program—drives down the wages of the local population of computer engineers. What, exactly, is the nature of the unfairness? A bad argument, I think, would be that it is unfair simply because the net effect of the migration policy is a lowering of local wages. While the lowering of the wages is the start of an argument, it is not a conclusion. We do not have, as it were, a human right to have our current wage preserved. A better argument, I think, might begin with the thought that distributive justice—in particular, the gap between the wealthy and the less well off—can be undermined because of the presence of these newcomers. If migration has the effect of lowering wages, while also lowering worker solidarity and increasing corporate wealth and power, a theory of justice that condemns such things would potentially be able to condemn the policy that brought these skilled migrants into society. (To make matters more complex, it might also be true that corporations can benefit from even nominally undocumented labor; some corporations seem to relish hiring the undocumented, precisely because of the vulnerability imposed upon them by their legal status.)[28] All this might ground a democratic decision to refuse to seek out certain kinds of migrants, in the name of distributive justice.

I do not want to say this is wrong; but I do want to make two moderating claims against this sort of argument. The first is that an argument that begins with distributive justice would have to acknowledge the force of distributive justice at the global level, as well as at the domestic one. I do not believe that distributive justice has the same meaning between states as it does within them; but this is not the same thing as taking it to have no meaning in the international realm. A theory that grounds the right to exclude on the needs of distributive justice, then, would have to figure out how to understand wealth and poverty at the global and at the local realm, and how to balance these two concerns—which means, in short, that it might be more difficult than we think to arrive at a single conclusion about how to defend distributive justice by means of migration policy.

The second moderating claim echoes this, but notes the empirical complexity of economic analysis here. As mentioned above, the actual effects of any given program of exclusion are complex. So, too, are the effects of any given program of inclusion, such as a preference for skilled labor. To be confident about the relationship between this program and distributive justice, we would have to know a great deal—more, I think, than we do—about the effects of migration on wages. At any rate, as before, we could not use these ideas to exclude the truly desperate unless we were willing to make the rather implausible claim that distributive justice ought to trump basic survival.

This leads us to the final way in which a preference for skills might be unjust: it might be unfair toward those among the prospective migrants who do not have those skills. Here, I believe the argument will find significant difficulty. What is wrong with such documents as the travel ban is that they seek to dress up mere animus in the clothes of a neutral concern for security. A preference for the skilled, however, is itself that sort of neutral concern. A preference for skilled physicians, for instance, seems to be a preference that does not in itself rest upon anything approaching animus or moral incapacity. It is possible, of course, that our *perception* of who has a particular set of skills might reflect something like animus. The permission to prefer those likely to do a needed job well does not cover the exercise of bias in predicting the future. (A family story might serve as an example: my mother was a computer scientist in the 1960s, and while at Jet Propulsion Labs helped program the Mariner missions to Mars. IBM sought her out for an interview, based upon her work, but then proceeded to tell her that it would not hire

her, since it could not predict what a woman computer scientist would do.)
Nor is a society immune from a charge of bias in its analysis of what sorts
of jobs are genuinely necessary; it is possible, for instance, that we might be
guilty of sexism in setting up the list of qualifications that provide prospective migrants with the right to move. It is also possible—as Lori Watson has
argued—that the skills themselves are distributed, at the global level, in accordance with biased principles.[29] If societies are predictably sexist, then
they can be predicted to spend more money and time on the education of
boys than on girls, with the result that the apparently neutral preference for
the educated can end up reinforcing—and benefiting from—global sexism.
All this is true, and global sexism might require countries to work together at
the global level—but none of this necessarily requires that *migration* should
be the site at which the resistance begins. If I am in need of an appendectomy
in a racist society in which only white men can be surgeons, I take it I have a
permission to hire a white surgeon. The obligation to resist racism, here, does
not entail the obligation to pretend that the skills of the surgeon are not rare,
nor that they are valuable. So, too, with the skills sought out by the society at
the border.

The preference for the skilled, in short, might have a tendency to reinforce
global injustice and might on occasion exacerbate domestic distributive injustice; but it cannot in itself be said to be an intrinsic injustice, as the preference for a particular racial or religious group would be. The one who is
refused in favor of a more highly skilled candidate is not treated unfairly, in
the manner discussed above. She is, instead, provided with a reason for her
comparative disadvantage that we can expect to motivate her—without it
relying, covertly or overtly, upon her own moral incapacity.

3. The Bigot's Veto

At this point, it is worth taking stock. The principles I have defended allow
the state to have some leeway in deciding which migrants to take. They are,
at the very least, more friendly to state agency than those whose principles
mandate open borders. These principles, however, seem also rather restrictive, at least in comparison to the world in which I write these words. The set
of people who have a right to cross borders—including the border marking
out the United States from Mexico—will be significantly larger than is recognized in current domestic law. Indeed, if the argument of the previous

chapter is correct, the United States—like all countries—may have an obligation to use its power to work abroad to undermine unjust and malignant forms of government, and as part of this effort might have an obligation to build ways in which those oppressed abroad can actually make their way to refuge in the United States. No country, moreover, may rely—either overtly, or as a pretext—upon racial or religious preferences in the determination of who may be admitted. No country, finally, can look only at domestic effects in deciding what pattern of skilled migration is best; a concern with distributive justice, I have argued, must entail a concern for both global and domestic distributive justice. What I write here, in other words, is rather restrictive. Even if what I write here is unduly conservative for many philosophical liberals, it would likely be felt unduly liberal if brought forward as the platform of a political party.

This, however, might give rise to a problem. I do not mean a problem from the standpoint of philosophy; what I say is right, or wrong, based upon what can be said about the arguments I provide. It is a problem, however, if what I say is simultaneously correct and incapable of being put into play in societies as we know them to be.

The past decade has demonstrated some uncomfortable truths about liberal democracies. Whereas John Rawls had assumed—blithely, in retrospect—that anyone raised in a liberal democracy could be relied upon to preserve the norms of liberal democracy, we have seen in the past decade a staggering resurgence of right-wing populism and authoritarianism.[30] Weak but existing democracies, such as those in Hungary or Turkey, have begun to twist into things closely approximating single-party authoritarian regimes. While it is an exaggeration to think of Donald Trump as a dictator, he has demonstrated an affinity for authoritarian methods—and for authoritarians themselves, as his friendships with Rodrigo Duterte and Vladimir Putin demonstrate. We have begun to see, I believe, how wrong Francis Fukuyama was when, in 1989, he forecast the end of history. Once the Soviet Union fell, rather than a global agreement on liberal democracy, we ought to have seen the resurgence of something altogether more nasty and tribal. The past decade has seen an increasing willingness, particularly on the part of white working-class citizens of wealthier societies, to think that their stagnant wages are ultimately the fault of people of color and foreign nationals. Frederick Harris and Robert Lieberman note that the rise in authoritarian politics in the United States has come precisely at the time that white working-class Americans have faced a decline in their standard of living; more than half of these people, moreover, agree with the assertion that racism against whites is as prevalent or more prevalent than racism against non-whites.[31]

All this, of course, is not philosophy. It might be shown to be relevant to philosophy, though, when we reflect upon the relationship between the increased diversity that begins with migration and the rise of popu-list movement that promises resistance against migration—and the return of power to those who perceive themselves as having lost it. The United States, of course, is one example; it is no accident that Donald Trump began his campaign by decrying migrants from Mexico. But this is by no means an American phenomenon. Take, for instance, the Nordic countries, tradi-tionally felt—by liberal North Americans like myself—to be bastions of so-cial justice. In the past decade, migration from the Middle East and North Africa to these countries has increased. The result has been a marked in-crease in policies and parties opposed to these migrants and to their forms of life. Denmark, for instance, has begun officially classifying some mi-grant communities as "ghettos" and has mandated that children raised in those communities spend several hours a week away from their parents.[32] In Sweden, the nationalist Sverigedemokraterna has made a surprising bid for power; the party was founded by neo-Nazis and is committed to re-ducing migration to Sweden.[33] We could, indeed, write a fairly long list of parties and politicians who have used fear of the unassimilable outsider as the basis of their political programs.

Why, though, is any of this a problem? The answer, I think, is in how it might give rise to a tragic choice for liberal theory. I want to make three distinct claims—all of which rest upon empirical evidence, but for which I think that evidence exists. The first is that we have seen, in the past decade, increased evidence that a great many people simply do not *want* to do politics with outsiders. The precise ways in which the line between the insider and the outsider is constructed are always distinct, of course; but that the line continues to exist, despite our nominal shared commitment to moral egalitarianism, seems hard to dispute. The second claim I want to make is that an increase in social diversity, when there is a backdrop of significant felt opposition to that diversity, may tend to undermine social trust. The Pew Research Center has been gathering data about trust in the United States for over half a century. In 1958, over 70% of their respondents reported feeling trust in the federal government; in 2015, only 20% said the same. In 1972, almost half of Americans said that most people could be trusted; the number is now slightly over 30% and falling steadily.[34] It would be too easy to say that all of this is the result of increased diversity; but increased diversity, and the racial resentment of whites who increasingly view themselves as the victims of programs designed to help racial minorities—including migrants—is undoubtedly one factor. At the very least, right-wing politicians have increasingly used this factor for political purposes. This leads to the third, and final, claim I want to make: a reduction of social trust is deeply worrying because the political system itself depends upon the voluntary action of a great many people for its preservation. The withdrawal of even a few people's labor can end up destroying the system, or at least its ability to adequately perform its job. Gene Sharp, the celebrated theorist of civil disobedience, noted this well; malignant societies can be brought to their knees by a relatively small number of people withdrawing their will to participate in the methods and norms set up by the state. The problem, though, is that this phenomenon isn't one that works only when the labor is withdrawn by activists. The state can be brought to its knees as easily by the nativist as by the human rights lawyer.

All this, I think suggests that the morality of migration might be rather more complex than we at first believed. I think it is possible that following the proposals I lay out here might increase support for populist and anti-immigrant movements. At the very least, I am confident that the more robust proposals of Kieran Oberman and Joseph Carens would do so. Carens, at one point, writes dismissively about the effects of increased migration upon domestic governance:

> We know how to admit immigrants. Despite occasional political rhetoric that the boat is full, no democratic state in Europe or North America can pretend that it could not take in many, many more immigrants it does now without collapsing or even suffering serious damage.[35]

This, however, isn't the point. It's not whether the boat is full; it's whether or not those already present in that boat will continue to *row*.

These worries reflect, I think, some of those given by David Miller; but, where he takes the particular and the local as reflecting the proper limits of ethics, I take this simply as a sort of human pathology. Terry Pratchett once wrote that humans had a natural design flaw—a tendency to bend at the knees.[36] To this, I would add another: a temptation to think that the word for *stranger* ought to be functionally the same as the word for *thief*.

I am not the only person to have had these worries. Hillary Clinton, speaking after the announcement by Angela Merkel that she would be stepping down, identified similar concerns:

> I think Europe needs to get a handle on migration because that is what lit the flame... I admire the very generous and compassionate approaches that were taken particularly by leaders like Angela Merkel, but I think it is fair to say Europe has done its part, and must send a very clear message—"we are not going to be able to continue provide refuge and support"—because if we don't deal with the migration issue it will continue to roil the body politic.[37]

Clinton is speaking, here, not in defense of a roiling body politic; she believes, we might imagine, that the resurgence of right-wing populism in Germany is an unmixed evil. She is, instead, merely asserting that Germany might be facing a kind of tragic choice. It can do justice for the world's most miserable now, but at the cost of undermining the very institutions that put it in place to do that good. It can, instead, preserve liberal democracy, but at the cost of excluding some people with very good claims against that sort of exclusion. What it can't do, says Clinton, is avoid sacrificing *something*. It can preserve its liberalism or act upon that liberalism; it cannot do both.

If all this is right, then, I think Germans—like the rest of us—have a tragic choice. By tragic, I mean not simply difficult, or vexing; I mean, instead, that there does not seem to be any morally rightful way forward—one without some significant moral cost, such that we ought to hesitate before accepting it. On the one hand, we could simply assert that liberal justice forbids racial or religious discrimination in migration. We might, that is, simply say: let justice be done, though the heavens fall. (A philosophical friend of mine, upon hearing these ideas, put this nicely: we're in the business of saying what the truth is about ethics—we're not in the business of worrying about idiots.) This is coherent; but it is potentially costly, as well. In the limit case, it might place stressors upon the preservation of the society in question, if a great many people were to cease to find that preservation morally appealing. As the old saying goes, the Constitution is not a suicide pact; we must not interpret it in a way that leads to the breakup of the Union. The same could be said, though, for the project of liberal justice itself.

So: we might try the other tactic. We do not do what justice requires in the space of migration, because doing justice would undermine the ability of our institutions to preserve themselves—and, indeed, to continue doing what justice they can. This would create, as it were, a sort of bigot's veto, in which the racist and the nativist are given a right to prevent the administration of justice, by threatening—implicitly or otherwise—to make the society itself ungovernable. This is unpalatable, of course. We do not want liberal justice to bow to the demands of the illiberal. But a liberalism that refuses to acknowledge these people seems arid and theoretical—a toy theory, useful in some contexts, but incapable of guiding us in the real and messy world we inhabit. We can say racists and nativists are wrong, after all; but we cannot claim that they do not *exist*—and any theory that does is doomed to irrelevance.

This, I think, represents a genuinely tragic choice. Neither option is appealing—and neither option leaves the one who chooses it free from the taint of serious wrongdoing. We might seek to make this tragedy less stark, of course. We might seem to increase infrastructure, including educational infrastructure, so that we are no longer so tempted to see the outsider as competitor. We might try to build educational institutions that work against nativism and racism. All of these might blunt the edge of the dilemma; I do not think they can eliminate it. Both solutions seem to regard people's aversion to outsiders as beginning in the world of reasons. The solutions try to change material circumstances, so that people no longer have a reason to be hostile to migrants; or they seek to demonstrate that hostility to migrants is irrational. The problem, I think, is that much of the hostility to migration emerges not from reason, but from something far less cognitive: we are hostile, I think, to what is unfamiliar, jarring, out of place, and we are most hostile when we are most acutely aware of our own vulnerability. If there is a way of overcoming this tragedy, it will emerge not from the space of reasons, but from the simple fact that what begins as unfamiliar can eventually become familiar. Take, as an example, the rather remarkable alteration in attitudes toward gay men and women in the last half of the twentieth century. Widespread social hatred and disapprobation gave way to something approaching social toleration; this last might not be enough, of course, but it is nonetheless extraordinary given the starting point. The explanation for this, though, seems to begin not in the space of argument, but simply in the fact of visibility; as more and more people came out as gay, more and more people became used to—and comfortable with—homosexuality itself.[38]

If there is a solution to the tragic dilemma here, I think it would have to make use of these ideas. Familiarity, and time, might eventually bring us to accept what was once alien and strange. The Chinese Exclusion Act is appalling, not only because of its immorality, but because it relied upon a demonstrably wrong premise; migrants from China were *not* hostile to the Constitution, and those who wrote that act should have known that truth, even then. We might do justice in migration, and hope that we look back upon the injustices of the present age—the travel ban among them—with a similar eye. What cannot be avoided, though, is the thought that even this is a risk; we are hoping, to put it bluntly, that time and familiarity are more powerful than racism and bigotry. I think the bet is worth taking; but I do not claim that it is not, in the end, a bet, that might go wrong. Liberal justice, we might conclude, is a risky undertaking, in any world that resembles this one. In order to create a just world, we must hope not only to be virtuous, but to be lucky as well.

7

People, Places, and Plans

On Love, Migration, and Documentation

In the previous chapters of this book, I have looked at what states cannot do to those who propose to move across their borders. Liberalism, I have argued, does not demand open borders; states may exclude some unwanted would-be migrants, and may use some forms of coercion in doing so. There are some individuals, however, who have a right to cross borders, simply because of what is happening to them within the borders they currently inhabit. Their lives do not include that to which they are entitled simply in virtue of their humanity, and they therefore have a claim against the rest of the world's states to something very much like asylum. The other states, at the very least, cannot rightly use coercion to keep those particular migrants from moving. The claims of these migrants, though, are general—in the sense that they speak to the set of states in the world, as a whole, and argue that what is happening to these migrants ought to be a matter of concern to all. People are, here, understood primarily with reference to the vulnerabilities and dangers faced by all humans.

Some migrants, though, can make more particular claims on particular states. Sometimes, this emerges because of what those particular states have done to the migrants themselves, or to people very much like them. I have already mentioned Michael Walzer's arguments that the Vietnamese displaced by the Vietnam War had a right to entry into the United States; these particular migrants, argues Walzer, were made American, in virtue of how American violence was brought to bear upon their country.[1] Other times, though, the claim of particularity emerges not from what the state has done, but from what the *migrant* has done—or what she would very much like to do. In this chapter, I will focus primarily upon this last form of particularity. Some migrants present themselves as having rights to particular relationships with a society in which they do not (legally, at least) belong. They seek to preserve what they have built in the past and to build something new for the future. There are, of course, many possible specific forms such

Justice, Migration, and Mercy. Michael Blake, Oxford University Press (2020). © Oxford University Press.
DOI: 10.1093/oso/9780190879556.001.0001

claims might take. In this chapter, I will examine only three: claims beginning with a particular *affinity* for a particular place; claims beginning with the rights and interests of the *undocumented*; and the claims that begin with the imperative of *family unification*.

The thesis of this chapter will be primarily negative: comparatively few of these particular claims are rightly thought to give rise to demands of justice. States can, in many cases, refuse to admit newcomers, even when the force of these particularistic bonds are very strong. Those so excluded are not treated unfairly, and so are not treated unjustly. This is not, I should emphasize, the same as saying that a refusal to accommodate a great many of these claims is morally praiseworthy. I will argue in the final chapter of this book that a morally adequate state will develop some policy instruments by which the particular claims of outsiders such as these are to be provided with the migratory rights they seek. A good polity, that is, will include a legal right to unify with one's spouse, a legal program allowing some people to move so as to make use of local resources and opportunities, and some program of amnesty or regularization for the long-term undocumented. These legal rights, though, are not best defended with reference to the norm of justice, but the distinct norm of mercy; and, while some of those seeking amnesty will have a right in justice to that amnesty, it ought to be granted to a number of those who have no such right. We show ourselves to be callous and unmerciful, I believe, when we do no more than merely refrain from injustice. In the present chapter, though, I want to make the negative case, prior to building this positive one. The migratory claims of many people with whom we are instinctively in sympathy are not themselves required by justice. If this is thought hard-hearted, I would like to reiterate that what I say here is not intended to undermine the moral importance of the claims under consideration. It is, instead, intended to impugn the assertion that such claims are only, or best, interpreted with reference to the idea of justice.

1. Particularity and Place

We might begin with the most conceptually simply, but most unrealistic, of the particular claims I will consider. Imagine that someone wishes to migrate to a new country, because that country has within it those things that are most required for her particular vision of what her life ought to be. The plans she makes might be bound up with the physical nature of the country itself; her plans might be, as Anna Stilz has it, *located*, and her located life-plan might involve some jurisdiction to which she has no particular title.[2] If I want passionately to become an oceanographer but have legal citizenship only within a land-locked country, I might seek the right to go to a particular country with a coastline. Other people might want to make use of the distinctive human institutions and relationships found within a particular place. Perhaps the place in question is one that would enable me to fulfill my religious duties, as I understand them. Perhaps, more simply, I *want* to go to that place; writers often want to settle in Paris, and we might want that fact itself to ground a claim that Paris should be open to their presence. Many academics, on a less romantic note, have sought out education or opportunities in countries not our own; I wanted to move to California for my doctorate, specifically because Debra Satz was (and is) in California, and my education and my career would both have suffered were I prevented from doing so.[3]

We will consider later what might be different if I have already begun to build a life within a particular place; we will consider, in the present section, only what claims I might make that look toward my desire that my future have a particular shape. Kieran Oberman, recall, differentiates between attachment and possibility, where attachment refers to what has already been built—and possibility refers to what is simply desired. Here, we are looking at (mere) possibility. If I want very strongly to move to California—if, indeed, I can make the case that my life, in the absence of the right to move to California, would be fundamentally worse than my life in the presence of that right—can we therefore say that I have a moral right to make that move?

My answer, not surprisingly, is no. The discussion here echoes what was said about Oberman's view, in chapter 2. One has a *right* to this sort of movement—one is treated unjustly if prevented from moving in these ways—only if one has a right to the greatest possible set of opportunities; and, as I have said, I do not think that right exists. Most notably, I do not always have the right to the cooperation of others in the pursuit of my particular goal. In moving to California, I did not only create a relationship with Debra Satz (and, for that matter, the various other students and faculty in the Department of Philosophy). I created, in addition, a particular relationship with the other people who were liable to the laws of the state of California—not to mention those people liable to the laws of the United States itself. The intensity of my desire to be a philosopher did not, in itself, create an obligation on the part of these people to let me in. If they had refused—if they had decided to vote for legislators who shut down the F-1 visa program—I could not claim that they had wrongly interfered with my freedom of thought, or freedom to pursue my education.

I would also note, moreover, that whatever these last freedoms mean, they do not in general make it wrongful for me to be sometimes asked to adjust my desires. We understand this, I think, when it comes to time. The United States, in the twenty-first century, has no particular opportunities available for town criers, shepherds, or for lamplighters. My freedom of opportunity is not denied when I am told to adjust my ambitions to that set of jobs available to me in the present. The same, however, seems to hold true across space, as well as time. If there were one remaining political community in which the town crier is a viable option, it does not follow that I have a moral right to enter into that community—no matter how much I would like to do the job. The intensity of my subjective desire for the job does not create an obligation on the part of that community's citizens to enter into political relationship with me.

All this, of course, is rather familiar; it echoes what I said earlier. It is, however, useful to be reminded of these conclusions, before moving on to more complex—but more realistic—cases of particular claims to migration. In both of these cases, I think, whatever rights we defend will have to rest upon factors distinct from mere intensity. If justice defends the right to migrate, in these cases, it will have to say more than that the right to migrate is *desired*.

2. The Undocumented

By the *undocumented*, I mean those individuals who are currently residing within a political community, without the legal right to be present within that community. The rights of the undocumented have been a matter of some political controversy—to put things rather mildly—for the last decade at least. Right-wing populism, in North America, Europe, and Australia, has been arguing for an emphasis upon border security; the undocumented are the greedy outsiders, come to take jobs from the deserving. The rise of populism has created its own antithesis, in which a nascent movement for the rights of the undocumented has insisted—in the United States, in particular—upon the rights of the undocumented to social equality; we are undocumented, as the saying has it, and unafraid.

This broad picture, of course, conceals a great deal of diversity; and the debate over the rights of the undocumented tends to ignore a great many potentially relevant differences. The undocumented exist not as abstractions, but as particular people residing within particular societies, each of which has its own history, and its own ways of coming to term with that history. The abstract category of the undocumented, after all, simply marks out presence without legal permission; it does not, in itself, differentiate between cases that are likely to provoke rather different moral reactions. Take, on the one hand, Angela Luna, an American citizen who in 2004 overstayed her Japanese visa by two weeks—thereby becoming, in the eyes of the Japanese government, present without right and guilty of a crime. Luna was held for several hours in a Japanese jail, before being barred from returning to Japan for five years— which she regarded as excessive:

> We were treated like criminals. . . . I am upset about it, especially since a lot of it is political and not a glitch in the bureaucratic system. The punishment certainly didn't fit the crime.[4]

In the same year, at least twenty-one undocumented Chinese workers drowned in Morecambe Bay while picking cockles. Morecambe Bay has treacherous tides; the Chinese workers spoke little English and could not understand the warnings from other cockle pickers that they were in danger of being cut off. The workers had paid human smugglers associated with the Snakehead gang to be transported from Fujian province to England's coast, only to discover that they were to be held in virtual slavery upon their arrival. Fujian is one of China's most impoverished provinces, and the men who were trafficked were seeking money for their families that remained in poverty. Li Hua, one of the few survivors of the event, now lives in witness protection in the United Kingdom; he was willing to testify in court against the gangmaster who supervised the workers, and his life therefore continues to be in danger.[5]

One problem, then, is that the category of the undocumented includes both Li Hua and Angela Luna—two people for whom, I suspect, we have wildly different degrees of sympathy. Li Hua paid a trafficker to move him to the United Kingdom, but did so as a result of Fujian's grinding poverty and the lack of alternative possibilities. Angela Luna, in contrast, chose rather arbitrarily to remain in a country without that country's permission—thereby becoming, for a week at least, undocumented. If we are to develop an adequate theory of justice for the undocumented, it will have to be one that reflects the fact that being *undocumented* is not enough for us to draw a strong moral conclusion.

One obvious difference between the two, of course, is the simple fact of *time*. Angela Luna spent a mere two weeks as an undocumented resident; Li Hua spent considerably longer. Joseph Carens relies on considerations such as these in his analysis of the ethics of amnesty. For Carens, the right to remain—even when one's entry is without right—is grounded in the fact of what he calls *social membership*. Those present in a place build a life for themselves within that place—and, over time, the line between the place and the life itself become blurred. The ties we build become so central to our identity that these ties ought to be preserved—even if we were not within our rights to have made those ties in the first place:

> Fifteen years is a long time in a human life. In fifteen years connections grow: to spouses and partners, sons and daughters, friends and neighbors and fellow-workers, people we love and people we hate. . . . We sink deep roots over fifteen years, and these roots matter even if we were not author-ized to plant ourselves in the first place. The moral importance of [one's] social membership ought to have outweighed the importance of enforcing immigration restrictions.[6]

Joseph Carens describes, to buttress his argument, the case of Miguel Sanchez, who was unable to pay the bills in his hometown, lived in fear there of police violence, and now resides without legal right in the United States.[7] Sanchez, argues Carens, has a right to remain because the life he lives now—under constant threat of deportation—is morally unacceptable. He is a member in fact of the United States, and what he has built within that country must be respected. Carens concludes that deportation, after a certain period of residence—he suggests three to five years—is inherently unjust.

This argument is a powerful one. It is not the only one that might be made. Adam Hosein has argued that the moral key to the rights of the undocu-mented is not simply time, but also agency.[8] In particular, the state must seek to justify its coercive law to all those so coerced—documented and undocu-mented alike. Respecting the agency of the undocumented, however, would require the state to provide those people with the ability to make plans and live in the knowledge that they will not be subject to the sudden and unex-pected destruction of everything they have built. Hosein shares with Carens the thought that living under the threat of deportation is a presumptively wrongful way to live; no one ought to be made to live with the constant threat that one might be ripped from everything that one loves. Where Carens emphasizes simply the pain of the deportation, though, Hosein argues that the threat of deportation makes the state's administration of its legal system unjust toward the undocumented. No one, asserts Hosein, could be rightly provided with what he calls at-will migration rights; being allowed to enter into a place, but then being subjected to the constant threat of being removed from it, is inherently a violation of the rights of the person. These rights, Hosein acknowledges, can be waived—but the waiver has moral weight only if made fairly and freely; Li Hua's decision to migrate, though, was neither. Nor, argues Hosein, can we think of the deportation as simply like removing someone from our property after a trespass. The state, unlike the landowner, proposes to rule over people, using coercive means; it cannot do that while reserving the right to deport long-standing residents.

There are, of course, any number of other arguments that might be used to ground the right to amnesty for long-standing undocumented residents; Hosein himself discusses such arguments as the economic contribution made by the undocumented and the moral imperative of working against caste structures. In the present, though, I will focus only on the argument from *autonomy* and the argument from *social membership*, since these arguments seem the most likely to me to be successful. I do not, however, think that either argument succeeds in justifying the claim that the undocumented have a right—after some suitable period of residency—to remain.

I would begin, though, by noting a point of agreement between Hosein and myself; we would both think that Li Hua's decision to migrate was the result of true desperation—rather than, as in Angela Luna's case, something more like voluntary choice. Li Hua's poverty may in fact be so grave that he has a right to cross borders in search of economic opportunities for his family; while I cannot demonstrate this, I believe this is likely so, especially in view of the horrendous conditions he accepted as a means of escape from those circumstances. I am less confident than Hosein is, though, that we cannot be held to have voluntarily alienated our rights to make certain sorts of plans, when we cross the border without the legal right to do so.

Imagine, perhaps, that Angela Luna stayed in Japan for five years, rather than two weeks. (This is not a fanciful case: Thailand recently announced the arrest of a German citizen who overstayed his tourist visa by nineteen years.)[9] What would be wrong, in this instance, with deporting Angela Luna? The deportation, of course, is unwelcome. That much is uncontroversial. (It was equally unwelcome, I imagine, to the German man made to return to Germany.) But the destruction of my plans does not count as injustice, when the plans rely upon what other people have no obligation to provide. Imagine, for instance, that I paint a lovely mural on the side of your barn. This mural is my masterwork, and the line between the painting and myself is (in some metaphoric sense) blurry. Imagine, further, that you did not give me the permission required to paint on your barn. You begin to paint over my masterpiece. Do you wrong me? I cannot see why. You are, I imagine, unmerciful; you are not unjust. What you do to me is what I knew, or should have known, you had the right to do. What you do, moreover, is not a punishment. You do not do it to teach me a lesson, or to impose pain. The pain, instead, simply comes about as a result of your doing what you have every right to do: to exclude me, and my paint, from what is yours, and not mine. If you induced me to come in, and offered vague promises about preserving my painting, then perhaps a claim can be made on that basis. But I think even that claim is unlikely to work, unless you did rather more than that. If you and I were both aware that you did not give me the right to make my art permanent, then I do not think you wrong me by destroying that art.

Something similar holds true, I should say, for even very fine (or very valuable) art; in 2009, Banksy's One Nation Under CCTV—painted on the side of a government building—was painted over by the Westminster City Council. The chairman of the council argued that, since Banksy had failed to acquire permission to paint on the side of the building, the council had "every right" to destroy his art.[10]. Many of us might wish the council had chosen to retroactively grant Banksy that permission; but I do not think the chairman was wrong in his assessment of that council's rights.

What's true of property, though, seems also true of other forms of human relationship. If I bring about our relationship by violating your rights, then that relationship is rightly severed. Imagine that I receive my job as a professor by means of a skillful forgery; I forge my degree, a package of glowing letters of recommendation, and so on. Imagine, further, that I demonstrate after five years that I am reasonably good at the job of being a professor: I publish, I teach, I show up to meetings, and so on. If my forgeries are discovered after my fifth year, I think it fairly obvious that I will be fired, and that I deserve to be fired. I never deserved to be hired in the first place, and the fact that my firing will damage my future plans seems largely irrelevant.[11] Hosein's argument seems to imply that the need for permanence is so great that even unjust relationships ought to be made permanent; and that, I think, simply isn't right.

These examples, of course, might be thought to miss the point. The key to Hosein's argument is not that all plans ought to be permanent, but that a government that proposes to rule justly must create the circumstances under which plans might be made permanent. What I mean the examples to tell us, though, is simply that one's plans can be ruptured—without injustice—when those plans are made without right. A state that deports Angela Luna does so without wronging her, even if it does so after several years. Hosein might argue that the state doing so is, actually, wronging her—by making it impossible for her to make her plans permanent. To this, there are at least two replies. The first is that the state is able—indeed, obligated—to give her the protection of the law, while she is present within that state's jurisdiction. She is temporarily a member of that state's community, while she is present without right; to be justified to her, the state must protect and fulfill her human rights, but it cannot be thought that these rights include either voting rights or the right to remain in perpetuity. The second thing to note, though, is that the state can also simply say that it *was* within Luna's power to make plans that are permanent. She could have stayed in the United States and made her plans there. What she builds in Japan—like what I built on the side of your barn—is built without right and may be destroyed. If she—or you—dislike that, you need only refrain from taking what isn't yours.

We can, at this juncture, return to Carens's analysis of social membership. Carens identifies a way in which being subjected to deportation is potentially rather painful: the one who is subjected to deportation cannot easily travel, experiences fear at traffic stops, and so on. What is painful, though, is not necessarily unjust in virtue of that pain. Carens uses the example of Miguel Sanchez—who, he tells us, couldn't make a living in his Mexican home and migrated without documents to the United States. Miguel Sanchez's vulnerability here, argues Carens, is unjust; why should he be made to experience this sort of pain when his native-born neighbors do not?

Carens might well be right about the claims Miguel Sanchez can make; but I believe he needs to tell us more than he does about the circumstances from which he is seeking refuge. To see this, examine the real case of Morgan, an undocumented migrant from Canada who resides in the United States. He has been, he says, resident in Portland for almost a decade; he works for cash and doesn't file income taxes, and is aware of his vulnerability, but chooses to take the risk because of his felt affinity for Portland, Oregon. He confesses to feeling nervous at traffic stops—"I'm always a little edgy," he says. But he has no thoughts of leaving, to return to Canada. His American-born friends, moreover, argue that he has a right to stay—and they make their arguments in terms rather similar to those of Carens:

> [Morgan's] friend Amber Whittenberg says Morgan's reasons [for staying] are even simpler. "It's because it's his home," she says. "He's here because Portland is his home." . . . [H]is friend Eric Roser says Morgan's dreams could be satisfied in Canada. "It really comes down to the fact that he wants to be here," Roser says. "Does it mean he has any less right to be here than, say, a refugee? Yes. But does it mean he shouldn't be here? I don't think so. I think there's room enough for him."[12]

My own reaction to Morgan, though, is rather different. On my view, Morgan has simply made a bet: he will build a life for himself in Portland, and if he has no legal right to do that, then he is making a bet that he won't be deported. But this is what Ronald Dworkin called *option luck:* someone is taking a gamble, and liberalism allows him to bear the costs and the benefits of that gamble.[13] Liberalism, for Dworkin, should be in the business of compensating people when they face bad *brute luck*—when bad things happen to them, or when they face pain that is brought about because of circumstance or the choices of others. It shouldn't be in the business of compensating people when they take a chance and what they hope for doesn't happen. The professor without a PhD is also taking a chance—but it seems (to me, anyhow) fairly clear that the costs of that choice are rightly borne by him. So, too, with Morgan. Liberalism, at least, is going to find it hard to say that, if Morgan is subjected to the pain of a deportation, he is treated *unjustly.* Even though he faces psychic pains not faced by his native-born neighbors, there is no unfairness in that differential; he chose to take a risk, and they did not.

All this, of course, is not intended to dispel the thought that the undocumented can make claims of justice. It is intended, instead, to force us to figure out how those claims might be rightly made—and to find a basis for the claim that goes beyond mere time, toward an analysis of the circumstances under which the choice to cross the border is made. I believe Morgan—like Angela Luna—is an example that forces us to be clear about the nature of the moral claim at stake. But I do *not* believe that all—or even most—undocumented people are actually in the position occupied by Morgan or Angela Luna. They more closely resemble Miguel Sanchez or Li Hua instead. This, however, is really the point: we have to dig a bit deeper into the one choosing, and the circumstances in which that choice is made, before we can adequately analyze what justice would in the present case demand.

So: let's do this, by looking at what is true about Morgan. He is an autonomous agent, or near enough—at least, he's the sort of creature generally thought capable of taking responsibility for his choices. He's coming from a set of circumstances that are morally perfectly adequate; he doesn't especially like Canada, it seems, but that's not the same thing as emerging from grinding poverty or the denial of basic human rights. And, if deported, his specific plans would be denied; his ability to make plans would not be. He would be deprived of a great deal—but he would continue to be able to live as a human among other humans, in a society that offered him adequate opportunity to make plans.

I think all three of these aspects of Morgan are often missing from particular undocumented claimants—with the result that the justification for deportation I am providing here simply won't work for them. Morgan, to begin with, is a full-fledged moral agent. Not everyone is. Children, in particular, occupy a peculiar—and under-theorized—position within our moral thinking. They are rights-bearing creatures, but they are not possessed of the full cognitive machinery that enables us to hold their decision-making against them. They differ in the degree to which they approximate it; the fifteen-year-old child is rather unlike the fifteen-day-old one, after all—although neither is rightly held to have the sorts of moral freedom generally ascribed to adults. I have claimed that it would not be unfair for us to deport Morgan; he made the choice to test his luck, and if he is unlucky, the pain he experiences is not unfair toward him. The same cannot be said of someone who crosses the border without right but does so while still a child. Children, in law and in morality, are not rightly held to have the same freedoms as adults; we do not let children drink alcohol, work for wages, join the military, and so on. This reflects the simple fact that children do not have the right sort of agency to make this sort of decision and to have that decision held against them. And yet, in discussing the program of Deferred Action for Childhood Arrivals (DACA)—which applies to the undocumented who crossed the border while children and therefore not full agents—Representative Steve King thought it was appropriate to hold children accountable for having committed crimes:

I believe we only encourage illegal immigration by discussing amnesty for the 12-20 million illegal immigrants living in the United States
today. . . Amnesty pardons immigration lawbreakers and rewards them
with the object of their crime—citizenship.[14]

This is, I think, morally somewhat absurd; if a five-year-old child sought
to join the armed services, King would be unwilling—I hope—to let that
child bear the consequences of his or her "choice." The same should be true,
though, about the "choice" of a child to migrate without legal right. Morgan
can be made to bear the consequences of his decision, as he would do were he
to choose to join the army. The child can do neither.

This is, I think, reason to think that DACA as a program is eminently defensible. Regardless of one's overall analysis of the undocumented, the fact
that the DACA recipients made no choice to break a law seems morally relevant to their particular claims. I would note, further, that children are entitled to more than simply our recognition of their inability to make this sort
of "choice." They are also entitled to access to particular other people who
will guide and form that child's agency. There is an analogy, here, between the
state and the parent. Human beings are vulnerable to one another and have
a right to live in a state that protects their most basic human rights. We have,
as Hannah Arendt had it, a right to have rights—which is to say, a right to
the social and political institutions needed to coercively defend our rights.[15]
The child, though, has a right not just to a state, but to parents or guardians.
The Obama administration proposed both DACA and Deferred Action
for Parents of Americans (DAPA)—on which American minor children
could be guaranteed that they would not have their undocumented parents
deported.[16] The rights defended here are not the rights of the parents, but of
the children; the child whose parents are deported loses her right to guidance
and protection, as surely as the adult made stateless. DAPA was enjoined
shortly after its introduction—but it seems to have a powerful moral logic;
the child has, in morality and in law, a right to particular people who will
love and guide it. The state ought to recognize the particular vulnerability of
the child, by protecting that child from the loss of its parents. There is, again,
a claim of justice here; the child is treated unjustly, to say the least, by being
deprived of the particular person with responsibility for the development of
her agency.

These facts, I think, are why the Trump administration's policy of separating migrant children from their families is so deeply abhorrent. These

children are placed in facilities that very much resemble those designed for criminal punishment.[17] The implied logic of these facilities is that the child has done something wrong; certainly, from the child's point of view, the experience of being locked up or caged cannot help but feel punitive. This logic, however, fails to respect the fact that the child has not done something wrong, because they—as children—are not possessed of the cognitive preconditions of doing *that sort of wrong*. What the Trump administration fails to respect the present conditions of agency for these children—and, given the long-standing damage done to these children's cognitive development, it disrespects their future agency as well.

This, then, is one clear case of someone who fails to look like Morgan. The child has made no decision and so cannot have that decision held against her. But we might also look at the circumstances against which the undocumented adult makes her decision. Miguel Sanchez looks distinct from Morgan here, as well. Miguel, in particular, might be thought to have no choice at all; his lawbreaking results from unjust circumstances, or something very much akin to them. These facts, then, might be used to ground a claim on the part of Miguel and those like him.

One very clear way in which this case might be made is if Carens's description of Miguel is taken literally. Miguel, writes Carens, "could not earn enough" to pay the bills in his Mexican home. These bills, presumably, are for the necessities of life; although Carens does not specify, it seems implausible to suppose that Miguel is in debt because he has particularly expensive habits. The logic developed earlier in this book, however, has argued that borders cannot be legitimately closed against those who are facing violation of their basic rights in their countries of origin. When I discussed the Convention, of course, our focus was on what the state was actively doing to harm its citizens; the concept of persecution involves an active decision by some agent to cause harm to some particular person. But I have also argued that the right to cross borders is held even by some people whose circumstances are not rightly described with reference to persecution. Those who face death by starvation, for example, are entitled to—at the very least—move across the world's surface without hindrance so as to preserve their lives. Any state that used force to return them to such a situation would be using force to preserve a morally inadequate status quo; I have argued that this sort of coercion is morally impermissible. These facts, though, have implications not only at the border, but within them. If someone's decision to cross the border would not have been rightly prevented, it cannot represent a morally deficient decision, such that the lives built by that decision are rightly placed at risk. Put more simply: if we would not have been morally right to coercively prevent the migrant from crossing, we have no right now to coercively expel that migrant from our society.

This seems clear to me—or, at any rate, it seems to be clearly implied by the theory I here defend. Things are more interesting, I think, if we read the idea of "could not earn enough" in a more capacious way. We might read this phrase as entailing not Miguel's inability to acquire the necessities of life—whatever we might mean by that—but by his inability to acquire what which he is *due*. Imagine, for instance, that on any plausible theory of global distributive justice, Miguel is entitled to a higher standard of living than he is able to acquire in his hometown. Imagine, further, that he is able to simply cross into the United States and thereby improve his standard of living. What he does in crossing into the United States seems to make the world more closely resemble the world imagined by our theorizing about justice. Miguel has raised himself out of morally objectionable poverty, without doing anything (we may supposed) that has made anyone else worse off. Is this enough of a reason to think that Miguel has a right to cross that border—and that he now has, after having spent time in the United States, a right to remain within the United States?

The answer, I believe, is no. As I will argue in the rest of this book, the United States would reveal itself to be deficient in moral character were it to deport Miguel; it would show an objectionable lack of mercy, as I understand that term. But that is not the same as injustice toward Miguel. Miguel is seeking to justify his decision to cross by citing the demands of global justice. The problem is, though, that the political community into which he is crossing—here, the United States—has a moral right to decide for itself how to accommodate those demands. The example of Robin Hood, as described in chapter 2, is intended to motivate this conclusion. Miguel is simply not the right sort of agent to determine which particular pathway is the one the United States shall take, in face of these global duties. Miguel, I believe, is in a morally similar position to Robin Hood in the example. He does not have the right to make the world more just by breaking laws; even if he is right—as I think he is—that the world after his lawbreaking is a more just world, that does not mean that he was justified in the lawbreaking. Miguel, in other words, cannot claim that he was right to break the law; and, accordingly, we cannot think that it is wrong—wrong because unjust—to unmake what he built by means of that lawbreaking.

I will have more to say about this sort of lawbreaking in the next chapter. I would note, in particular, that nothing I have said here involves the claim that Miguel demonstrates a deficient character in breaking these laws. He doesn't. But this is a fact about our moral reaction to lawbreaking; it does not tell us anything about whether the law preventing him from crossing the border is one he had an obligation to obey.

I will close with one final way in which Miguel might be distinct from Morgan. Morgan, in being sent home to Canada, will find his particular plans unmade. He will find it hard to keep up friendships in the United States, see the sights he is used to in Portland, and so on. But he will likely be able to continue his agency—he is, we can assume, possessed of both the skills and the circumstances needed to rebuild a life for himself. The same, though, cannot be assumed true of Miguel—and, I suspect, it might not be true of a great many people. If this is so, then the decision to deport would count as a decision to destroy not simply what is built by agency, but agency itself; and this, I believe, is a decision that we cannot rightly make. Even if we are sometimes permitted to make people bear the costs of their decisions, we generally balk at letting people *annihilate* themselves. This is controversial, of course; liberals disagree about the extent to which we ought to respect a voluntary choice to destroy one's ability to choose. But most of us recognize this as distinct, if nothing else—and, in this context, we might think that a claim of justice would emerge from the fact that certain deportations would entail not simply pain, but something more as well.

Some examples of this are clear; we cannot rightly deport people to situations in which they are literally going to be annihilated, whatever the circumstances of their arrival. Thomas Mann, for instance, arrived in France in 1933 and was told on his arrival that it would not be safe for him to return to Germany.[18] In some cases, the decision to deport would be a literal sentence of death; we cannot, I have argued, rightly engage in such deportation, regardless of the circumstances of entry. But I think more can be said. There are some people for whom the project of rebuilding a life in another country is simply so difficult that it might be morally tantamount to the destruction of the person. Extreme differences in language and culture, for instance, might make the process of developing plans and projects very nearly impossible. These aspects seem to take on more gravity for the elderly; as we age, our ability to begin again naturally seems to atrophy, and our ability to learn (or relearn) the language and norms of a new place begins to fall away as well. Carens, in defending these ideas, discusses the case of

Marguerite Grimmonds, who was nearly deported at the age of eighty to the United States, after moving at age two to Scotland.[19] Grimmonds was, we might think, immune from that deportation because the decision to move without legal right to Scotland was not rightly her own; but we might also point out that the deportation of an eighty-year-old woman is tantamount to the destruction of her agency. Similar considerations might hold true for the current case of Francis Anwana, a forty-eight-year-old deaf man with cognitive impairment facing deportation to Ghana, after being brought to the United States as a child. (He faces deportation only because the managers of his group home failed to file a renewal for his visa.) Anwana has been able to build a flourishing life for himself in the United States; it is unlikely that the same could be said of him were he to "return" to Ghana, where he would have no family nor any system of social support.[20]

I do not want to overstate the case; people do, after all, move to wildly different countries regularly, and for that matter eighty-year-olds have been known to voluntarily pick up and migrate. The key, though, is that we might sometimes think that what they are doing here is demanding—so demanding, indeed, that being made to do it might count as the destruction of the person herself.

3. Love and Family

We can conclude with an examination of family unification. Bringing families together is a key part of the narrative that undergirds American immigration law; the United States has traditionally been exceptionally open to the provision of migration rights to relatives of current American citizens or permanent residents. We have, of course, also seen in recent years a counternarrative, on which family unification represents the unjustified immigration of an indefinite number of foreign nationals; the Trump administration, in particular, has begun using the phrase *chain migration* to denote the perceived excesses of American willingness to assist family. Both of these ideas, though, depend upon particular visions of why it is that the unification of the family is a good thing; and it is worthwhile spending some time trying to figure out what the family actually *is*, and how the family might ground a claim of justice. We are, again, trying to figure out whether or not the claims of family members are best understood as claims of justice, or as undergirded by some other moral notion such as mercy.

The family, though, is itself susceptible of being understood in a multi-plicity of ways.[21] When we speak of the family, we often mean to refer to one of two related, but distinct, notions. The first is *dependency*; the child is de-pendent upon its parents, and the family's unification might be defended with reference to the moral imperative of the child's development as an agent. The second is *affection*; the family is a site for love, or something like love, and we are bound by justice to respect those relationships that bring that love into the world. We can examine these two ideas in turn.

The claims of dependency, I believe, are fairly clear. Adults, as I have discussed, are entitled to the conditions under which they are able to exer-cise their agency. Children, in addition, are entitled to the conditions under which their developing agency is nourished and developed. This means that—as Carens emphasizes—there is a need for sites and institutions within which the young are able to act as political agents within their societies.[22] But most importantly, it means that there must be particular people who are committed to being present within those children's lives, so as to guide and foster the agency developing within them. This means that the relationship between parent and child cannot be severed, except at the cost of illegitimate destruction of the child's agency; the child has a right to their parents' pres-ence in their lives. This, I have argued, undergirds the moral importance of policy measures such as DACA and DAPA—although I would note that even these programs are likely insufficient; agency, as Hosein emphasizes, requires the ability to make plans, and both DACA and DAPA portray themselves as mere temporary deferrals of deportation. The fact that I have disagreed with Hosein's analysis of the justice of deportation does not mean that we disagree about the centrality of the ability to make plans.

I would argue, moreover, that the claims of dependency might potentially be extended beyond the child. The child has a need of particular care for her agency; so, too, might the elderly, or those suffering from cognitive impair-ment, or any number of other people whose agency requires not simply a society of laws but the presence of a particular person playing a particular role. These claims, I would argue, are claims of justice as strong as those made on behalf of minor children. We would act wrongly, were we to deport the particular people required for the effective exercise of agency—or, for that matter, those people whose agency is in question.

Things become more complex, though, when we start to look at the claims of love. If the unification of a loving relationship is to be taken as a claim of justice, it must be that there is something special about love. We act wrongly, on this analysis, when we make it harder for this sort of relationship to grow and develop in the world. We act more wrongly, further, in undermining this sort of relationship than we would the relationship between friends, coauthors, or business associates. These last forms of relationship, after all, are given no special status in migration law; familial relationships—and, in particular, the relationship between spouses—are given extraordinary deference. The question, though, is whether or not something special can be found to justify this unique status. Luara Ferracioli has argued that we cannot find an adequate moral justification for this status; the deference to love is the result of historical accidents—not philosophical reasoning:

> [O]nce we acknowledge that an array of special relationships should be allowed to flourish in a liberal ethos, it becomes clear that the immigration policies of liberal states cannot arbitrarily favour some of these relationships at the expense of others. The upshot is that either immigration arrangements ought to be designed so as to include all sorts of special relationships that give meaning to people's lives, or none at all. The current philosophical and practical consensus that familial and romantic relationships enjoy *unique* immigration status cannot, on reflection, be justified.[23]

This represents the first challenge to the thought that family unification reflects a claim of justice; if claims of affection, or claims of biological relation, cannot be regarded as morally distinct from other sources of value, then the liberal state cannot rightly differentiate so as to prefer spouses to friends. If I want to be unified with my best friend, and you want to be unified with your spouse, I am treated unfairly—and, hence, unjustly—by a state that gives you but not me what is desired.

I think this is a powerful worry about the justification for family unification. I believe other worries might be added to it. One of these is that, once we move away from considerations of dependency, we face a complex relationship between the good we are pursuing—affection, or something like it—and the categories we use. Why, for instance, should the law provide a US citizen to sponsor her mother-in-law for purposes of migration, but not her cousin? The answer is, presumably, because the relationship of mother-in-law is likely to be backed by something like a personal relationship of affection, while the cousin is somehow more "distant" in lineage and therefore in affection. There is, however, no reason to think in any individual case that this is so. Affection is, after all, a rather unpredictable thing, and it has a habit of ignoring the categories we build to constrain it.

The Trump administration ran into these difficulties when it tried to specify the set of people who had a "bona fide relationship" with a US citizen or permanent resident. The administration declared that the relationship of mother-in-law was bona fide but that a great many others were not. The Ninth Circuit thought this arbitrary and enjoined the administration from using its rules:

> Stated simply, the government does not offer a persuasive explanation for why a mother-in-law is clearly a bona fide relationship, in the Supreme Court's prior reasoning, but a grandparent, grandchild, aunt, uncle, niece, nephew, or cousin is not.[24]

This is true—but the judge here does not notice that the same problem generalizes, to encompass all relationships. If there is no bright line separating the mother-in-law from the cousin, then there is presumably no bright line between the cousin and the more distant cousin, and eventually between that cousin and the one so distant from us that we cannot accurately figure out the degrees of removal, and so on. There is, in other words, a stark lack here of bright lines. If we want to make a claim of justice, though—if we want the mother-in-law's migration to be required by justice, but not the distant cousin—we are in need of a bright line, so as to explain the difference in rights. The law necessarily works with arbitrary differences; we accept that we can drive at sixteen, or drink at twenty-one, because legal rights need clear lines. Moral claims, though, need stronger foundations, and if we are required to treat the cousin differently from the mother-in-law, the cousin is entitled to know why.

All of this is intended to undermine the thought that family members have a unique and powerful claim to reunification. To this, we might also add the thought that what the state does in refusing the migration of the foreign spouse isn't really to coercively prevent the emergence of love or a loving relationship. Instead, it is to refuse to provide a home for that love. The United States, for example, would be making things more difficult for me if it failed to provide migration rights to my foreign-born spouse. But it cannot be said to be preventing me from having a loving relationship with that spouse— as it would if, for example, it made it illegal for me to marry (or carry on a romantic relationship) someone of a particular gender.[25] The failure to provide the means needed for a relationship is not the same as coercive interference with that relationship. Say, for instance, I were to fall in love with a woman who works at the University of Miami—but that I could not move to Miami, except to work at the University of Miami (my skills being limited to the doing of philosophy) and that the University of Miami has no interest in hiring me. Does the University of Miami interfere with our relationship, when it refuses to provide me with employment? The answer is, I think, no; it fails to provide me with the tools needed to pursue that relationship, but it was under no obligation to provide those tools. So, too, is it with spouses holding foreign citizenship. The state that refuses to allow that foreign spouse to migrate makes it more difficult for the marriage to continue. It cannot be said to be coercively preventing that marriage—a fact that, I think, makes the thought that affection provides a claim in justice even more difficult to make out.

One final consideration. We are often called upon to adjust our desires to what is compatible with the rights of others, and with the resources available to us. It is difficult to think of love as falling within this category. That does not mean, however, that we should not do so. Indeed, I think we are often called upon to be cognizant of the ways in which our particular relationships might be constrained by the rights of others. We are not, as it were, passive victims of our hearts; while Woody Allen famously argued that the heart wants what it wants, many of us wanted to reply that the heart can be expected to control itself. We expect those who supervise graduate students to control their emotions and their actions; falling in love with one's graduate student excuses nothing. We expect soldiers, or diplomats, to return home after lengthy periods abroad, regardless of the friends they leave when they do so. We are, in short, obligated to take charge of whom and how we love. How can my relationship with my spouse, then, be taken as a trump card, used to demand rights that are denied to other forms of human relationship?

I want to be clear, at this point, that I am not arguing against a law offering migration rights to spouses, or to other family members. I would not want to live in a country that did not do just that. I am arguing, instead, that it is unclear why this law is demanded by justice. The love we have for our spouses may be special, to our spouses and to ourselves. It is simply not clear, to me, why it should be taken as special from the standpoint of justice.

The best version of the claim, I think, comes from Matthew Lister, who situates the claim with reference to the desires and interests of the citizen—rather than the foreign national.[26] Lister argues that the right of that person to her spouse is different in kind from the right of the people around her to be free from having to deal with that foreign spouse; certainly, he argues, we tend to think the marital relationship is deeper than the mere relationship of fellow national. My interest in living with my wife, that is, is more important than your interest in not having to run into her in the market.

I am not confident that this is incorrect; Lister's argument seems like the strongest possible basis of the claim to special status. It is worth noting, though, that even if Lister is correct, then Ferracioli's problem remains, when in particular cases other relationships are as important to the claimants in question as the spouse's is to her. But I am not confident that Lister's argument is correct. Imagine, for instance, that I fall in love with a woman from Italy who has never set foot in the United States. This is, perhaps, unrealistic; but it is conceptually clean. Imagine, further, that the United States refuses to allow her to enter into the United States. Imagine that I then argue, with Lister, that this is a violation of my rights; my love is more valuable to me than whatever it is that my fellow citizens are seeking to accomplish by means of the exclusion. It seems to me that my fellow citizens have a reply ready: you have the right, they say, to a society in which you are treated justly. That precludes us treating you as morally inferior, in our domestic law. We couldn't make your marriage illegal. But we don't do that when we refrain from offering rights to the particular outsider you love. We do not demonize your love or claim that it is lesser than ours. We are refraining from offering something that we have no obligation to provide—to you, or to anyone. We do not stand in the way of your love; but neither do we choose to provide these goods to you—or to anyone whose chosen spouse is not already part of this particular relationship.

This may, or may not, succeed as a strategy. I believe it might succeed, although I am open to being convinced that it does not. The reply, however, undoubtedly looks heartless. And so it is. But in face of this heartlessness, there are at least three replies. The first is to say that the reply is both heartless and unjust: it is unjust because the intensity of the desire for my spouse makes it different in kind, or because it is so damaging to be deprived of my spouse that my agency is impaired. The second reply is to say that most marriages don't look like the marriage I propose with the woman from Italy. That marriage is, as it were, all possibility—most marriages involve people having lived in the same country together for a long time, so that they combine both possibility and attachment. This might be true; but we would have to say, once again, why these facts matter—why these difference are ones that demand migration rights as a matter of justice. The final response, though, is to say that the moral problem with the proposed response isn't to be found with its purported injustice, but with its heartlessness. This is, of course, what I want to say. I can complain—and complain loudly—if my spouse is not provided with the rights in question. But not all moral complaints are complaints in justice, and our conceptual vocabulary is rich enough to allow my complaint to be made precisely. The next three chapters will attempt to do just that.

8

Reciprocity, the Undocumented, and Jeb Bush

The previous chapter ended with the thought that not all moral complaints must be made in the language of justice. We can, I think, rightly describe policies as vicious—as reflecting decisions to be cruel or heartless—without requiring that our complaint necessarily entails the doing of injustice toward a wronged party. Over the next three chapters, I want to develop and articulate a concept of political mercy, which I think might be one way of making clear how that sort of complaint might be made. I will begin this task, though, by changing gears, and talking about the morality of undocumented migration—not from the standpoint of the state, but from the standpoint of the migrant and our evaluation of his or her agency. We ought to differentiate, I will argue, between what we can legally seek to prevent, and our moral attitude toward those who seek to avoid our laws. We can, that is, seek to exclude people from moving across our borders—even, perhaps, fairly needy people—but that does not permit us to regard those who move nonetheless as morally bad people. This may seem like cold comfort; but I think it may have surprising implications, both for what we are able to do through our migration policy, and for what the purposes of that policy ought to be.

As a way of introducing this, I want to recall the words of Jeb Bush, as he campaigned for the Republican nomination for president:

> But the way I look at this—and I'm going to say this, and it'll be on tape and so be it. The way I look at this is someone who comes to our country because they couldn't come legally, they come to our country because their families—the dad who loved their children—was worried that their children didn't have food on the table. And they wanted to make sure their family was intact, and they crossed the border because they had no other means to work to be able to provide for their family. Yes, they broke the law, but it's not a felony. It's an act of love.[1]

Justice, Migration, and Mercy. Michael Blake, Oxford University Press (2020). © Oxford University Press.
DOI: 10.1093/oso/9780190879556.001.0001

We have not spent much time in this book focused on the morality of the migrant: whether, most importantly, the migrant has the obligation to obey the law that excludes her. This is, in one way, understandable: the state is more powerful than the migrant, and we are most often worried with those agencies that can do the most damage. In another sense, however, this is a problem. Much of our popular political discourse begins with the morality of migration in this first-personal sense. Recall the frame of argument we began with in the first chapter: the right wing in the United States uses the ritual invocation of illegality as immorality for rhetorical purposes: what part of *illegal*, runs the question, don't you understand?[2] The left wing, for its part, speaks back with a dismissal of any relationship between legality and morality: no human, runs the reply, is *illegal*.[3]

In this chapter, I want to try to offer some preliminary reflections on the morality of breaking an exclusionary law. This will require me to offer some account of what, in general, could give us a moral reason to obey a legal command. This is a fairly large topic, with a venerable history; I cannot deal with all of it here. Instead, I will limit myself to analyzing this topic with reference to two visions of how the legal system in question might be shown to have a hold on us. Following Andrew Lister, I will distinguish between a *Humean* account of obligation, on which its hold on us is related to the moral imperative of reciprocity in the allocation of the benefits and burdens of cooperation; and a *Kantian* account, on which its hold relates instead to more abstract notions such as the duty to support just institutions.[4] My first thesis is that the latter sort of ground is more promising than the former; the former offers us a way of showing that the migrant need not obey the law that excludes her, but at the cost of permitting forms of international lawbreaking we have reason to condemn. My second thesis, however, is that even the second sort of ground cannot offer us an easy means by which to condemn those who migrate without legal permission. We must distinguish between the duty to support a just institution, I will argue, and the costs that must be incurred in the course of fulfilling that duty; circumstances might exist under which we can insist upon a duty to obey, while acknowledging that the particular costs of obedience are ones that any person would find it difficult or impossible to bear. Under these circumstances, I argue, we have no right to morally condemn those who fail to comply with the duty in question. We do not make a moral error when we insist that the duty persists, that is, but we make a significant moral error when we attribute a defective character to the one who fails to abide by that duty. This means, in the end, that a legitimate state might be right to insist both on the right to exclude certain migrants *and* that no particular moral defect should be ascribed to those who migrate without right.

To get to this conclusion, however, I will have to make some assumptions. I will assume that the state trying to exclude is the right sort of state to issue authoritative commands; however we are to identify the line of decency below which states lose the right to expect obligation, our state is above that line. What this means, of course, is that there exists some set of states capable of imposing valid moral duties upon agents by means of legal pronouncements, and that the state with which we are concerned is among that set. I will assume, of course, that the earlier arguments in this book have succeeded, and we there is no general right to cross borders; the arguments of Joseph Carens and Kieran Oberman, in short, will be taken as wrong, such that there is nothing inherently unjust about trying to exclude some unwanted would-be migrants. I will assume, further, that the law in question actually does mandate that some set of people that want to come into the country may not do so, and insists that those who come nonetheless have committed a criminal action.[5] I will need to assert that we are not dealing with people who may have a particular, rather than a general, claim against the state; we are not dealing either with long-standing undocumented residents, or with those who can make valid moral claims against the state in virtue of its particular history or actions abroad.[6] Even a state which has the right to exclude, after all, might lose that right in virtue of particular actions, and particular people will have the right to migrate even against the wishes of that state. I will *not* assume, finally, that the law mandating exclusion is itself just; I will merely assume that the state is the sort of entity that might create an obligation to obey that law, regardless of whether or not that law is just.

I am, in short, assuming quite a lot, both about facts and about ethics. Many people will believe that one or more of these assumptions fails to hold true—either everywhere, or in some particular political context. This is not, I think, a problem; my aim in this chapter is not to argue that potential undocumented migrants have a universal obligation to obey the law precluding migration, but to show how that obligation could be understood and where it might be asserted—and how it might be limited even under the most idealized circumstances. I want, in short, to see what limits might be placed on what we expect from potential migrants under even the best of circumstances. If these limits can be found, then we might at least understand the space within which further normative argument might be undertaken.

So: let us assume that the assumptions I have made are worth exploring. We are facing a state that is the right sort of creature to create obligations by means of commands. That state issues a command, to nonresidents of that state: you shall not cross this border. What reason do those nonresidents have to obey that command?

1. Hume and Reciprocity

It is a striking fact about the law of exclusion that those over whom it asserts authority have no part in the making of that law. If reciprocity is a moral requirement, and if that reciprocity requires fairness in the allocation of the burdens and benefits of cooperation, then this fact might give rise to some troubling conclusions. We might be tempted toward radicalism about exclusion; Arash Abizadeh, as described earlier in this book, takes these ideas to entail the illegitimacy of any individual state's engaging in unilateral exclusion.[7] Even those of us who do not go this far might be tempted to think that this failure of reciprocity undermines the obligation to obey. The excluded might simply say: if this law offers me burdens, without some degree of benefits—let alone a substantive say in the process of lawmaking—then what reason can I be given to mandate voluntary compliance with that law? Why, in short, should I listen to a law that claims to be obligatory, but which provides me with neither political voice nor justifying benefits?

This vision of obligation, I should specify, asserts that the obligation to obey the law ultimately rests upon fairness in the allocation of the benefits and burdens of cooperation with that law. To see how this works, we might examine the notion of reciprocity animating the contractualism of John Rawls. Rawls's criterion of reciprocity holds that we can only reasonably propose political rules to others when we can "think it at least reasonable for others to accept them, as free and equal citizens."[8] This criterion of reciprocity guides us in developing the social and political rules we can expect to be both just and stable over time—including what particular sorts of inequalities can be rightly accepted among citizens. Rawls's own distributive principle—the difference principle—is defended by him as one that reflects this idea of reciprocity; it provides the least advantaged with the sorts of justification for the inequality that accept and reflect the moral equality of all citizens.[9] These ideas are not used by Rawls to ground an obligation to obey the law; as I will discuss in section 2, Rawls defends in his mature work instead a natural duty to promote just institutions. We might, however, use such ideas to directly ground an obligation to obey the law, in at least a just society reflecting this sort of reciprocal concern: you ought to obey the law, in short, because that law reflects both your reciprocal right to be listened to in the making of the law, and a fair distribution of the benefits of cooperation.[10]

This vision of obligation may or may not be attractive; what it can't do— or, at any rate, can't do easily—is ground an obligation to obey the law of migration. That law, after all, is pitched against those who are by definition nonmembers of the society in question. What they are excluded from is membership itself. Thus, a vision of obligation which starts with the creation of a reciprocal political community is unlikely to provide any analytic help to the question of obedience to migration law. It is entry *into* that reciprocal community that is sought, and which that law refuses.

This might be, of course, exactly where we want to end up. One might take this analysis of reciprocity to offer the possibility for both justification and criticism of social institutions. It might give us reason to respect and obey so-cial institutions that reflect this sort of reciprocal concern—and to condemn those that do not. In a similar vein, Jeffrie Murphy argues that the retributive theory of criminal punishment is formally correct, but cannot under current circumstances justify the widespread imprisonment of the racially and eco-nomically marginalized:

> Consider one example: a man has been convicted of armed robbery. On investigation, we learn that he is an impoverished black whose whole life has been one of frustrating alienation from the prevailing socio-economic structure—no job, no transportation if he could get a job, substandard ed-ucation for his children, terrible housing and inadequate health care for his whole family, condescending-tardy-inadequate welfare payments, harass-ment by the police but no real protection by them against the dangers in his community, and near total exclusion from the political process. Learning all this, would we still want to talk—as many do—of his suffering punish-ment under the rubric of "paying a debt to society"? Surely not. Debt for what?[11]

Murphy's purpose is to argue that the state in question may not rightly punish; but a parallel argument might be made that the individual in ques-tion has no obligation to obey the law in such a society—or, at any rate, that he has no obligation to obey the law *because it is the law.* (He might, or might not, have an obligation to avoid armed robbery, simply in virtue of the rights of others to be free from being threatened with guns.) We might make similar arguments, though, for the lack of an obligation on the part of prospective migrants. If we were to insist that the law of exclusion has given them some form of historic benefit, and that they have built up a debt of obedience because of that benefit—they may be as entitled to say: debt for what?[12]

These arguments, however, might prove entirely too much. Critics of Rawls's own vision of justice as fairness have noted that his analysis of justice, unless modified or clarified, would make those who are not participants in the basic structure of society invisible to concerns of justice; since the severely disabled, for example, may not be able to participate either in the market economy or in political deliberation, a theory of justice focusing on fairness in the allocation of the benefits of cooperation might have nothing to say about the justice of policy affecting those persons. They are not participants in the process of building the advantages and so have no claim to be heard in the discussions of how our social institutions will distribute them.[13] Here, however, we want to say that such implications provide us reason to reject Rawls's theory—or, at any rate, to demand its clarification or revision.[14] Such individuals are rightly understood as having rights under justice, regardless of how they do or do not participate in the creation of benefits distributed by justice. This, however, might seem to apply as easily to *obligations* as it does to *rights*. We are tempted to say that those who are not benefited by a law have no obligation to obey it; saying this, though, comes entirely too close to saying that the morality of law is concerned only with the interests and obligations of those who are able to participate in the activities coordinated by that law—which is a conclusion we rightly want to avoid. If we want to insist that some individuals who do not participate in political society nonetheless have rights to be heard before that political society, we might also have to accept that some people who are not participants in that society might have obligations before that political society.

We can support these conclusions by noting how we might have obligations to respect the laws of a foreign society. There seem to be, for instance, some cases in which I have some obligation to obey the law of a country to which I have never been and from which I receive no particular benefit. Take, for an example, the law of Australia regarding video games. The game *Blitz: The League* is currently banned for import or for sale in Australia; it depicts a no-holds-barred football league within which steroid use is not only possible but beneficial to the performance of one's virtual avatar.[15] (It should go without saying that the game is easily available for purchase in the United States.) I might believe that Australia's decision to censor this game is pointless and regressive. Imagine, though, that I were to frustrate the Australian decision by opening a service smuggling copies of *Blitz: The League* into Australia, which I provide for free to Australian gamers. Might I be thought wrong in doing so? Perhaps, if those games were to find their ways into children's hands; but the question persists even if I take steps to prevent that from happening. (Perhaps I simply smuggle copies of the game into Australia and give them to mature—but easily amused—Australian friends.) Were I to do this, I think I might still be charged with a lack of respect for the Australian political community. The Australian political community, after all, is at least as democratic as my own, and I might be thought to show an objectionable lack of respect for the Australian reciprocal process of political deliberation when I simply reject the law as foolish and then reject its hold on me. I disobey the law that insists that copies of *Blitz: The League* not be brought into Australia, and I might be thought to encourage others to disobey the law that precludes the domestic sale of that game. I believe I have an obligation to obey those laws, not because they are wise or important—I think they aren't—but because I have some degree of respect for the political community from which those laws have emerged.

What this means, though, is that I might have some obligation to obey not only those laws that offer me reciprocity in the process of lawmaking or in its outcomes, but to obey the law of (some) other countries as well, because of how they provide that sort of reciprocity for their own members. I may be obliged to obey laws that treat me as an equal in the making of law; but I might also have some obligation to respect the laws of *other* communities as well—at least when those communities are of a particular character. The latter obligation, though, cannot be grounded directly in my own claims to reciprocal justification of political authority; we would have to ground them in a more general obligation to respect the process of seeking to build responsive and justifiable states. We should, I think, therefore reject the thought that there is no obligation to obey migration law, since that law does not treat the migrant as an equal in the distribution of benefits. As we have now seen, that a law is capable of offering us benefits—whether those benefits are understood against current status, or with reference to some moralized baseline—is not a necessary condition of that law's being obligatory.

There are, of course, any number of responses here. One is simply to bite the bullet and to assert that those who are excluded from the process of lawmaking have no obligation to obey that law; this is, as I have indicated, not without some costs. Another is to assert that the excluded migrant does, in fact, participate in some sort of cooperative activity with the state that excludes her, which enables us to ask about fairness in that cooperative activity. There is, on this account, a cooperative activity in international relations, on which states voluntarily participate in mutual activities of respect for one another's territorial sovereignty and political activity; we might ground the obligation to obey an exclusionary law in the fact that states are engaging in such an ongoing project as a cooperative venture.[16] The problem, though, is that even if this were true, it would seem to create obligations on the parts of states, rather than individuals. States, presumably, have interests in being free from other states taking charge of their territory or political independence; that might create some obligation of obedience to international law, when that law is understood as justifiable with reference to reciprocity. But nothing here gives the individual person an obligation to obey the law of exclusion. The reciprocity at issue here is between states, not people. We might assert that the individual has an obligation to respect that reciprocity; but, once again, we're now focused not on reciprocity as the independent ground for obligation, but on an independent obligation to respect and promote reciprocal relationships between other agents. We are back, once again, to the thought that we might be obligated, not because this community treats us as a moral equal by means of reciprocal justification, but that we are obligated to protect and preserve some *other* community's ability to act in a manner reflecting the concerns of reciprocity.

It therefore seems appropriate for us to examine the second ground for a potential obligation to obey: the Kantian vision, on which we are obligated to protect and preserve just institutions. This vision of the obligation, I will argue, can provide would-be migrants with some obligation to obey an exclusionary law. If I am right, however, then such an obligation depends upon particular factual premises; and, even where such an obligation can be shown to exist, it may not serve as justification for the sorts of policies states like the United States are currently deploying. It is to these concerns that I now turn.

2. Kant and Natural Duty

As mentioned earlier, John Rawls did not ground the obligation to law directly upon reciprocity; we have a duty to obey the commands of a just state not because of fair dealings, but because we have a natural duty to support just institutions.[17] The concept of reciprocity, as I have discussed, still has a home in Rawls's account of what a just state looks like; but reciprocity itself is not taken to explain why that state's commands are obligatory. Rawls is the most prominent defender of this view, but emphatically not its only defender; there are a number of theorists who have recently put forward versions of this duty.[18] There are, naturally, important differences between these thinkers, and they each defend importantly distinct visions of what particular actions this sort of duty would demand. For the moment, though, I want to ignore these differences, and ask instead what would be implied by any such duty for the would-be migrant. If the migrant who proposes to break an exclusionary law does wrong, it seems plausible that such a wrong is best understood with reference to a natural duty to obey just institutions. The one who breaks the law, after all, makes the institution that created that law less authoritative; insofar as we are able to break the law with impunity, that law is made less law-like overall. The lawbreaking may have concrete effects; widespread disobedience to law, after all, may make the very enterprise of deliberative politics impossible.[19] But concrete effects need not be demonstrated; it is enough to say that the one who violates the law has failed a broad duty to promote and preserve the just institutions that created the law. We might say something similar in the particular case of migration. Widespread disobedience to an exclusionary law might have negative effects upon our ability to do politics together.[20] But we need not even demonstrate that it will; it would be enough for us to say that the one who violates the exclusionary law makes the just institutions that wrote that law less authoritative—and that doing so violates a standing duty to those institutions.

This vision of an obligation to obey is more plausible; it is not, however, without its difficulties. The first, and most obvious, is that it is clear that this duty is at most a prima facie duty of obedience; such a duty is, of course, compatible with principled forms of lawbreaking, such as civil disobedience. For the moment, though, I want to ignore this sort of lawbreaking and focus instead on what this prima facie duty might actually do, in some particular fact patterns. My contention will be that the duty of obedience might be less powerful than it first appears; the obligation to obey the law may not provide the clear and easy moral condemnation of illegal migration that many on the right wing assume. I want to defend this conclusion with reference to three fact patterns, in descending order of moral gravity.

a.   *Abraham* is subject to violations of international human rights in his
country of origin. He has the ability to walk across the border into a rights-
protecting country, which has nonetheless passed a law forbidding him
from doing so.

I take it as fairly obvious that Abraham does not have an all-things-considered
obligation to refrain from walking across that border. There seems, to me, to be
a simple reason Abraham can cite in defense of his decision. The violation done
to the just state through the breaking of its laws is vastly less important than the
violation done to Abraham through the breaking of his body. I find it hard to
offer justifying reasons to explain why this should be so; but I suspect that any
reason I might offer would be less convincing than the conclusion itself. One
who disagreed would seem to place the conceptual well-being of the state ahead
of the continued existence of a particular human person, understood as a rights-
bearing entity. At the very least, considerations like this are what gave rise to the
modern law of asylum, which is often taken to have emerged after the horrors of
the Second World War. States are legally precluded from excluding people like
Abraham; the state's right to exclude, however that is to be grounded, is taken
as less morally pressing than the right of people to escape particular forms of
radical evil. If we see this not from the standpoint of the state, but from that of
Abraham, we might think of him as subject to two duties: to respect the laws
of the (otherwise) just state that wishes to exclude him, and to respect his own
continued right to survive as a rights-bearing individual. To insist that Abraham
select the former duty would seem wrong-headed, to say the least. Indeed, an
Abraham that chose that duty might rightly be charged with showing himself
inadequate in self-respect.

These considerations get more contentious, though, the further away we
get from the sorts of human rights violations that animate the modern law of
asylum. To see this, examine a case in which the rights at stake are the more
controversial ones not currently taken to ground a right to asylum: the right
to be free from undemocratic and tyrannical forms of governance.

b.   *Bobby* is subject to mere tyranny in his country of origin. He has the
ability to walk across the border into a right-protecting country, which has
nonetheless passed a law forbidding him from doing so.

This case is more complex, I think, for a variety of reasons—not least because the right to democratic governance is more controversial as a source of

international right.[21] Under international law, Bobby cannot be said to have a right to entry into a country of refuge; mere tyranny is not sufficient to overcome the general presumption that states may control entry onto their territory. It is worth noting, however, that the legal concept of *complementary protection* offers some possibility of granting Bobby, and those like him, some limited immunity from exclusion—although that form of protection falls far short of what is guaranteed by the covenants setting up norms of refuge and asylum.[22]

Our question, however, is moral, rather than legal; and, following the arguments I have made in this book and elsewhere, I would argue that Bobby does have a right to be free from the sorts of tyranny he faces in his state of origin, and that other states have no right to use coercion to insist that he continue in these unjust forms of relationship. From the first person, though, we need not even ask that question; we need only ask whether, and how, Bobby ought to take the exclusionary law as authoritative over him. Whether or not the law excluding him is unjust is not necessarily central to that story; we can have obligations to obey an unjust law, when it issues from an otherwise just political regime. Does Bobby's obligation to the regime in question entail listening to its commands, when what it commands is his exclusion?

I do not think so; instead, I think we face here two distinct visions of how to support and promote just institutions. One of these is to listen to the particular commands of that state; the other, though, is to increase that institution's reach, by bringing more of the human world within its coercive grasp. We rarely separate these two ways of thinking of our duty toward institutions. We generally take the set of people over whom the state governs for granted and ask only what we must do as members of that set to preserve the state's power. In cases of migration, though, we cannot make this assumption. We might help the cause of just institutions, not by listening to them, but by making them more authoritative over the world—by, in essence, giving them more people to govern. We might, that is, think that the duty to promote just institutions can be satisfied by bringing more of humanity within the world governed by those institutions. If this is right, though, then it seems Bobby faces a conflict from within the natural duty to preserve and promote just institutions; he might either listen to those institutions when they seek to exclude him, or—by ignoring those institutions when they seek to exclude him—expand the reach of those institutions, by giving him an additional person over whom that institution might be authoritative. If, in short, we are obligated to build stronger institutions, one way of doing that might be to increase the number of people over whom those institutions rule; and it is at least open to Bobby to say that his decision to migrate does just that.

This argument, I must admit, looks a bit like a trick. At the very least, it has the whiff of internal contradiction: I shall respect and preserve these just institutions by ignoring their attempts to exclude me! Nonetheless, I think these materials might actually justify Bobby's decision to migrate. If we like, we might rephrase this argument with reference to the moral disvalue of relationships of tyranny. We might think of the duty of justice as a duty to reduce the prevalence and power of totalitarian regimes. We might, however, think that one way of fulfilling the latter duty would be to remove people from the grasp of such regimes; and there is no reason in principle why the person I save from tyranny cannot be *myself*.

Much more, of course, might be said here; but I think these ideas offer at least the beginning of a justification for Bobby's decision to violate the exclusionary law. He is able, I think, to argue that the duty to preserve and promote just institutions does not reduce to a duty to obey each particular command of those institutions; in cases involving the movement of people across borders, it is possible that a violation of a particular command might be less morally significant than the creation of a new, and just, political relationship. When Bobby enters into a just society, after all, he will become possessed of rights against that society simply in virtue of territorial presence; the world is made more just, as it were, simply because he has moved across the border.

The most pressing—and, I suspect, controversial—case, however, involves not objectionable tyranny, but simple economic disadvantage. I must be clear here that we are not dealing with a case of poverty so significant that the impoverished face significant hurdles to their ability to build lives of dignity. There can be cases of deprivation so severe that they are best assimilated— in ethics, if not in law—to one of the cases discussed earlier. I am, instead, dealing now with mere economic inequality, whereby an individual might make a radical improvement in her life-chances simply by means of crossing an international border.

Carla is impoverished, but not facing avoidable death or impairment as a result, in her country of origin. She has the ability to walk across the border into a rights-protecting country, and will radically improve her standard of living by doing so. That country has passed a law precluding her from doing so.

Carla, of course, is markedly similar to Miguel Sanchez. Carla—and those like her—are often referred to as "economic migrants"; the term is sometimes condemned, since it often seems to downplay the ways in which material deprivation can be as destructive as state persecution.[23] What I want to insist upon, though, is that Carla's case does not seem one in which there is—at least absent some other part of the story—an adequate justification for her to break the exclusionary law. That law disadvantages her; but all laws disadvantage *someone*, and we do not in general take that fact to legitimate lawbreaking. The law is perhaps unjust; it may be that the best theory of global justice would describe this particular sort of poverty as morally illegitimate. That fact, however, does not seem sufficient to ground a right to break the laws of a just regime. We do not, in general, await moral perfection before asserting moral duties; even if the distribution of wealth in the United States is unjust—and I know very few people who don't complain about at least *some* aspects of that distribution—it doesn't follow that the property rights created by the United States are not rightly owed some degree of deference. The proper response to this sort of injustice is, if the United States is an entity deserving of some sorts of deference as a political structure, political speech, rather than lawbreaking. Even if a just society would have rather different allocations of property, it doesn't follow that you can simply take my car in *this* society. Similarly, the fact that the world right now is unjust, and it is unjust toward Carla, does not—not yet, at any rate—give Carla a right to break the law excluding her.

These conclusions are unsatisfying, to say the least. There are, however, many ways in which we can go from here. We might want to find some way to reject the thought that Carla has a duty to obey the exclusionary law. We might, for instance, want to say that Carla cannot be excluded from the wealthy country, because that country has gained its wealth by means of global exploitation and colonialism that produced Carla's poverty.[24] Even if this were true, however, it is not clear that this would justify Carla's lawbreaking; it would help us to see why the exclusion is unjust, but it would not thereby render the exclusionary state incapable of issuing authoritative commands. We could start speaking of civil disobedience toward the state; but even that, on most accounts of civil disobedience, is best understood as fulfilling a particular duty of obligation toward that state—civil diosobedients, after all, are not anarchists. For my part, I think we should go in a different direction. I want to talk not about the duty of obedience, but the costs of *compliance* with that duty. This conversation will return us to considerations similar to those discussed under the heading of reciprocity; we cannot rightly expect compliance with a duty, I will suggest, when the burdens of compliance with that duty are so significant that we could not anticipate ourselves—or, indeed, anyone—being able to successfully live up to its demands.

I want to begin this by distinguishing what the duty demands we do, with the concrete effects of the performance upon our own particular situation. A particularly powerful way of looking at this is drawn from the novel *Smilla's Sense of Snow*. In the novel, Smilla—a Greenlandic Inuit—is threatened with imprisonment; because Inuit form of life is built against the backdrop of unlimited land and distant horizons, imprisonment holds a particular terror for her, and for those like her:

> "Imprisonment," he says slowly, "in a little soundproof room with no windows is, I've been told, particularly uncomfortable when you've grown up in Greenland." There is no sadism in him. Merely a precise and perhaps faintly melancholy understanding of the instruments at his disposal. There are no prisons in Greenland. The greatest difference in the administration of the law in Copenhagen and in Nuuk is that in Greenland the punishment is more often a fine for offenses which in Denmark would have resulted in imprisonment. The Greenlandic hell is not the European rocky landscape with pools of sulfur. The Greenlandic hell is the locked room. In my memories of my childhood it seemed as though we were never indoors. Living in the same place for a long time was unthinkable for my mother. I feel the same way about my spatial freedom as I've noticed men feel about their testicles.[25]

If we are retributivists about punishment, then Smilla's imprisonment is rightful if it is merited for her crime; we have no reason, at the bar of justice, to ask about her *particular* dislike of imprisonment. If Smilla commits the same crime as Dennis—a former monk who actively likes small rooms—then we might rightly imprison them for the same period of time; Dennis will suffer less than Smilla, but our goal in imprisonment is justice, understood as something like the forfeiting of unjust advantage, not the perfect harmonization of psychological pain. There seems to be nothing unjust about Smilla's punishment, even though most of us would hope to have a criminal justice system in which justice is not the only virtue given significance. What this means, though, is that justice might relate to what it is we are right to do; the particular psychological burdens justice creates are, by and large, not a part of the story. In face of Smilla's story, I think we might begin to start thinking that the notion of mercy, as applied in the criminal law, is worth revisiting. Even if Smilla is not wronged by her imprisonment, we have a good moral reason to refrain from punishing her in this way.

I think something similar might be said not just about punishment after lawbreaking, but about compliance with the law. It is undoubtedly true that there are differences in how costly we will find it to comply with law. One who is not interested in punching others will find the law precluding battery easy to live up to. One who wants to punch *everyone* will experience a great deal more personal difficulty in seeking to obey the law. This does not, in itself, give us any particular reason to think that the law is optional; there is a good reason for the law to exist, and we understand that the costs of complying with that law will be distributed unequally. If the duty to obey that law exists, then the fact that its costs will be distributed unequally will not cause that duty to cease its hold upon all.

We might, then, apply this analysis to Carla. Imagine that Carla would triple her income by moving across the border. This is not entirely fanciful; while people rarely choose to migrate simply for economic reasons, it is undoubtedly a part of the story—and those who migrate from Mexico to the United States, for instance, do in fact often increase their income by a factor of between three and six.[26] The costs *to Carla* of compliance with this law are, to put it mildly, significant; especially once one recognizes that this income is not merely her own, but is very often relied upon by family members who do not participate in the market—including both children and the elderly. One way of responding to these facts is to say that the law excluding Carla is unjust. Our current question, though, is not with the justice of the law, but with *whether that law ceases to oblige Carla*. If what I say here is correct, the answer is no; Carla will be burdened by that law, but the particular burden it places on her does not make the law's obligation cease to hold.

This all looks rather heartless; and, if nothing more were said, it might be rightly condemned as inhuman. I think, though, we might go a bit further. Even if Carla has an obligation to obey the law, we might nonetheless ask what moral consequences follow from that obligation. It might, after all, be entirely possible for this duty to be trumped by particular obligations to particular others; it is at least possible that Carla's obligation to a child or parent might rightly trump that of her obligation to the excluding state. (Jeb Bush's quote lends itself naturally to this thought.) I am more interested, however, in how these considerations of costs might affect our evaluation of Carla's moral *character*. In this, I think notions of cost and reciprocity might come back into their own; not as a way of grounding the obligation to obey the law, but as a way of gauging the moral character of one who violates that law.

There are, here, at least two possibilities. One might be to ask about the relative costs of compliance with this sort of duty for the residents of the wealthy and of the more impoverished society. Migration law allows the wealthy and the poor countries to exclude outsiders, in the same equal way that the law forbids both the rich and the poor from sleeping under bridges. In fact, of course, the burdens faced by the wealthy are considerably less onerous than those faced by the poor. The wealthy by and large have fewer reasons to seek to migrate, and considerably more ease should they choose to do so.[27] It is open to us to think that this sort of lack of reciprocity, at the very least, might open the way toward some idea that failure to live up to the obligation here by the impoverished might be more comprehensible—and, thus, perhaps less indicative of a deformed moral character—than such failure on the part of the wealthy.

Another way of getting at this, though, would argue that there are some burdens in the face of which almost any normal person would fail to live up to a particular duty. One way to start here would be to start with the famous case of *Regina v. Dudley and Stephens*. This case, familiar to most law students, involved the murder and cannibalism of a cabin boy by the more experienced sailors of a shipwrecked British vessel. The question put before the judges in this case was whether or not necessity was a defense for murder; whether, that is, the fact that the murder was needed to preserve the lives of the sailors was adequate to defend that murder as legally permissible. Their answer was that it wasn't. What I am interested in, though, is a strange acknowledgment made by the judges that they, were they in the boat, would have acted just as the sailors themselves acted. This, in their view, did not make the act itself rightful:

> It must not be supposed that in refusing to admit temptation to be an excuse for crime it is forgotten how terrible the temptation was; how awful the suffering; how hard in such trials to keep the judgment straight and the conduct pure. *We are often compelled to set up standards we cannot reach ourselves, and to lay down rules which we could not ourselves satisfy. But* a man has no right to declare temptation to be an excuse, though he might himself have yielded to it, nor allow compassion for the criminal to change or weaken in any manner the legal definition of the crime.[28]

This is a remarkable statement; it announces that there are some moral tests that we can expect any normal human—even a judge—to fail. This does not, however, render the duty in question any less real. If the burdens of compliance are too strong, the situation calls for the application of mercy, perhaps— the judges in *Dudley* thought as much—but compliance itself does not cease to be required.[29]

This might seem deeply strange. If it is, the strangeness might emerge from the thought that morality is intended to guide our actions; we might find it hard to assert both that a thing *ought* to be done, and that it *won't* be done, by good people as we understand them to be. But it seems right—to me, at least—that the world can provide us with moral tests we can predictably be expected to fail.[30] Most of us would, I suspect, eventually choose to slap an innocent child, if the alternative entails deep pain for ourselves. This does not mean that we are monstrous; merely that we are human. Nor does it means that the child has somehow lost the right to be free from bodily assault. The assault is, perhaps, excusable—which is to say, that the ordinary sorts of punitive responses are inappropriate, but that the conduct itself continues to be wrongful. The narrator of Jonathan Littell's *The Kindly Ones* describes this well:

> Once again, let us be clear: I am not trying to say I am not guilty of this or that. I am guilty, you're not, fine. But you should be able to admit to yourselves that you might also have done what I did. . . . If you were born in a country and at a time not only when nobody comes to kill your wife and your children, but also nobody comes to ask you to kill the wives and children of others, then render thanks to God and go in peace. But always keep this thought in mind: you might be luckier than I, but you're not a better person. Because if you have the arrogance to think you are, that's just where the danger begins.[31]

The narrator's analysis is self-serving, perhaps, but that does not mean it is incorrect. The world may have spaces in which the ordinary person will fail to perform what ethics would demand; the thought that no such space could exist reflects privilege, rather than morality.

Things are different, perhaps, for Carla—certainly, the obligation to obey the exclusionary law is weaker, to put it mildly, than the duty to avoid murder or cannibalism. But the structure of the argument is the same. The personal cost of compliance with the duty may become so strong that we would, ourselves, expect failure were we in the situation. But that failure is, still, moral failure; it does not become rightful merely because it is inevitable. Its being inevitable, though, does make *some* moral difference. We are not allowed to condemn others as morally second-rate, when they fail tests we ourselves would fail. We cannot mark others out as uniquely immoral, when their crime is one that would expect ourselves to do, were we in their shoes.

The idea that there is a limit to how much we can expect people to be motivated by duty alone is a long-standing one within political philosophy. Rawls discusses it under the heading of the strains of commitment; a political society is only rightful when it is based upon principles we could imagine everyone accepting as motivating.[32] We cannot expect a society to persist, were that society grounded on principles that would require some people to sacrifice a great deal for the benefits of others; hence, Rawls's rejection of consequentialism, which he argues would demand such excessive willingness to sacrifice for others. These ideas might seem to help us escape from the conclusion that Carla has an obligation to obey the law. That law might cease to oblige were compliance with the law psychologically implausible. I think this conclusion, though, would be too hasty. Rawls's ideas here are concerned to provide the basis on which the political coercion at the heart of the modern constitutional state might be justified to those subject to that coercion; he wants, in other words, to figure out how people can continue to do politics together over time. The strains of commitment provide a constitutional democracy with some limits on what might be expected to do the job. These considerations, though, do not tell us that a given use of legal power is always wrongful, simply in virtue of the fact that failure to comply with that law is predictable. It is, at the very least, open to us to insist that the exclusionary law is just, or not just, on its merits; and that the obligation to obey that law persists, even when lawbreaking is both comprehensible and predictable.

3. Obligation and Migration: On Jeb Bush and Donald Trump

At this point, we might ask what has been gained. I have defended the thought that the law of exclusion might be rightly ignored by a great many people—including those whose countries of origin fail to provide them with the rights they are due as persons. I have also argued that this law, regardless of whether or not it is just, would continue to oblige a great many other people—but that we cannot expect the obligation here to actually be effective, for people of normal moral sensitivity; even if there is some obligation to obey the exclusionary law of a foreign country, that is, there is some degree of difference to standard of living past which *anyone* would make the decision to disobey that law. There is, in other words, no demonstration of an inferior moral character in the decision made to leave a relatively impoverished society and migrate without legal right to a wealthier one. Jeb Bush, in the remarks quoted at the start of this chapter, makes this point well. The migrant did break the law, and that is not a matter of moral indifference; the lawbreaking, however, was not one from which we can infer anything negative about that migrant's character. Quite the opposite, in fact; the migration is more often done to benefit particular others, those dependent on the migrant—hence, the thought that it might be an act of love. Bush, in this analysis, occupies an odd space within public discourse: he argues simultaneously that a society may rightly exclude the migrant and that the migrant's action should be viewed as a comprehensible, if not praiseworthy, act.

This speech doomed Bush's campaign; Donald Trump's campaign released a video titled "Act of Love," in which mugshots of undocumented migrants—together with a description of their violent crimes—were played as Bush spoke his words.[33] Trump's campaign had a fairly blunt view of migrants, whether documented or undocumented. His campaign promised a new "Deportation Force," potentially focused on deporting all undocumented migrants—Trump famously repeated, "They have to go," whenever discussing that population—coupled with the infamous wall along the southern border.[34]

These are familiar facts; what is their relevance here? It is tempting to think that Jeb Bush is incoherent—and Trump, while perhaps morally monstrous, was and is coherent. I think this is mistaken. Trump's analysis runs together two distinct questions: first, what states may do to deter undocumented migrants from entering the United States, and second, how we ought to understand the moral character of those who migrate without right. Trump's view is simple: we can do what we need to do, because these are (as he has it) bad hombres. Bush's analysis says that the question of what may be rightly done by a state to prevent migration is distinct from what we ought to think about those who manage to migrate nonetheless. I think Bush's vision, while also subject to criticism, is at the very least coherent. A country might seek to exclude some migrants, without thinking that those who migrate nonetheless are worthy of moral condemnation. The considerations given above can explain why this should be so. If the United States is a society capable of creating binding obligations on people in virtue of its laws, then its laws against undocumented migration can—until overcome by some more important moral consideration—oblige foreign citizens to refrain from such migration. Those who are not deterred, however, have not shown any moral failing we would not make under the same circumstances. Morality compels us to recognize that the costs they would bear, in refraining from migration, are costs we would similarly be unwilling to bear in the name of that sort of moral duty. Undocumented migration is not an act of depravity; it is an act any normal human would do, were they placed in the situation migrants themselves inhabit.

What, however, follows from this? The biggest conclusion, I think, is that there is nothing incoherent about defending the right to exclude, while refusing to offer moral condemnation to the undocumented. The former right may or may not be legitimate; that is a question for another time. But if that right exists, we might use it to justify some policies designed to make migration without documents more difficult. The latter part of the story, though—on which we must recognize the absence of bad character involved in undocumented migration—has its own role to play in the development of policy. I will here examine only two implications of recognizing these facts.

The first is that the act of migrating without right is, even if a violation of law, not in itself indicative of a moral defect; accordingly, the conventional apparatus of criminal law is poorly applied to the situation of the undocumented migrant. I will borrow Joel Feinberg's analysis here: much of the criminal law is designed to offer a space within which the state offers an authoritative disavowal of the criminal's action. Incarceration, in particular, offers not simply an unwelcome result for the incarcerated, but a sort of spectacle, in which the criminal's action is held up for an authoritative disavowal. In contrast, other forms of unwelcome treatment—such as fines, even if rather large—do not tend to involve this symbolic form of speech. We reserve incarceration for those cases in which we want to communicate to the criminal, and to the world, that the action done is not only illegal but morally reprehensible.[35] (This fact can also explain, I think, the anger felt by many people that no banking official spent a day in jail in the United States as a result of the 2008 recession.) This means, though, that the increasing willingness to treat undocumented migrants through the lens of incarceration is morally wrong in a profound way. Migrants are increasingly subjected to detention either in prison-like facilities or in prisons themselves. This might be wrong, of course, simply in virtue of the specific wrongs often accompanying the prison experience in the United States.[36] But I think it might also be wrong simply from the inappropriate message communicated through the ritual of imprisonment. We mark out the undocumented migrant as morally depraved by subjecting her to the same rituals used to stigmatize violent criminals. If we acknowledge that the migrant, in choosing to break the law, commits no wrong we would not ourselves also choose, we would be more averse to using this sort of policy implement; the message it sends is not one we have the right to communicate.

The second implication I want to address is the continued relevance, for conservatives about migration, of the idea of rewarding lawbreaking. This is sometimes spelled out with reference to the moral wrong involved in undocumented migration itself. We have seen, in an earlier chapter, Steven King's thought that DACA rewarded the wrongdoer. He was not alone in his assertion; Tom Tancredo, a conservative congressman from Colorado, consistently rejected any program of regularization, since that would "reward people who have broken the law."[37] Sometimes, such ideas are developed in a more future-directed way: the suggestion is made that the act of migrating without legal authorization speaks to a malignant character—from which we can expect anything from poor citizenship to outright criminal activity. Jeff Sessions, Trump's first attorney general, argued repeatedly that sanctuary cities such as Chicago protect "criminal aliens"—by which he seemed to mean, simultaneously, that the alien is a criminal in virtue of his migration and that violent crimes can be expected from him in the future. In a similar vein, the Trump administration has recently introduced a hotline—the Victims of Immigration Crime Engagement (VOICE) hotline—on which one can provide information about "crimes committed by individuals with a nexus to immigration."[38] This rather odd locution similarly elides the distinction between crimes that show one's character to be deformed, and the action of violating migration law. This elision, however, implies—wrongly—that one's status as undocumented is predictive of one's proclivity to violence. As the father of Mollie Tibbetts noted, her daughter was not killed by an undocumented migrant; she was killed by a human who happened to have the legal status of being undocumented.[39]

Most powerfully, the policy by which the children of undocumented migrants were separated from them at the border was justified with reference to the thought that the parents themselves were exceptional in their moral depravity. Katie Waldman, a spokesperson for Immigrations and

Customs Enforcement, argued that these separations were required by the best interests of the child. It would be, she asserted, better for those children to be placed in custody than left in the care of criminals:

> [ICE has] a legal obligation to protect the best interests of the child whether that be from human smugglings, drug traffickers or nefarious actors who knowingly break our immigration laws.[40]

This, of course, relies explicitly on the thought that there is something nefarious indeed about crossing the border without right; the parent who breaks migration laws is a bad person, and the child must be protected from that parent. None of this, however, is true. The separation of families at the border assumes that the parents of those families are pernicious people, from whom children ought to be separated. But that elides the decision to break the law, under extreme deprivation, with the displaying of a uniquely depraved character. What I say here can, if nothing else, offer a way of speaking back to this moral elision. Even if the law excluding Carla creates moral obligations, it is a law that we ourselves—were we in her situation—would be unable to fulfill. That should provide us with some degree of humility—and, perhaps, the willingness to compromise—in our political deliberation surrounding migration. At the very least, we might be able to reject one fairly common version of this thought: that by regularizing undocumented residents, we would thereby be rewarding a uniquely immoral set of people now, with an influx of immoral people expected to come. What created the migration, in the end, may have been the simple fact that such migration was vastly rewarding for those who undertook it.[41] The people who chose to migrate—and those who may still choose to do so—are not responding in a uniquely immoral way, but a manner that most reasonable humans should find comprehensible. Immigration policy might seek to acknowledge these facts and adjust its vision of ethics accordingly; or it can refuse to do so and engage in the continued demonization of migrants and those who work with them.

It is, of course, an unfortunate reality that much of the world will continue to choose the latter option. The rights of migrants are under attack throughout most of the highly developed countries. The views of figures like Trump are clearly on the rise. I do not, in response, claim that views such as that of Jeb Bush are correct, all things considered. Those views may, of course, rest upon a view of the right to exclude that cannot pass scrutiny. But I do believe that those who defend the right to exclude—including myself—ought to be much more careful about what they take that right to entail. In particular, I think those who reject open borders ought to nonetheless recognize a great many limits on what can be rightly done to undocumented migrants. Whether or not the decision to migrate without right is an act of love, it is emphatically not an act of moral depravity; and our ongoing debate about the morality of migration is impoverished by words and deeds of those who insist that it is.

One question, of course, is left open by this chapter. If we would be wrong to regard the undocumented migrant as displaying malignancy of character, might we not have a reason not simply to avoid asserting her moral depravity, but also to refrain from excluding or deporting her? Might we not, in other words, think that we have reason to change not only what we say about the migrant, but what we do, as well? The answer, I think, is yes—but we can only reach that answer after examining more closely what the virtue of mercy actually entails; and it is to this task that I now turn.

9

On Mercy in Politics

I have, in the preceding chapters, frequently mentioned mercy as a particular sort of virtue. I have not, however, said very much about what that virtue is. It is now time to become slightly more specific about what mercy is, and about how we might deploy the concept of mercy within political life. The present chapter will try to do this, as a precursor to discussing the relationship between mercy and migration in the following chapter. I want, in particular, to do three things. The first to is to explain why I take the concept of *mercy* to be the appropriate one to use in our discussions of migration. The second is to explain why the appeal to mercy is neither perverse nor sectarian, despite the fact that it might at first seem to be both. The final section is to explain why liberals—even political liberals—might have reason to adopt some notion of mercy as a distinct political virtue. Liberalism, I will argue, has reason to think that even a just state in which mercy is not practiced is a very poor sort of state—and, indeed, is unlikely to remain just for long.

Before any of this, though, I will have to spend some time explaining why it is that mercy is even a plausible candidate for a political virtue. Much of political philosophy, since John Rawls's *A Theory of Justice*, has been dominated by a concern for justice—for, that is, the definition and defense of rights, and a rightful political order. Rawls, indeed, identifies justice as the first virtue of political institutions, much as truth is of mathematics; laws and institutions, "no matter how efficient and well-arranged," must be altered or abolished if they fail to do justice.[1] This philosophical concern, of course, follows on the political struggles of the 1960s, in which a great many social conflicts—including, notably, the civil rights struggles in the United States—were comprehensible as fights over justice; as fights, that is, by those deprived of right for a world in which their rights are defended. This legacy is essential to understanding both philosophy and activism today. The same legacy, though, can become a conceptual prison. The state can do a great many things that are worthy of moral censure; not all of them involve a failure to treat people as moral equals, in the institutional settings in which those conflicts arise. Rawls himself understood this. While he identified justice as the first virtue

Justice, Migration, and Mercy. Michael Blake, Oxford University Press (2020). © Oxford University Press.
DOI: 10.1093/oso/9780190879556.001.0001

of political institutions, he never argued that it was the *only* such virtue—and, indeed, later made clear that a great many other virtues might be rightly part of a morally defensible and stable set of political institutions. A state can be unjust, of course, if it fails to provide individual people with those rights and goods that are required for the effective exercise of their agency, or if it otherwise fails to provide people that to which they are morally entitled. But a state that does *only* that—which never violates rights, but which never goes out of its way to help those whose plans and projects might be helped—is guilty of moral infirmity. To repeat Jeffrie Murphy's point, which began this book: the one who carefully avoids wronging others cannot be accused of injustice. But it that is *all* he does for his fellow humans, he can certainly be accused of *something*; he is, at least, hardly a good example of what a good human should be.[2]

I understand mercy, then, to be the virtue of not giving someone the harsh treatment we are permitted in justice to provide them, out of a moral concern for the effects of that treatment upon the recipient of that harsh treatment. Adam Perry analyzes mercy in similar terms.[3] In cases of mercy, Perry writes, there exist two possible options; we might—without injustice—choose to treat a particular agent with either harshness or leniency. Mercy, as a virtue, is shown when we choose the lenient option and refrain from imposing the harsh one. Importantly, though, mercy as a virtue finds a home only when the imposition of the harsh option would not be morally wrongful. As Perry has it: one never *has to* act mercifully. Nevertheless, Perry argues, the state has a reason to act mercifully through its criminal law; practices such as leniency in sentencing—and, importantly, pardons—may reflect valid moral concerns. The showing of mercy, indeed, might enable the state to "model the virtue of mercy for its citizens."[4] I would like to extend this idea, beyond the criminal law to the law preventing individuals from moving across borders. We might think that mercy tells the state that some people, who would not be treated unjustly by exclusion or deportation, ought nonetheless be free from such practices. In this way, the state might both live the virtue of mercy and demonstrate the sorts of virtues that undergird democratic stability.

This, then, is the core of the virtue I will defend: the thought that we have moral reasons, as individuals and as states, by which we might help the individual people around us pursue and develop their plans, even when the success of those plans is not something for which we have responsibility in justice. We have, in other words, a good moral reason to work for the success of the lives of other people—even when those other people could not claim injustice, were we to refrain from helping. I use the language of mercy to express this, but the same virtue might be described with reference to kindness, or the avoidance of cruelty, or perhaps simply moral decency. However we describe this virtue, it entails the principled insistence that we ought to take care of the needs of those who do not have a particular claim on our assistance. The goods they seek are ones that could be brought into the world through our assistance. They do not have a particular claim on our help; they are not facing the destruction of their agency, or some particular relationships such as equality of citizenship that might make that help mandatory. We could treat them harshly, without treating them unfairly. They are, instead, simply needy, and in a position where we might help fulfill that need. We might, without injustice, turn away from such people. Where we consistently do so, though, we reveal ourselves to be morally deficient; we are not unjust, but we are certainly unmerciful.

I want, in short, to defend the idea that a society can be criticized as unmerciful, when it refuses to go beyond justice. Many people, I suspect, will accept in general the thought that some virtue like mercy ought to be present within political society—as part of the discursive toolkit by which we evaluate, praise, and condemn particular sorts of policy. Many people, though, are likely to think that the word *mercy* is the wrong one to use; and so it is to a defense of this language that I now turn.

1. Mercy and Perversity

Why, then, should we understand this virtue under the heading of the word *mercy*? I cannot, I suspect, convince everyone that the term is the correct one; but I can at least explain why it seems right to *me*. There are three reasons why the term seems to me the correct one to use. The first is that the one who presents herself at the border is, in a rather literal sense, *at the mercy* of those who are guarding that border. The concept of being at someone's mercy, of course, is a recognition of a radical inequality of power; I am at your mercy when I can be utterly destroyed by your decision-making, and you in turn are immune from my own. This utter difference—in which the individual, as a natural person, presents herself to a political society, whose armed officers offer her threats should she attempt to cross a line—is one that ought not be ignored, or papered over by vague language. The migrant, we should remember, is at the mercy of the country to which she seeks admission, and the language of mercy might be one way of keeping these facts before our eyes.

The second reason, though, is to recognize the standing relationship between religion and the morality of migration. Many religions have a concept of something like mercy. The Islamic notion of *rahmah* is understood in terms strikingly similar to that of the Christian notion of mercy; in Buddhism, too, the figure of Guanyin is understood to be the bodhisattva associated with compassion or mercy. In the history of North American and European thought about migration, the Christian ideal of *Misericordia*—mercy—has had a significant role to play.[5] I am not claiming, of course, that politics, in a just society, should reflect specifically Christian norms. I am, instead, making a rather more contextual and moderate claim: those who have fought for legal protections for the migrant have often done so, in Europe and in North America, for theological reasons, and those of us doing political philosophy might learn from work. The sanctuary movement, for instance, began with a theological commitment that those fleeing violence in Central America should be given a home within the United States—despite that latter country's refusal to do so. John Fife, minister at the Southside Presbyterian Church in Tucson, opened his church to those fleeing oppression and cited the Christian ideals of both justice and mercy in doing so:

> We are writing to inform you that Southside United Presbyterian Church will violate the Immigration and Nationality Act, Section 274(A). . . . We believe that justice and mercy require that people of conscience actively assert our God-given right to aid anyone fleeing from persecution and murder. . . . We beg of you, in the name of God, to do justice and mercy in the administration of your office.[6]

Today, the seeds planted by Fife and others have blossomed into a new sanctuary movement—one devoted to resisting the deportations undertaken by the Trump administration. Here, too, the devotion to the thought that justice must be accompanied by mercy—by the will to be moved by the need of the outsider, even when we might turn away—continues to inform Christian activism. The thought that Christian mercy ought to affect how a state uses its borders is, then, both long-standing and powerful. (Indeed, one history of Catholic teaching and activism on migration is simply called *Mercy without*

Borders.) The United States Conference of Catholic Bishops has recently reiterated this call to combine justice and mercy:

> A country's regulation of borders and control of immigration must be governed by concern for all people and by mercy and justice. A nation may not simply decide that it wants to provide for its own people and no others. A sincere commitment to the needs of all must prevail.[7]

I should, of course, reiterate that I do not expect political philosophers to use this term *because* Christian social teaching has used it. I want, more modestly, for those of us who write about political philosophy to be open to the possibility that the Christians are, here, on to something important—and that we can use the language of their faith, without committing ourselves to that faith itself. Even a political liberal, that is, can be open to the possibility of acknowledging the rhetorical power of adopting the Christian terminology—so long as it is possible to use this terminology without thereby invoking the comprehensive values found within Christianity itself.

In the next section of this chapter, I will try to demonstrate that this can be done. But the third, and most important, reason I use the concept of mercy is the fact that the criminal law itself uses often has occasion to deploy the concept of mercy, and uses it in contexts rather similar to the ones in which I mean to use it here. Recall the case of Smilla, or the sailors in the case of *Dudley and Stephens*. These individuals faced particular punishments, for particular crimes; there would have been no injustice involved in the imposition of the punishments in question. But, in both cases, the evil done to the particular person seems excessive. The state that put them in prison—or, for the sailors, hanged them—would not be wronging them; but it has a good moral reason to avoid the punishment nonetheless. (The sailors, we should note, received conditional pardons from Queen Victoria, despite her aversion to the practice of pardons more generally.) What the state does in giving mercy to the criminal, that is, is to refrain from doing what justice permits it to do—in the name of the particular good of the person against whom that state action would be brought. The criminal is treated mercifully when his crime is not met with that punishment which justice would permit for that crime. So, too, is the migrant. If her deportation or her exclusion is not unjust, we should not think that the moral question has been entirely decided. We can, in short, think that mercy itself might intervene to prevent the state from doing what is just and yet cruel—much as in the criminal law itself.

This, however, might bring us to the issue of perversity. There are ways in which my defense of the language of mercy might be thought to assume exactly the sorts of relationships that a moral theory of migration ought to undermine. There are at least three of these. The first takes off from the analogy with the criminal law. The one who is treated with mercy, there, is identified as a wrongdoer; she receives mercy, as it were, only because justice provides her with a condemnation. This seems, though, to presuppose that the one crossing borders without right—or the one presenting herself at those borders without a claim in justice—is somehow a wrongdoer in need of forgiveness. That, to put it mildly, seems perverse. The second sort of perversity begins with the notion of gratitude. The one to whom mercy is provided, we might think, has some obligation of gratitude; the court has, as it were, done something for him that he did not deserve—and the morally appropriate response, we might think, is gratitude. But we might think that something is rather wrong when there is a call made for gratitude to be expressed by people like, in the example of the previous chapter, Carla. She is born into relative poverty and has crossed a line into relative wealth. She is rightly deported, let us imagine, but the state refuses to do this. Does it not seem, at the very least, a little bit self-serving for the state to insist upon her gratitude? She was, recall, born into poverty, just as many of those now awaiting her gratitude were born into wealth. Is there not something perverse about the expectation that the impoverished owe gratitude to the wealthy, when the wealthy refrain from utterly decimating the lives of the poor? We might, finally, return to the theme of Christianity, and note that the giving of mercy is ultimately the domain of God; those of us who show mercy in this world do so in a self-conscious imitation of God and his love. But is there not something rather horrible about taking the citizens of a wealthy society to be godlike, doling out their mercy to the relatively impoverished citizens of the developing world? Is the goal of political philosophy, in short, not to overcome this sort of vicious inequality—rather than seeking new ways to rein in its excesses?

All of these are powerful worries. I do not think any of them are sufficient reason to refrain from using the language of mercy. We might start with the issue of wrongdoing; it is true that the most frequent home for the norm of mercy is in the criminal law, but that merely reflects the fact that the criminal law is the place in which states most directly and obviously inflict violence upon particular persons. Mercy itself, though, seems to be applicable to any context in which someone who might inflict hard treatment upon another nonetheless has a strong moral reason to refrain from doing so—a reason that begins with the importance of that person's good to her, and the ways in which we would destroy that good were we to do what justice permits. It might be good to consider this by focusing on what it is that the state would do to the migrant, were it to use force to push her across the border or to keep her from crossing that border. It is going to use coercion—which is another way of saying that it proposes to use violence, or the threat of violence. The purposes of that coercion, the Supreme Court has repeatedly said, are unlike those found in punishment; deportation, on current American law, may be unwelcome, but it "is not punishment for crime."[8] For the one being deported, though, that legal nicety might seem somehow irrelevant. The state, in deporting, is doing something profoundly damaging to an individual person, and the individual person might react as though it were a punishment indeed. And if it can be understood in these ways, it seems possible also to allow the concept of mercy to be applied here, to tell the state why some deportation or pattern of deportation is morally disreputable.

The issue of gratitude is, perhaps, more complex. I cannot provide any theory here of when we ought to feel grateful—or of how we might rightly express that gratitude. But I think two things might be said, to make the worries expressed less damaging. The first is that the proper form of gratitude in a political community might involve nothing more onerous than doing one's part to maintain and preserve that political community. As things stand, I have no particular duty to preserve the institutions of French democracy—although I would, if I were to move to France, and I might have stronger duties here were these institutions to become marginal or endangered. (Certainly, I accept that I have a duty to avoid *damaging* French political institutions, although this duty rarely makes a difference in my day-to-day life.) We might think that whatever gratitude ought to be showed by the migrant could be limited to these, fairly uncontroversial forms. The second thing to note is that, even if we were to think that particular forms of gratitude were appropriate, the virtue of gratitude would likely come with an expiration date. When I was hired at my university, I felt enormous gratitude to all those who had chosen to provide me with a scarce and valuable thing—and did my best to express that gratitude. When I became an American citizen, I also felt a surge of gratitude toward a country in which I have a home, a family, and a career. In both cases, though, the felt gratitude was not incompatible with—in very short order—the felt right to criticize the practices and decisions of both my university and my country. When one is chosen to join a community of equals, one might show one's gratitude—but one has to, in short order, get down to the messy business of *acting* as an equal. Gratitude, at least when it is taken to mean something apart from an ongoing duty to preserve the institutions in which one is found, might be an inherently temporary virtue.

The final worry here is perhaps the most profound: isn't there something morally strange about arguing for the obligation of the United States (say) to demonstrate mercy in its dealings with strangers? The goal should be justice—which, in a cosmopolitan vein, we might think entails the abolition of borders themselves. There are, again, two answers to this. The first is found in the earlier part of this book; there, I argued that there are no good reasons to think that liberalism itself requires open borders. If this is true, though, then there will always be cases of people who want to go to places but who have no particular right to do so. The moral question to be asked— does mercy allow us to understand what ought to be done, in the face of such migrants?—seems one that would arise even in an ideally just world. If, for instance, we arrived at a world of global economic justice—however you might define those terms—there might still be a need for an account of mercy. The second reply, though, goes to the point of political philosophy in the first place. Even if the radical is right, and the world we ought to be building is one without borders, the fact remains that here and now our world is shot through with borders, all of them guarded rather jealously by heavily armed men and women. We stand in need of moral principles for precisely this world, with those armed men and women. That these principles might be irrelevant in a world without borders does not negate their power in this world. Bertolt Brecht's "A Bed for the Night" expresses these ideas; the one who provides beds for the homeless does nothing, says the song, to alter the material conditions that gave rise to the homeless. But it does something, here and now, and that's worth celebrating:

> It won't change the world
> It won't improve relations among men
> It will not shorten the age of exploitation
> But a few men have a bed for the night
> For a night the wind is kept from them
> The snow meant for them falls on the roadway.[9]

So, too, with the idea of mercy for the migrant. We could imagine a world so thoroughly transformed that no migrant is at the mercy of the state to which she seeks entry—or to the global forces that produce wealth and poverty. But, while waiting for that world to arrive, we might as well get on with the business of figuring out who must be helped and how and why we are the ones to help them.

2. Virtues in Political Life

I want to return to the thought that mercy might be an inappropriate basis for public discourse about political ethics—not because it would be perverse, but because it would be *sectarian*. John Rawls, after all, developed in his concept of public reason a particular vision of a society capable of stability over time, despite the presence within that of multiple distinct comprehensive doctrines of ethics. The society would be stable, argued Rawls, precisely because matters of basic justice and constitutional essentials would be justified with reference to a political conception of justice—which, Rawls emphasizes, does not depend upon the truth of any particular comprehensive doctrine.[10] Rawls calls upon us, in short, to develop a discursive practice for political life that does not depend upon the particular virtues or vices present within comprehensive doctrines. What I am doing in this chapter and the next, though, is arguing for a discursive practice in which a particular concept of mercy can be used for the evaluation of migration policy. Does the power of my argument here depend upon the rejection of Rawls's own?

The answer is, I think, no; there is space within Rawls's political liberalism for what I propose to do here. There are two reasons for this, if we were to stick quite close to the vision of liberalism defended by Rawls himself. The first is that Rawls limits his most demanding test of political ethics to matters of basic justice and constitutional essentials; once these are satisfied, it is possible for political agents to use discursive materials that would not be appropriate for use in these more foundational contexts. Put more simply: we need not reason from public materials in all political contexts—and, while this might be a matter of some interpretive complexity, it is not clear that Rawls would regard all migration policy as constituting a matter of basic justice. The second thing to note, however, is that Rawls himself acknowledges the importance of particular political virtues. These political virtues might be accepted into the political conception, so as to provide additional materials by which the society in question might come to grips with the ethics of public institutions:

Even though political liberalism seeks common ground and is neutral in aim, it is important to note that it may still affirm the superiority of certain forms of moral character and encourage certain moral virtues. Thus, justice as fairness includes an account of certain political virtues—the virtues of fair social cooperation such as the virtues of civility and tolerance, of reasonableness and the sense of fairness (IV:5–7). The crucial point is that admitting these virtues into a political conception does not lead to the perfectionistic state of a comprehensive doctrine.[11]

Rawls emphasizes, here, some particular virtues; but I think it is open to us to introduce our own. I believe we might think that mercy itself—or some political conception of mercy, suitably shorn of all its comprehensive implications—is one such virtue.

It could only perform that role, though, if it were possible for it to be shown to be potentially compatible with a variety of comprehensive doctrines. I believe that it can indeed be thought to do just that. In the rest of this section, I will discuss only three forms of comprehensive doctrine, each of whom have materials that might be used to ground a political conception of mercy. The goal, here, is to show that we might follow Rawls's own invitation, and think that there is a place even within his system for a virtue such as mercy. If that were true, then the concept of mercy might play the discursive role I have discussed; it might be something we could invoke, in public discourse, as a means of defending or criticizing particular forms of migration policy.

2.1. Christianity

I have discussed Christianity to some degree above, and so will try to be comparatively brief in what follows. The Christian tradition explicitly identifies mercy as a virtue, and applies that virtue to political life. How this virtue is lived and understood, of course, varies tremendously; there may be no such thing as the uniquely Christian position on any particular matter of social importance. The concept of mercy, however, is central to more or less any Christian worldview; the death and resurrection of Jesus Christ is understood as a form of gift, rather than as what is demanded by justice. What the fallen sinner is entitled to, in justice, is damnation; she is saved by the mercy of God—not by his justice. Hence, the emphasis in Christian theology of mercy as a social norm that ought to guide God's children in the present world. The papal encyclical *Dives in Misericordia*—rich in mercy—articulates the need to temper justice with mercy:

> The experience of the past and of our own time demonstrates that justice alone is not enough, that it can even lead to the negation and destruction of itself, if that deeper power, which is love, is not allowed to shape human life in its various dimensions. It has been precisely historical experience that, among other things, has led to the formulation of the saying: *summum ius, summa iniuria.* This statement does not detract from the value of justice and does not minimize the significance of the order that is based upon it; it only indicates, under another aspect, the need to draw from the powers of the spirit which condition the very order of justice, powers which are still more profound.[12]

The continuing relevance of mercy here has influenced Christian teaching on migration, as already mentioned. But I would like to emphasize that this teaching does not emerge only within Catholic thought; it is, instead, found in any number of Christian traditions, and in any number of sites of resistance to unmerciful forms of migration control. Roger Mielke, a senior official of the Evangelical Church of Germany, argued that the German openness to the refugee (*willkommenskultur*) reflected the Christian virtues of mercy:

> [We] are to receive and care for the lost, the wounded, and those in need of protection. In every suffering human face, the body of Christ is to see Jesus himself. The church is to encounter each person with an unconditional commitment that extends far beyond the circle of fellow Christians, reaching out to include every person as a creation of God who, though lost, is someone Jesus came to save. As Matthew 25:40 teaches, "Whatever you did for one of the least of these brothers and sisters of mine, you did for me." . . . In accordance with this ethic, there is only one possible way for the body of Christ to respond to the vulnerable and marginalized, including today's refugees and migrants: with unconditional love. In a nutshell: we must practice mercy.[13]

Pope Francis has recently used similar language in speaking about the migrant. On July 6, 2018, Pope Francis said a special mass for migrants. Speaking on the anniversary of his visit to Lampedusa, the pope emphasized the need to approach the migrant in the spirit of mercy:

The Lord promises refreshment and freedom to all the oppressed of our world, but he needs us to fulfil his promise. He needs our eyes to see the needs of our brothers and sisters. He needs our hands to offer them help. He needs our voice to protest the injustices committed thanks to the silence, often complicit, of so many. I should really speak of many silences: the silence of common sense; the silence that thinks, "it's always been done this way"; the silence of "us" as opposed to "you." Above all, the Lord needs our hearts to show his merciful love towards the least, the outcast, the abandoned, the marginalized. . . . Before the challenges of contemporary movements of migration, the only reasonable response is one of solidarity and mercy.[14]

Much more could be said, of course; the Christian concept of mercy is complex, and I cannot claim expertise in the theology required to understand it fully. But I hope to have shown at least this much: the Christian, if motivated by ideas such as those discussed here, will be able to enter into a public political discourse about how and when mercy ought to be shown to the stranger. Rawls's *Political Liberalism*, after all, begins in some ways with the difficulty of democratic deliberation across divides of religious commitment, and Rawls hoped to have shown that this deliberation could be done. The political conception of mercy I defend, then, might be accepted by the reasonable Christian and used to enter into political discourse.

2.2. The Ethics of Care

I believe something similar might be said about the ethics of care, as developed in the last half of the twentieth century. I want to be careful, here; I am writing in the tradition of John Rawls, for whom considerations of right and justice were primary. It was exactly this sort of vision that the ethics of care often sought (and seeks) to either modify or reject. Many ethicists of care—although by no means all—argued that the concept of justice itself might be, at the very least, demoted from its position of importance in the work of philosophers such as Rawls.[15] There are, moreover, many distinct visions of the ethics of care, and they disagree about important issues—such as, among others, whether or not care describes primarily an emotional state or primarily a particular sort of work or practice.

These differences, though, come with certain common themes, which demonstrate that a public norm of mercy might be accepted by many ethicists of care as a reasonable addition to our public discussions about migration. Virginia Held describes three of these themes.[16] The first is that the ethics of care demands the acknowledgment of the particular, rather than subsuming that particular under some abstract category. What is morally primary is the actual encounter with the particular person, rather than the bloodless abstractions we might develop to sort and categorize people. The second is the thought that ethics itself resists subsumption under broader principles of justification. An example might help: Held notes that analytic political philosophy would allow us to have friends—so long as the principle allowing that friendship can be shown to be justifiable to all humans, both friends and not. This, Held argues, is an inadequate basis for moral life— not to mention a rather weak foundation for friendship. The ethics of care is particularly associated with feminist scholarship and emerges from the conviction that the distinct social roles assigned to women—homemaker, mother, caregiver—have moral demands to care for others; the power of these demands has often been invisible to men. This leads to the final aspect of the ethics of care: the primary principle is the recognition of need, and vulnerability, and the common human need to be cared for. The default philosophical agent, argues Held, is the atomistic man, who is identified with his choices and his freedom. The lives of the vulnerable—the child, the elderly— are pushed to one side, to be either ignored or treated as problem cases to be dealt with later. The ethics of care brings the marginalized to the fore and argues that ethics demands that we work to care for the vulnerable—rather than first developing abstract principles by which these vulnerable people might be analyzed.

This, of course, is a mere sketch of a complex family of views; but I think it might suffice to get us started. The ethics of care seems to begin with the considerations quite similar to those that motivate the virtue of mercy, as I understand it here. Like mercy, it seeks to go beyond a concern to the administration of formal justice; instead, it looks to the particular ways in which particular people will be affected by what we do. Indeed, it seems to begin precisely with the thought that radical need—that the vulnerability of some people, when they present themselves at the border—might be an independent basis for moral evaluation. The concept of mercy seems to begin with the idea that we should not, in ethics, simply rely upon abstract reasoning, but should enquire about what we can do for those who are vulnerable to our decision-making. The particular vulnerability of those at the border has, indeed, already been examined by feminists working within the care tradition; Eva Kittay, for example, analyzes the migration of relatively impoverished women from developing countries to developed ones through the lens of care—and argues that this sort of migration, which does violence to the relationship between the woman and her family, is a site of distinct moral wrongs.[17]

The notion of care, of course, can be taken to constitute a radical challenge to the entirety of the project of liberal justice. It might, for instance, be taken to have genuinely revolutionary implications, at the global level. In applying her own vision of the ethics of care to the international realm, for instance, Virginia Held argues that we might find—in a world in which individuals genuinely cared for one another, across international borders, and used that care to build relationships and practices of mutual respect—the use of concepts like human rights might simply become unnecessary. We should, at any rate, be willing to demote the notion of right, rather than analogize all of ethical value to some version of justice.[18] But I think those who endorse the ethics of care might also endorse the political virtue of mercy—even if they do so only in the full recognition that it does not constitute the more radical alteration they seek. The virtue of mercy, at the very least, reflects the need to be concerned first with the need of the particular other, rather than with the abstract question of whether or not that other has a claim in justice to what she seeks. As such, it seems at least potentially possible for those who endorse this form of ethics to accept the political conception of mercy.

2.3. Kantian Ethics

The ethics of care is often developed by opposition to Kantian ethics—and there is good reason to think that the two visions of ethics begin with distinct premises. The ethics of care, after all, begins with the particular and mistrusts principle; Kantian ethics, in contrast, insists upon the principled test of the categorical imperative and mistrusts the sorts of empathy and particularity endorsed by the ethics of care.[19]

Nevertheless, it seems plausible that some version of mercy might be accepted by a reasonable Kantian, as a way of living the distinct Kantian vision of beneficence. Kant, of course, is no less complex than any of the other theorists of justice considered here, and much of what I will say might be challenged by those who know more than I do about Kantian thought. But perhaps a rough outline of Kantian ethics could suffice.

Kant divides his ethical thought between the doctrine of right and the doctrine of virtue.[20] The former is the realm of justice and of rights—rights which are, in principle, susceptible of being defended by coercion. Hence, the obligation to refrain from murder is a duty of justice, and the state is right to coercively punish those who fail to abide by this duty. The doctrine of virtue, however, defends moral duties which are distinct in a number of ways. These duties are not duties of justice, and they do not identify agents that might make claims of right upon us. Hence, the duty of beneficence— the duty to work for the particular plans and ends of some other people, not for our sake but for theirs—is not a duty that produces rights on the part of the beneficiaries of our beneficence. Those over whom we might exercise this duty cannot claim to have been wronged when we refrain from doing so. The duty is, instead, an *imperfect* one. The duty is, moreover, not rightly defended by means of coercion; the state could not mandate that its citizens act in a beneficent manner toward one another. Even if that were possible—and it is difficult to see how we might be forced to demonstrate this form of virtue—it is not the right sort of duty for this sort of coercion. We are, instead, given space within which to decide for ourselves how and when to develop a plan with which to assist the needy and the vulnerable. We have, as Kant has it, a certain "playroom" (*latitudo*) within which we might decide for ourselves how to be beneficent.[21] Nevertheless, the failure to be beneficent—the failure to demonstrate this virtue, by developing some plan within which the ends of others might be assisted, by being integrated into our own—is indeed an ethical failing. The one who fails to be beneficent fails to abide by the categorical imperative, and the maxim of his action is incapable of being justified:

> Yet a *fourth*, for whom things are going well while he sees that others (whom he could very well help) have to contend with great hardships, thinks: what is it to me? let each be as happy as heaven wills or as he can make himself; I shall take nothing from him nor even envy him; only I do not care to contribute anything to his welfare or to his assistance in need! Now, if such a way of thinking were to become a universal law the human race could admittedly very well subsist, no doubt even better than when everyone prates about sympathy and benevolence and even exerts himself to practice them occasionally, but on the other hand also cheats where he can, sells the right of human beings or otherwise infringes upon it. But although it is possible

that a universal law of nature could very well subsist in accordance with such a maxim, it is still impossible to will that such a principle hold everywhere as a law of nature. For, a will that decided this would conflict with itself, since many cases could occur in which one would need the love and sympathy of others and in which, by such a law of nature arisen from his own will, he would rob himself of all hope of the assistance he wishes for himself.[22]

The duty of beneficence, then, is a duty that falls upon us all. It does not find its source—as it does in the ethics of care—in the emotional life of the human. Indeed, Kant distrusts emotion and argues that the only sort of love that can be commanded by duty is the rather cold love that emerges from practical agency:

> For, love as an inclination cannot be commanded, but beneficence from duty—even though no inclination impels us to it and, indeed, natural and unconquerable aversion opposes it—is *practical* and not *pathological* love, which lies in the will and not in the propensity of feeling, in principles of action and not in melting sympathy; and it alone can be commanded.[23]

These differences, though, conceal a deep similarity. In both the ethics of care and in Kantian ethics—as, for that matter, in Christianity—we are commanded to take care of the vulnerable, to develop some plan of beneficent action by which some individuals are understood as objects of our principled concern. We are, that is, commanded to help some individuals, by making their projects and plans principles of action for ourselves. In none of these are the particular objects of our actions entitled to the beneficent actions we perform for them. We have the freedom to decide what and how we might help, and no potential beneficiary of our help is wronged when we refrain. But we are rightly criticized when we *never* go beyond the commandments of mere justice and instead seek to be justified solely with reference to the fact that we respect the particular rights of other people. For Kant—as for the ethics of care, and Christianity—we are commanded to do more than justice.[24]

These thoughts, of course, are often developed in the context of providing particular goods to particular other people; Kant, of course, focuses on the provision of material goods by the prosperous to the less wealthy. But there is no reason to think that these ideas are limited to the context of charitable giving. Instead, I think these ideas might be used to ground the political concept of mercy I have been describing. All these comprehensive doctrines, indeed, might accept a political society in which we are capable of using the concept of *mercy* in public life to critique, to defend, to justify and to propose particular pieces of policy. I have, in this book, focused upon the implications of mercy upon migration policy; but it is worth remembering that a society exhibiting the virtue of mercy might have to demonstrate that virtue throughout its legal and political institutions—and not simply at its borders.

3. In Defense of Mercy

The question we still have to answer, though, is *why* the state should be merciful. Perry, of course, has provided one important answer, which I will expand upon below. But it is worth asking, more directly, what it is about the state that makes it appropriate for that institution to display the virtue of mercy. There are plausible reasons to think that it shouldn't. Take, for instance, the skeptical argument of Xan, the ruler of a future United Kingdom in a world facing universal sterility. Xan's brother Theo argues in favor of opening the borders; Xan resists the thought.

> Theo thought: *They even speak alike now. But, whoever speaks, the voice is the voice of Xan.* He said: "We're not talking about history. We've no shortage of resources, no shortage of jobs, no shortage of houses. Restricting immigration in a dying and underpopulated world isn't a particularly generous policy."
>
> Xan said: "It never was. Generosity is a virtue for individuals, not governments. When governments are generous it is with other people's money, other people's safety, other people's future."[25]

Xan's ideas, of course, have strong echoes in modern conservative thought. Margaret Thatcher said, famously, that the problem with socialism was that eventually you ran out of other people's money. Why, though, should we not think that mercy—or beneficence, or any similar virtue—is best expressed by individuals, rather than states?

There are, to this, two distinct answers. I will call these answers the arguments from *democratic emotion* and from *democratic agency*, and will deal with these in turn. The first argument—that of democratic emotion—begins with a simple fact: democratic self-rule is a fragile thing. In particular, while we have very little information about how to build a flourishing society from the outside, we have some very good information about what sorts of things a flourishing society must have for that society to persist. One thing such a society must have, it seems, is a sense among the citizens that the game of electoral politics is worth playing, and worth playing even when the results of that politics do not go one's own way. In a flourishing democracy, stability is provided by some sort of commitment to doing justice within that state—rather than, as it were, simply taking one's toys and going home when one loses an election. John Rawls's account of stability shifted over the course of his career; what did not shift was his conviction that we cannot have a democratic society unless people have, as individuals, an existing and felt moral reason to continue to support that democratic society, and to support it even when that society does not give us the results we would choose. But, as I emphasized in discussing the bigot's veto, it is possible for a society—or a large part of it—to cease to feel this sort of felt affinity. Certainly, we may sometimes rightly worry about the stability of a society when the sorts of empathetic identification with other people is made more difficult or opaque.

What, then, is required for the existence of this sort of stability? Once again, it is easier to say what is corrosive of it than what would create it. One key argument comes from Susan Moller Okin, whose *Justice, Gender, and the Family* argues that the family is a key site of justice.[26] There are many reasons for this; the norms of gender and divorce law, for instance, create relationships of differential power within the home, which in turn create differential ability to acquire power outside the home. More importantly, though, Okin was committed to the thought that doing justice was a *skill*—that it required moral education, and that the family was itself a school in which that skill was either reinforced or undermined. Okin's critique of patriarchal liberalism is far-reaching, but one aspect of that critique is important for our purposes: we cannot, says Okin, be good agents of justice in one sphere if we live in a society that consistently denies it in another. If the family is allowed to remain a sphere of injustice, then, this is wrong both in its concrete effects on women's lives, but also because of the effects it has on the moral personalities of girls and boys growing up in those unjust families.

Okin's argument, though, can also tell us something about the development of moral personality even outside the family. Doing justice within society, Okin said, is a skill; it is a skill, though, that rests ultimately upon the continued willingness to see humans as worthy of moral concern.[27] We are creatures that are liable to moral corruption—to reinterpreting moral matters until they give us reason to do what we already wanted to do. We are prone to biases, implicit and otherwise, in how we understand the lived experiences of other humans. The exercise of empathy, though, is required for us to continue the process of electoral politics; we must remember the moral nature of our opponents, to continue doing politics with them—and the moral reality of those citizens we may never meet, in order for us to avoid self-interested ways of ignoring their complaints. What Okin's argument establishes, though, is the fact that lessons learned in one sphere have effects on skills within the political sphere. It is hard to be a political egalitarian, when the family is patriarchal. But so, too, I argue, it is hard to be continually motivated by the goods of those with whom we share a society, when that society regards the goods of outsiders as unworthy of moral concern.

What I mean by this is that we need virtue as well as law in order for society to flourish. Virtue, however, must be modeled. Virtue requires, at the minimum, a constant recognition of the moral reality of other people, and a willingness to consider them as morally significant creatures, whose goods are worthy of being taken seriously. In the absence of this sort of empathetic identification, we are likely to fall into a variety of pathological states, none of which seem to lead to stable forms of self-government. At the macro level, there is the simple fact that one must be committed to the thought that those with whom one disagrees are rational humans, rather than devils, in order to continue the process of political deliberation with them. The political polarization of the ongoing election is not itself a problem; a democracy might survive polarized views, if those views are capable of respecting and negotiating with their opponents. What is more problematic, I think, is the ways in which the recent election frequently involves the demonization of one's opponents, up to and including threats of imprisonment—and the threatened refusal to concede to an election that does not go one's way.[28] Political deliberation requires the continued sense that one's opponents are not demons made flesh, but reasoning creatures like us, with whom we have moral reasons to do politics. Rawls notices, too, that virtue is a plant that needs tending. He analogizes our will to do politics in a spirit of mutual respect to a sort of capital that can be expended or preserved.[29] A polity that begins with the will to do justice can cease to do this when it is not provided with a constant reminder that other people are real, and that we owe them the sorts of moral respect that are due to creatures such as them.

What does all this have to do with migration? The answer, I think, is that how a state treats those who are outside that state provides some lessons for how we are obligated to treat people generally. A polity that refused to take the goods of other people seriously—that avoided violating rights, but did no more—would be an inadequate polity, simply in virtue of the fact that it failed to remind the populace of the society that human goods are worth taking seriously. We need regular spaces in which we rehearse the moral reality that outsiders are human, too, and that they matter as much as our own neighbors. I cannot claim that this sort of ritual will defeat the profound forces that have tended to make us look at migrants and see threats and invaders. But the absence of the ritual tends toward the absence of belief.[30] We are sometimes skeptical of this sort of moral education; does anyone, we might wonder, look to migration policy to determine their moral outlook? Perhaps not—but there are some sorts of migration policy that can reliably be felt to undermine our skill at living up to our moral views. An explicitly racist immigration regime, for instance, would give comfort to domestic racists, and would exacerbate those racist ideas lurking below the surface in democratic society. Similarly, an unmerciful policy—one that did ignored the goods of outsiders and refused to take them as worthy of moral concern—would exacerbate our own tendencies toward moral corruption and selfishness. The skill of empathy is required for particular acts on the part of citizens toward newcomers; the acts of several Republican governors in suing to keep out Syrian refugees, for instance, has certainly given moral support to those who have no desire to assist in creating some sorts of mutual accommodation to those refugees.[31] The point, however, is more general than this. In refusing to listen to the pleas of those outside the state, the state makes it easier to refuse to listen to the pleas of those with whom one disagrees.

At this point, though, I want to transition to my second argument—the argument from democratic agency. This argument is more easily stated, but perhaps more complex in its details. The thought is this: we generally speak as if the state were an agent in its own right. Even those of us who are suspicious of assigning metaphysical status to collective or group entities tend to think that we are right to think of the state as taxing, governing, and so on. If I am subjected to a tax, it is a mistake for me to focus my resentment on the tax collector; he is only the agent of the state, and it is the state to which my resentment is rightly directed.

Now, we might actually dissolve all this and refer only to natural persons; after all, some individual person proposed the tax bill, people voted on it, and so forth. But we often want to propose some sort of agential structure for a state, one that endures over time and is distinct from the individual persons currently occupying roles within that state. For this to be possible, though, we have to be able to understand the state as having agency in its own right; and for us to be able to do that, we have to understand the state as having the burdens of agency, which include ethical obligations toward those over whom it has power.

This, of course, seems a long way to go for a weak conclusion; no one thinks that the state does not have *some* ethical duties. What I want to specify, though, is that most of these duties can be rephrased as political duties. The state wrongs me when it violates my right to practice my religion, for instance; this is because the conditions of its being a just state prevent it from exercising this sort of coercive power over me. The state also wrongs me, sometimes, when it fails to provide me something necessary for my agency; a state that does not keep and maintain an adequate police service renders my life less secure than I have a right to expect.

Both of these, though, go to whether the state is exercising its power in the right sorts of way. They go to legitimacy, or justice, as a state. The point I am trying to make in the present context is broader than that. I think the state has some ethical duties, not because it is a state, but simply because it *exists*, as a sort of agent to which ethical duties apply.

The reason I want to insist upon this is that I think we cannot think of the state as an agent without thinking that it has some duties toward those whose goods it has power to promote or deny. These duties are not the same as the duties of justification toward those over whom it exercises coercive power; the state has these, as well, but I am not concerned with them at present. Instead, I want simply to note this fact: if we are going to speak of the state as having its own agency, then that agency must accept the burdens of fulfilling the duties that are incumbent on all agents—namely, to exist in a community with other agents, and to develop plans within which they promote the goods of some other agents. This means, though, that the state cannot be fully moral as an agent without developing some plan with which the goods of other people—those to whom justice owes nothing—are made part of its own plan.

To these thoughts I want to add one last idea: our ethical duties are often made most plain when they are pressed by those with no power to act on their behalf. Sirius Black, in *Harry Potter and the Goblet of Fire*, makes the point succinctly:

If you want to know what a man's like, take a good look at how we treats his inferiors, not his equals.[32]

We might blanch at the thought that the prospective migrant is in any way inferior to the one already resident within the society; but the moral logic of this quote depends upon reading *inferior* here simply with reference to power, not virtue—and the migrant is, simply in virtue of her situation, deprived of power held by those already present. How we respond to the need of such people demonstrates our character in a profound way. In domestic politics, after all, there is an admixture of self-concern in many of our duties, despite the importance of solidarity and empathy; we often have the thought that we owe our opponents good treatment precisely because we might someday be subjected to their rule. This means, though, that we have an obligation as individuals and as members of a state—to be very careful to live up to our duties toward those who are most powerless toward us. The state, I think, is defined as a moral agent most powerfully and directly by how it treats those to whom it has no particular obligations, and who themselves possess the least power to contest what is done. This means, though, that migration might indeed be a more important site of mercy than we might have thought. It is possible, as I will discuss, for mercy to be extended in domestic politics; but what is striking about migration is that those to whom rights of migration are given are, in general, not already members, and therefore not especially able to influence that state's policies or use its power to benefit or harm another. If agents are marked by how they treat those who are unable to resist—who are, literally, *at one's mercy*—then migration is an area in which we might find out a great deal about the character of wealthy states and the character of those who guide those states.

10

Migration and Mercy

In what has gone before, I have defended the thought that a society ought to do more than simply avoid injustice. It should, instead, act in accordance with the distinct demands of mercy—which I understand to involve a principled reason to refrain from certain forms of harsh treatment, even when one might engage in that harshness without injustice. The merciful act is done out of a recognition that the one who is vulnerable to us is human; her plans mean as much to her as ours do to us. The practice of mercy represents a way in which this fact is brought home to us, as citizens and as persons. It reflects the ongoing need to see human beings as valuable, as worthy of consideration—rather than as mere burdens, or as somehow morally unlike ourselves. The concept of mercy, moreover, can be developed into a public norm, useful in argument about how the power of a democratic society ought to be deployed. This norm can be accepted, I have argued, by a number of reasonable comprehensive doctrines; the norm itself is neither sectarian nor incompatible with the political form of liberalism endorsed by John Rawls. Mercy, in short, can help us come to grips with the ethics of policy, by extending our ethical toolkit beyond the concepts of justice and of moral right.

What remains, though, is to see precisely how the concept of mercy might be used in argument about migration policy. I want to be careful here not to give the impression that only one form of policy is defensible by a society in which such a norm is respected. What I have defended is a form of *argument*, rather than a particular form of conclusion. And, what is more, the concept of mercy does not demand that there be only one way of living up to its demands. By its very nature, it is compatible with multiple different forms of policy instrument. What I can say here, then, is limited by these facts; I cannot demonstrate that any given policy is the only way in which mercy might be lived by a political community, and will not try to do so.

It might, nevertheless, be possible for us to get some sense of how the ideas I defend might be used to justify particular forms of migration policy. Recall, as before, that mercy involves benefits given to those who cannot claim those benefits as of right. Mercy, that is, involves a decision to care for the goods

Justice, Migration, and Mercy. Michael Blake, Oxford University Press (2020). © Oxford University Press.
DOI: 10.1093/oso/9780190879556.001.0001

of particular other people; those other people do not have a claim to assistance, but those who fail to make the decision to care might nonetheless be rightly subject to criticism. We might, though, say more. It seems as though there might be two forms, at least, of merciful action or policy. On occasion, we face a particular person, who might be utterly unmade by the action we might perform—without injustice—against her. Smilla might be made to suffer greatly by imprisonment, and such suffering might be excessive for the minor crimes she has committed. Here, there is an individual person picked out, and we can point to her, specifically, in explaining the operation of mercy. We might call this *negative mercy*: mercy involves the refusal to do, to this particular person, a terribly damaging thing that justice would let us do. The doing of mercy is still discretionary, in the moral sense; we could refrain from showing mercy to Smilla, without being guilty of injustice. But she is the rightful site of mercy—or, at least, we can explain our failure of mercy simply with reference to how she is treated.

This might be contrasted with those cases in which there are any number of people who are potential sites for the operation of mercy. Take, for instance, the set of people who might want to enter into a given country, so as to improve their careers. If it is right that none of these people has a right, simply in virtue of their desires, to move, then we might not be unjust in keeping all of these people out. We would be, however, deeply unmerciful, given the extent to which we might make some people's careers vastly more successful by allowing them to migrate. I think we might describe this as *positive mercy*; the set of people to whom we might show mercy is large, and we might show ourselves to be merciful even if not all members of that set are given the migratory resources they desire. This kind of mercy is positive, I think, because it seeks to give some—but not all—of the people in question a positive benefit; there is no individual whose plans are so vulnerable to our decision-making that it is with reference to her, in particular, that we are merciful or not.

The line between the two kinds of mercy, I think, are likely porous. There are, perhaps, always people within a set of applicants for positive mercy who can present themselves as cases of negative mercy. The two categories, then, are perhaps best represented as ideal types for the operation of mercy in migration. There are some times when individual people present themselves to us for rescue; and if the rescue here is not the sort demanded by justice, it nonetheless is enough for us to encounter these people for the demand of mercy to come into play. There are other times, though, that it seems as though we might want to build programs and methods to help outsiders enter into our societies—even though we do not think that we would be unmerciful to any particular person by refusing them. The key, for both, is that we do no wrong to the one we reject in refusing her admission. That admission should be granted, in particular cases and by means of particular policies; but the failure to do what should be done is morally distinct from the kinds of injustice with which states have traditionally been charged.

All this, I think, can help us get some purchase on the cases previously discussed. In chapter 7, I described three cases of migrants who might be thought able to make claims of rights: those with a particular affinity for a place or its people; the undocumented; and those married to citizens of foreign societies. There I argued that there is nothing unjust in refusing the claims of such individuals. While some among their number might have claims of justice, those claims do not emerge simply from the fact of their situations as I have described them. In the present chapter, I will try to show how the concept of mercy might provide us with tools to explain why those persons—or, perhaps, some among their number—might be taken as particularly appropriate sites for the exercise of mercy. I will go through these examples in order and will conclude with some thoughts about the reasons for pursuing a project like my own.

1. Claims of Affinity

We rarely ask why there should be any migration in the world, apart from that migration demanded by justice; what would the world lose, that is, were there to be borders closed except to those fleeing violence or deprivation? People move across borders for any number of reasons—but a chief one is the simple fact that some things are found, or found in more abundance, inside a particular country. We might move because our careers require us to move to a new country—or, more broadly, those careers might flourish in that new place. We might move because of the geographic features found in only a particular place; surfers might want to move to Australia and volcanologists to Hawaii. Whatever the reason, we might want to move because our plans would be more successful were we allowed to do so. What the absence of migratory rights would entail, then, is the absence of the sorts of goods this sort of migration could bring into the world.

In what has gone before, I have argued that such claimants can be refused without injustice being done to them. Those whose agency would be destroyed by exclusion may not be rightly deported; but many people subject to deportation cannot make that claim. They claim, instead, that the plans they have made with that agency would be undermined by this exclusion. This, however, is a weaker claim. The one who claims affinity with a place presents herself as someone who might be helped by being given what is present only within some particular other country. That other country does not have an obligation in justice to give what is requested. But on the analysis I have given of mercy, that country would show itself to be unmerciful were it refuse to develop some program by which some people are able to make their lives better by using the resources found inside that country.

I take this to be an example of positive mercy, as described above. The state in question might be taken to be obligated to develop some particular policy measure, by which some people in other countries are given the right to migrate. This sort of policy might benefit both the newcomer and the country to which she migrates; indeed, in the general run of things we can expect exactly this to happen. The one who moves to a new place facilitates the exchange of information, acquires new knowledge for herself, builds transnational relationships and strengthens transnational institutions, and so on.[1] But the obligation to help some part of the world's population, by giving migratory rights to some outsiders, does not depend upon these benefits. If a given society were to decide that no non-refugee migration were to take place, I think we might not think that society was guilty of injustice. But many of us, I think, would regard that society as morally deficient. No individual person has a right to admission—any more than I did, in seeking to travel to the United States for education and then remaining there for employment. But the refusal to provide these tools to *anyone* speaks to an objectionable failure of mercy. To use Kantian language, we might describe this as a failure of beneficence. If we are attracted by more informal language, we might simply describe it as *mean*.

It is worth noting, though, that there are some important implications of the way in which the moral argument here is described. There are a great many sorts of people who might benefit from migration into a particular country. To restrict attention to the United States: aspiring actors might benefit from the right to go to Hollywood, while aspiring paleontologists might benefit from the right to go to Utah.[2] The United States, however, need not be open to all those who might benefit from permanent residency within the

United States. It can decide, I think, on who and how to admit. Its decision-making is not unconstrained; it can, as discussed above, make distinctions in a way that marginalize or demonize people in ways that violate the norms of equal treatment. A discretionary power is still one that can be exercised well or poorly. But precisely because there is no right to entry, some people may be refused that right—while others receive it—with some degree of freedom. The United States, for instance, might decide it prefers actors to paleontologists—or vice versa. I presume that it might, consistent with both mercy and justice, develop policy instruments that privilege the one group over the other. It could not, as before, prefer one ethnic group to another, because of the ways in which that sort of distinction depends upon covert and unjustifiable beliefs about the disfavored group. But paleontologists cannot make the same claim as the members of the disfavored ethnic group; we can seek their exclusion without violating their rights.

This, then, is the first implication of grounding these migratory rights upon mercy: they are legal rights, but no one provided with them has a moral right to be provided with them. It would not be unjust or unmerciful for us to offer greater rights to one particular type of person, if what we do here does not violate the particular rights to equal treatment such people hold. A second implication follows on from this first: there is nothing wrong in principle with pacing numerical limits upon the number of people benefited by the policy instrument in question. The United States, for instance, allocates only sixty-five thousand H-1B visas each year, with an additional twenty thousand allotted to those who have advanced degrees from American universities.[3] These visas, which allow the holder to reside within the United States and to intend to adjust to permanent residency, are often gone by April. There is nothing, however, unjust about this fact; those benefited by that program are the beneficiaries of mercy or something very much like it, and those who are not so benefited can make no similar complaint. A numerical cap, in short, seems in principle permitted by mercy. The Trump administration, however, has recently announced a plan to cap the number of refugee admissions at thirty thousand.[4] This seems markedly unlike the case at issue. The one refused because she applied after all thirty thousand have been provided to others can, I think, make a claim that she is treated unjustly. Certainly, if her claim to refuge reflects the sorts of considerations that undergird the Convention, then it would seem unjust to force her back into such malignant circumstances. Mercy, it seems, is compatible with numbers and limitations on the basis of numbers; justice isn't.

One final distinction between justice and mercy: the unjust state is, in principle, subject to external coercion in virtue of that injustice. Certainly, the injustice must be of the right character; those who have written about international justice have been keen to avoid countries coercing one another for trivial or minor concerns. But the refusal to do justice is, in principle, capable of grounding the justification of coercion. Kant, of course, makes this a key part of the doctrine of right: the perfect duties are susceptible, in principle at least, of being defended by coercive means. A failure to be merciful, however, cannot even in principle be made the basis of legitimate coercion. Kant applies these thoughts to the domestic realm; but they might as easily be applied to migration. A state that refuses to take care of the world's refugees is, perhaps, in principle rightly subject to coercion. (Whether or not such coercion could ever do the job it intends, of course, is another matter entirely.) A state that refuses to be merciful, though, violates no rights—and no outside agency seems entitled to intervene. There is, at any rate, no particular person whose rights might ground that intervention. The other states of the world can judge the exclusionary state as selfish, mean, and unmerciful; but they cannot hold it to account for these failures, any more than we can be held as criminals domestically for our failures of beneficence.

2. The Undocumented

I want to return to the undocumented, by reminding us of the case of Morgan. Morgan has crossed the border from Canada into the United States without legal authorization for doing so. He now resides in Portland and has built a life there; he has a job, friends, and all the usual things that make up the life built within a particular place. He has, it seems, lived in Portland for several years—more years, at any rate, than Joseph Carens would mandate for him to be provided the right to remain within the United States. I have argued that Morgan is not wronged by deportation. His life, and the plans within it, would be radically undermined by the decision to deport him. And yet, I have argued, this sort of pain is not rightly held as the basis for a right to remain within the United States. Morgan made the decision to violate the law preventing him from using this place to build his life; the pain he faces is a pain he cannot rightly regard as unjust. As time goes on, doubtless his pain at deportation would increase. And yet this pain is rightly imposed upon him, were he to be apprehended and subjected to deportation. He made a bet that he would not be discovered; his pain when that bet fails to hold is a pain he is rightly made to endure.

I believe these thoughts to be correct; but I also believe that the United States would show itself to be unmerciful were it to deport Morgan in this way. (I should emphasize that this is no hypothetical; the United States does deport people like Morgan, and people with much better claims, with appalling regularity.) Morgan, it seems, represents a case of negative mercy. Those who, like him, have built lives within a place might rightly be presented as uniquely appropriate sites for the exercise of mercy. At the very least, we might be able to criticize the state as acting without mercy when it chooses to deport Morgan and those like him. These thoughts, or something like them, have been motivating to a number of unlikely figures: Ronald Reagan, in his 1984 debate with Walter Mondale, explicitly defended amnesty for long-standing undocumented residents:

> But it is true our borders are out of control. It is also true that this has been a situation on our borders back through a number of administrations. . . . I believe in the idea of amnesty for those who have put down roots and who have lived here even though some time back they may have entered illegally.[5]

These ideas led Reagan to support the provisions of the 1986 Immigration Reform and Control Act, which gave legal residency rights to those who had continually resided in the United States for four years—regardless of their reasons for crossing the border.[6]

More recent conservatives, of course, have been less willing than Reagan to think that the deportation of long-standing residents was objectionably cruel. Representative Steve King, for instance, argued that the undocumented had made a choice—which, presumably, should be respected—to live "in the shadows":

> They came here to live in the shadows and we're not denying them the opportunity to live in the shadows. . . If they're encountered by any law enforcement officials, the law requires that they'd be placed in removal proceedings.[7]

King's argument assumes—rather than defends by argument—that amnesty is immoral; the undocumented, because they have violated the law, cannot be rightly pardoned. But there is a simple response to King, which is the same response given by Reagan: there are circumstances under which a pardon, or some merciful policy response, is the morally rightful response.

King has, of course, also argued vehemently that any program of regularization or amnesty for the undocumented would lead to future waves of undocumented migrants. There are, here, two responses: one empirical and one philosophical. The empirical response might be, as was discussed in chapter 8, that some undocumented migration happens simply because of the gap between wealth and poverty; it is unlikely that the primary consideration of the undocumented migrant is whether or not there might be, decades down the line, a policy response to provide them with regularization. But the philosophical response emerges if we assume that King, or those like him, are correct, and the response here would be to increase the number of migrants crossing the border without right. One response, I think, is to acknowledge that we cannot always do what would maximize obedience to law when what we propose to do violates moral duty. We see this, I think, in other contexts of law; if we could eliminate jaywalking simply by instituting mandatory execution for the first offense, we would not therefore think that the death penalty was a rightful response for jaywalking. We might think that this sort of penalty, of course, is unjust; whatever the jaywalker does, it does not legitimate the administration of death. But we might think that similar considerations hold even when the policy response is not unjust. Even if we could stop jaywalking through the public humiliation of jaywalkers, we would not immediately conclude that such humiliation was morally acceptable. Something might be, instead, both effective and morally wrongful—or, more broadly, that something might be both effective and indicative of an impoverished sort of moral character, insufficiently attentive to the virtues that ought to animate a human life. The response to King, in short, might be to simply say that a future increase in undocumented migration might be the price we ought to pay to avoid an objectionable lack of mercy in the present.

I want to close this section by reiterating that all this only applies to a subset of the undocumented residents of a particular place; a great many of those people chose to cross because of unjust circumstances in their countries of origin, or would face such injustice were they to return in the present. Those people have a claim of justice, and we ought to remember that claim in the design of policy. I would only reiterate that moral considerations affect even how we ought to treat those who can make no such claim of justice.

3. Family Unification

In discussing the unification of family, I will focus only on the unification of spouses; minor children, as I have noted, have distinct claims, rooted in their agency and the need for particular people to guide that agency. I have argued that it is at least possible that a state can rightly refrain from offering admission to the foreign spouses of domestic citizens. Certainly, I believe there is nothing inherently unjust toward the foreign spouse in doing this. If there is injustice, it is to be located in how the domestic citizen's claims are treated in comparison to the claims of those with whom she shares citizenship. Even here I am not convinced that there is any injustice to be found; a state that simply announced that it would refuse, in the future, to provide such rights would be announcing to its citizens that they have good reason to build such relationships with only those already provided with residency rights. This is, of course, cruel; but I do not yet think it is unjust. We do, again, demand that people take charge of their romantic relationships; we are told, rightly, to avoid engaging in romantic relationships with our students, our employees, or—most broadly—those over whom we have power. Love, to put it simply, isn't something that just happens to you; and if we acknowledge this fact, we can similarly acknowledge that your love of a particular person doesn't yet require the rest of us to provide him with a home.

To refuse to provide this home, of course, seems deeply unmerciful; and, indeed, the foreign-born spouse seems like the more obvious case of negative mercy. The spouses are making a particular kind of claim on the rest of us, which reflects the unique and powerful character of romantic love. If we were to try to make these claims ones of justice, we would run into the difficulties described by Luara Ferracioli: what make us think that these sorts of relationships are the only ones that reflect this kind of value? Might there not be other relationships—co-authors, best friends—that are as meaningful, as powerful, as these?

One response to Ferracioli, I think, is to simply say that she is right; but that the moral rightness of permitting spouses to migrate, but not best friends, is not thereby impugned. That is because we might take the reunification of spouses to be one site in which we might choose to be merciful—both to the citizen and to the foreign-born person with whom she seeks to build a life. If mercy involves the willingness to build something—some program, some policy instrument—by which the state provides value for the world, by giving to people the rights they cannot claim in justice, then the unification of spouses seems an unusually promising place to begin.

Spouses are special, on this account, not because there is something found in all marriages that is absent from other relationships; there isn't. Spouses are special, instead, because of the simple fact that spouses are *usually* more important in our lives than best friends are. When we make claims of justice, we have reason to be suspicious of *usually*. We cannot, I think, treat people justly when we sort them in accordance with predictive categories. Justice requires something more bespoke than this. We can say that those seeking asylum from the United States in Canada are usually not entitled to what they seek. But, in the rare occasion that someone can make a valid case for protection, we would wrong them by subsuming them within the category of American. (This is not an entirely fanciful case; Denise Harvey was recently provided with a stay of deportation to Florida on the basis that she had such claims.)[8] We cannot, when we are dealing with justice, rely upon predictions and broad tendencies; we have to figure out what Ferracioli demands we figure out—namely, how each relationship, in each individual case, is actually experienced by the individual person.

In mercy, however, we are more able to use predictive information, precisely because no individual person has a claim to have her lot ameliorated. Imagine that there is a set of people seeking admission to a given country, none of whom have an antecedent right to entry. All will be benefited by that; some of them, indeed, will benefit profoundly and will bring similarly profound benefit to particular people already present within the society. Those people, we might think, are picked out as natural sites for the exercise of the virtue of mercy. But a state that refused to give them those rights would not be wronging them, and it would not be wronging the citizens they seek to marry. The state that refused to provide them with such rights would be guilty of a lack of mercy, rather than injustice, in its refusal. Indeed, it might not even be guilty of that; if it could make the case that its migration policy elsewhere adequately respected the value of mercy—perhaps they have an exceptionally generous policy for some other category of foreign national— then they might not be guilty of anything at all.

Of course, in practice any country refusing to allow the unification of spouses is likely going to fail that duty; the unification of spouses is, as it were, the lowest-hanging fruit of mercy, given the near-universal respect given in human cultures for monogamous romantic relationships. But saying this is not the same as saying that the unification of spouses is a requirement of justice.

Instead, we can respond to Ferracioli's challenge by denying the conditions under which it arises. If we ground the legal right to spousal unification in mercy, rather than in justice, then it does not matter so much if there are other sorts of relationship that might ground something as valuable as a marriage. The best friend whose claim to migration is denied is not denied something to which she is due, because neither she nor the foreign-born spouse can claim migration as their due. So long as there is no pernicious distinction between spouses and best friends, then there is nothing wrong with seeking to fulfill the duty of mercy with reference to the former and not the latter.

Of course, it is always possible for us to try to establish that there is something pernicious in this distinction. We might claim, for instance, that the preference here reflects an illegitimate bias in favor of the monogamous and permanent relationship over alternative forms of relationship or community.[9] That might be enough to start us down an argument that the rights given to the spouses here reflect something morally impermissible. I think something like this would be clearly true if, for instance, these rights were given to all and only straight marital relationships; gay men and women would rightly feel that they were being treated as lesser citizens were their relationships held to be somehow less worthy than those of their straight compatriots. We might make a similar claim as regards alternative forms of human relationship; but I confess I think this sort of claim is unlikely. The greater rights given to marriages, in comparison to other forms of relationship—whether sexual or otherwise—might simply reflect the predictive fact that these other relationships are less likely to be as valuable, for as long, as the marital relationship. Grounding the legal right to spousal unification on these predictions seems, I think, to reflect empirical fact more than mere animus. (Certainly, it seems rather distinct from the sorts of animus that have tended to undergird the refusal to recognize gay relationships as equal to those of straight relationships.) What I say here, though, is open to the possibility that there are hidden forms of bias here that deserve excavation. Grounding these rights in mercy, at least, has the advantage of telling us what sorts of excavation we would have to do.

4. Mercy and Justice in Public Discourse

All the above has been to explain how mercy might be used to argue about migration policies that are not themselves required by justice. I would note, however, that the concept of mercy might also have a role to play in the criticism of policies that are unjust as well. Apart from its philosophical value, the concept of mercy has a powerful rhetorical pull. Mercy tells us who we do not want to be; what we are permitted to be, without the violation of right, but should nonetheless refuse to become. These ideas can help us make the case when what is proposed is both unjust and unmerciful.

Take, for instance, the response by former First Lady Laura Bush in response to the Trump administration's decision to separate children from their parents and to house those children in facilities that resemble prison camps. Bush argues that this policy is best understood with reference to our abhorrence of cruelty:

> I appreciate the need to enforce and protect our international boundaries, but this zero-tolerance policy is cruel. It is immoral. And it breaks my heart. . . . Recently, Colleen Kraft, who heads the American Academy of Pediatrics, visited a shelter run by the U.S. Office of Refugee Resettlement. She reported that while there were beds, toys, crayons, a playground and diaper changes, the people working at the shelter had been instructed not to pick up or touch the children to comfort them. Imagine not being able to pick up a child who is not yet out of diapers. . . . In 2018, can we not find a kinder, more compassionate and more moral answer to this current crisis? I believe we can.[10]

What was done to these children—and what is, as of this writing, still going on—is profoundly unjust. But we can use the language of mercy, which is also the language of virtue, to highlight the first-personal aspects of the issue: we do not want to become the sort of country that could do *this*. Bush also highlights the importance of vulnerability; the child, whose needs are profound for both human guidance and human love, is wronged profoundly by the policy that takes those away. The language of mercy can sometimes help us make sense of this. We do not need to engage in theorizing about justice in order to make the case. We can, instead, announce simply what we will not choose to be. When Senator Ted Cruz proposed that the United States prefer Christian refugees to Muslim ones, President Obama did not begin with a discussion of political justice, or the constitutional importance of equality before the law. He simply noted: that's not who we are.[11]

It is, of course, still possible for us to think that we are doing something disreputable when we defend what is just by means of virtues such as mercy.

There is a faint whiff of something like government-house utilitarianism; the actual justification for the policy is made separate, in a troubling way, from the reasoning provided to the public.[12] But I think the appearance of impropriety here is flawed. What is done to the children, after all, is both unjust and unmerciful; it deprives the children of that to which they are entitled, and the decision to treat children in this way demonstrates a deep lack of concern for those vulnerable to our political decisions. Under these circumstances, it seems, we can sometimes use any number of reasons with which to defend that which justice demands. John Rawls, at least, argues that the tradition of political liberalism includes the ability to propose multiple reasons for particular policies; Martin Luther King Jr. used both reasons drawn from abstract considerations of political justice and theological reasons drawn from scripture—often in the same paragraph.[13] Rawls notes that this sort of argumentation is permissible, on his account; what matters is that the reasons drawn from public reason might be made along with the others. What we might do with mercy is, if anything, less worrisome even than that; the concerns of mercy are, I have argued, themselves compatible with public reason, and a public conception of mercy might be introduced—so what we propose to do, here, involves nothing more than the use of multiple distinct forms of public reason.

This, however, leads to a question that must be asked at this point in the book: who, exactly, is this book for? To whom am I offering advice? I think, drawing on what has been said here, that this book is intended to offer advice to two distinct sets of readers. The first are philosophical authors—or, at least, philosophers who are like me in their rejection of open borders as a necessary implication of liberal theory. Some of us reject open borders because we think these borders protect something valuable and want these borders defended. Others of us think of these borders with less affection; liberalism doesn't rule them out, but the world might be better in their absence. However we think about them, there are a great many of us who are not ready to demand the opening of the border in the name of liberal justice; and this book is directed in the first instance to these people in particular. The fact that liberal justice allows us to exclude, I think, really only begins our conversation. We can have the right to keep people out without thinking that there are no moral principles on which that right is used well or poorly. I believe the philosophical literature would benefit from more direct engagement, not with the justice of migration policy, but with how it reflects the political virtues we have reason to prize.

The second set of readers, of course, are those who able and willing to engage in politics within the borders of the liberal state. I take what I have written here to be a way of reminding those people—who include, of course, myself—that we have a reason to avoid cruelty, as well as injustice, in what we do through politics. We are, as recent events show, in danger of slipping into something very nasty; if not outright illiberalism, then at least an increased hostility to the claims of the needy.[14] If not constantly reminded of the humanity of the marginal, we run the risk of forgetting their humanity, simply because it makes things easier for us to do so. I believe a public norm of mercy might go some way toward stopping this slide. Although I cannot think this norm sufficient, it might nonetheless be of some small use in keeping this flame of awareness alive.

5. Conclusions

I first presented these ideas, or their ancestors, at the University of Durham. Before giving my talk, I walked out toward Durham Cathedral. On the door of this cathedral is a magnificent bronze knocker, used in the medieval period to announce the intention to seek asylum within the cathedral itself. I remember thinking how marvelous this was. The knocker, polished by generations of hands, was a vivid reminder of the will to preserve the vulnerable. Those who sought refuge within the cathedral were a varied group; some were seeking to escape from justified punishment, while others were seeking immunity from deeply unjust forms of abuse by feudal masters elsewhere. But the cathedral knocker spoke to me then, as it does now, of the will to listen; to be attentive to the particular circumstances of the one seeking assistance, and to take the provision of asylum as virtuous response to these claims of need.

It was only later, of course, that I began to read more about sanctuary and discovered the limits that were placed upon the decision to seek that sanctuary. The one who sought sanctuary in Durham Cathedral was required to don a plain black garment, on which was present the yellow cross of St. Cuthbert, and then to leave England within thirty-seven days.[15] The departure, moreover, was permanent. One who returned, after being so expelled, was subject to execution. The cathedral, in short, would provide sanctuary—but that sanctuary was temporary and ended in expulsion, and the crime of being present without right after being granted sanctuary was somehow more unforgivable than any crime that might have originated one's desire for sanctuary.

These two sides of the sanctuary story tell of two distinct desires, both of which can be found in the medieval period as well as in our own. There is, on the one hand, the desire to help; to help the needy outsider, to bring him within, to provide what is needed for him to avoid the destruction of his person and his plans. There is, on the other hand, the desire to not have to be burdened with taking care of people; the desire, that is, to be free from being the one who is obligated to engage in a particular relationship with the unwanted outsider. I have, in what has gone before, defended the thought that the second desire is not inherently wrong; we do, I think, have some permission to avoid becoming the agents charged with the defense of another's rights, when those rights are adequately defended in that other's country of origin. But this limited permission is, and ought to be, bounded by the constraints of justice. And, more broadly, it seems as if, in recent years, the strength and vitality even of this first desire—to help, to do what we can, even when we are not obligated to help—has begun to wane. Our political leaders are increasingly willing to celebrate indifference—even hostility—to the claims of need that come from outside the borders. And, what's worse, we might suspect that the claims themselves are likely to increase in volume in the near future. Climate change, which I have not discussed in the present context, is likely to increase both economic inequality and the number of people seeking to migrate to countries of wealth.[16] For that matter, advances in communications and transportation technology have made the decision to migrate more available to more people. To repeat the quotation from Kishore Mahbubani that began this book: the Mediterranean has become a mere pond—and who would not move across a pond if it meant the difference between wealth and poverty?

We have, in short, a set of circumstances in which the desire to help is increasingly likely to be drowned out by the claims that we don't *have* to help, that these others have nothing to offer us, that the quality of their lives is of no concern to us. These trends are going to continue, and I do not think anything that can be written by a philosopher could possible stop them from doing so. But that does not mean it isn't right to try.

I want to end this book by deferring to Kurt Vonnegut Jr., whose book *God Bless You, Mr. Rosewater* described a future in which we have lost our ability to look at humans and see creatures worthy of defending. Vonnegut— through his character, Kilgore Trout—argues that we will soon face a fundamental problem, likely to be the most important one of the future: how can we love people who are *of no use to us?* Vonnegut's conclusion is that, if we don't start finding ways to love people—to treasure them, not because of what they can do for us, but simply *because they are human beings*—then we cannot imagine that we will survive. Vonnegut's characters—in that book, as elsewhere—continually arrive at what Vonnegut felt was the central insight of human value: that we ought to be kind, to people, because they are people:

> Hello, babies. Welcome to Earth. It's hot in the summer and cold in the winter. It's round and wet and crowded. At the outside, babies, you've got about a hundred years here. There's only one rule I know of, babies—"God damn it, you've got to be kind."[17]

I believe Vonnegut is correct; and that there is a serious risk of losing sight with the moral reality of those people who seek to cross borders, as their number increases in the years to come. What is real about these people is that they are agents, who have used their agency to build lives for themselves, and that the success of those plans is as important to them as our own plans are to us. We need, I think, to be steadily reminded of these moral facts, if only to avoid falling into the trap of seeing these outsiders as inconveniences rather than as people. Those of us who already live in relative comfort are at risk of becoming cruel—of ceasing to care about mercy, or kindness, or any other virtue that might give us pause before we go to the limit of what can be done in the name of exclusion. I believe, in short, that we may become deaf to the knocking, even as those who knock become more insistent—and their claims more urgent. I would like to believe that we will listen to them, and that this book might be of some small use in reminding us of why we should do so. I cannot claim to have any faith that we will do so. I am unsure that we will resist the darker urges of our nature, or that the virtue I defend here will continue to find a home in politics. But we can, if nothing else, continue to assert the importance of both justice and mercy, and to live in hope of a world in which these values are made real.

Notes

Chapter 1

1. The literature on colonialism is vast, although comparatively few philosophers have engaged with it in a systematic way. Two important recent exceptions are Ypi (2013) and Lu (2017).
2. Mahbubani (2001) at 61.
3. Much recent philosophical work has asked about the degree to which the decisions of wealthy consumers and political agents are causally implicated in oppression abroad. See, most prominently, Wenar (2017) and Pogge (2008).
4. Oberman (2016b), Oberman (2015), and Cole (2002) have begun the task of integrating a concern for the legacy of colonialism into the political philosophy of migration.
5. There is now a flourishing philosophical literature on global justice. See, for instance, Beitz (1999), Blake (2013), Blake (2001), Brock (2009), Caney (2006), Hassoun (2012), Miller (2007), Miller (1995), Nussbaum (2006), Pogge (2008), Rawls (1999b), Risse (2012b), Tan (2014), Tan (2000), and Valentini (2012).
6. These issues are discussed in Ngai (2010).
7. Bacon (2009) provides a good overview of these dislocations.
8. This idea is most closely associated with the work of Joseph Carens. See Carens (1987). Ayelet Shachar has developed the idea of an unjust birthright lottery in her own work. See Shachar (2009).
9. For an overview, see Collier (2013) and Borjas (2001).
10. United States Commission on Civil Rights (1980).
11. Even here, though, the effects are likely to prove complex. See Borjas (2017) and Borjas (2001).
12. These effects are discussed in Card (1990).
13. The constitutionality of the act was litigated in *Chan Chae Ping v. United States*, 130 U.S. 581 (1889), often called simply the Chinese Exclusion Case.
14. See Pérez-Peña (2017) for an overview of Arpaio's conviction.
15. See Mendoza (2017), Mendoza (2011), Reed-Sandoval (forthcoming), Reed-Sandoval (2015), and Reed-Sandoval (2013) for discussions of these effects.
16. Popular metaphors include disease, military invasion, and natural disasters. See Shariatmadari (2015).
17. The story is recounted in Alexievich (2017) 392–393.
18. Alex Sager (2018) is one of the only philosophical works to engage seriously with the first-person perspective of the migrant.
19. Cited in United States Commission on Civil Rights (1980).

20. Améry (1980) 46–47.
21. Bioxham (2005) discusses the background to the Tehcir Law in more detail.
22. The Wannsee Protocol uses the metaphor of deportation throughout. A translation of the protocols is available at http://www.ghwk.de/fileadmin/user_upload/pdf-wannsee/protokoll-januar1942.pdf.
23. Walzer (1986) 49.
24. I discuss my reservations in Blake (2014).
25. Murphy and Hampton (1988) 176.
26. Hence, Thomas Hill's thought that someone who accepts as a gift what is demanded by justice demonstrates an objectionable lack of self-respect. See Hill (1973).
27. See, for instance, Cabrera (2004).
28. Fisher (2013) xi.
29. See Blake (2013) and Rawls (1999b).
30. Risse discusses the world state in Risse (2012a) and provides what I take to be conclusive reasons against that state as a global ideal.
31. On the former, see Cohen (2009); on the latter, see the discussions of guest workers in Carens (2013), Lenard and Straehle (2010), and Walzer (1986). I am also glossing over the fairly important question of plural and transnational forms of citizenship. On this, see the work of Rainer Bauböck, including the conversations curated in Bauböck (2018a) and Bauböck (2018b).
32. See, on this, Carens (2013), and Miller (2016).
33. Gillian Brock and I discuss this issue in Brock and Blake (2014).
34. My idea of autonomy is influenced by Raz (1988).
35. See generally Rawls (1971) and Rawls (1989).
36. Bratman (1987) provides a powerful vision of how planning structures agency over time.
37. Rawls (1971) 358.
38. Blake (2013).
39. Scarry (1985) provides a powerful account of how the body can be used against the person inhabiting that body.
40. See Hightower (1997).

Chapter 2

1. The speech is described in Ross (2016).
2. Donald Trump's inaugural address can be found at https://www.whitehouse.gov/briefings-statements/the-inaugural-address/.
3. The language of illegality is rejected in Gambinno (2015) and Chomsky (2014).
4. The State of Washington sought to prevent the ban from coming into effect, and sought to demonstrate that it was (among a great many other defects) likely in violation of the Fourteenth Amendment to the Constitution. See brief at http://agportal-s3bucket.s3.amazonaws.com/uploadedfiles/Another/News/Press_Releases/Complaint%20as%20Filed.pdf.

5. Gil Martinez is cited in Adler (2007).

6. McWhorter (2012) describes the rise of Juan Crow as a concept.

7. The rejection of refugees has become a key part of Matteo Salvini's political identity. See Mead (2018).

8. Scoones et al. (2018) describes some of these movements and provides some analysis of how they might be addressed.

9. Miller (2016) 3.

10. Rawls (1971) 3.

11. Rawls (1971) 5.

12. The egalitarian plateau is discussed in theorists such as Dworkin (2000) and Sen (1992).

13. The importance of Lincoln to Rawls is difficult to overstate. For an overview of Rawls's life, see Pogge (2007).

14. This is why the pardoning of Arpaio was taken as so disheartening by many Latinx. See Romero (2017).

15. See Reed-Sandoval (2005).

16. The legal duties of police are a matter of complexity; it is not clear that the police are legally liable in the event that they fail to provide adequate protection. From the standpoint of morality, though, it seems clear that the failure to provide that protection is morally wrong.

17. *Plyler v. Doe*, 457 U.S. 202 (1982), internal citation omitted.

18. This is, I should note, not the only story that one might tell about international human rights. See Moyn (2010).

19. Not all migration, of course, is from colony to metropole. Africa is currently seeing profound changes brought about by migration (or temporary movement) of Chinese citizens into East Africa. See French (2014) for a discussion of these trends.

20. Kukathas (2012) 656. See also Kukathas (2010) and Kukathas (2005).

21. Nett (1971).

22. This thought is expressed well in Christine Korsgaard (1996).

23. Versions of this argument may be found in Carens (2013), Carens (1987), Dummett (2001), Kukathas (2012), Kukathas (2005), Oberman (2016a), Schotel (2012), and Wilcox (2009). Bertram (2018) provides a particular vision of this argument, which arrived too late for me to integrate into this book. (The same is true for Owen [forthcoming]). I am ignoring Huemer (2010), since his argument focuses on the right to move when one must move in order to avoid starvation; as will become clear, one need not defend open borders in order to defend the right to cross borders so as to preserve the conditions of one's agency.

24. Carens (1987) 252.

25. Clemens (2011) provides the canonical vision of the economic gains that might emerge from open migration.

26. The moral relevance of these remittances are a key point of disagreement between Gillian Brock and myself. See Brock and Blake (2014).

27. Oberman's work on poverty and migration is worth examining in this context. See Oberman (2016b), Oberman (2015), and Oberman (2011). Thomas Pogge (1997) provides a counter to Oberman's analysis.

28. Carens (2013) 239.
29. Oberman (2016a); see also Freiman and Hidalgo (2013). Freiman and Hidalgo's title nicely encapsulates their view; their article is called "Liberalism or Immigration Restrictions, but Not Both."
30. Gillian Brock, in Brock and Blake (2014), disagrees to some extent; as does Stilz (2016).
31. Ypi (2008) 393.
32. Wellman and Cole (2011) 198–199. Cole is here citing an earlier argument from Ann Dummett.
33. See Blake (2001).
34. Carens first uses this language in Carens (1987).
35. I say "frequently" coercive, to reflect the argument between David Miller and Arash Abizadeh about the nature of coercion at the border. For the moment, I will simply note that exclusion *often* involves an implicit threat of violence and that this fact should be sufficient to get the argument under discussion going. See Abizadeh (2008), Miller (2010), and Abizadeh (2010).
36. Abizadeh (2008).
37. Carens (2013) 258–259.
38. Blake (2013).
39. Rodríguez (2013) 2–3, emphasis added.
40. There are an extraordinary number of economic analyses of migration on offer. See Borjas (2017), Borjas (2001), Chiswick (1988), Clemens (2011), and Collier (2013).
41. Higgins (2013).
42. Oberman (2016a) 38.
43. Oberman (2016a) 39.
44. Hosein (2013) makes this case well.
45. John Rawls divides, accordingly, between liberty and the worth of that liberty. The former represents what we cannot be prevented from doing; the latter, the means that are at our disposal. See Rawls (1971).
46. *Masterpiece Cakeshop v. Colorado Civil Rights Commission*, 581 U.S. __ (2017).
47. See Calhoun (2018) and Calhoun (2015) for an explanation of how Calhoun understands the relationship between time and agency.
48. I should note, to ward off misunderstanding, that Miami is about as far within the United States as you can get from my own residence in Seattle.
49. Carens (2013) 239. See also Bauböck (2011).
50. Carens (2013) 242.
51. Carens (2013) 243.
52. Brock and Blake (2014).
53. Miller (2005); see also Miller (2016).
54. Cole, in Wellman and Cole (2011) 204.
55. Carens (2013) 250.
56. Carens (2013) 257.

Chapter 3

1. The thought that the child cannot be taken as a full moral agent is an ancient one; the legal notion of *doli incapax* denied the possibility that children under fourteen were capable of the sorts of discretion and intelligence required for criminal culpability.
2. Brian Kilmeade is the co-host of *Fox and Friends*. A discussion of his remarks can be found at http://nymag.com/daily/intelligencer/2018/06/fox-host-defends-trump-these-arent-our-kids.html.
3. See, on this, Bacon (2009) and Faux (2017).
4. Mendoza (2015) and Mendoza (2017) feature discussions of this issue.
5. Cafaro (2014) makes the case that the global environment would be harmed by an increased number of people living the American lifestyle—and emitting American quantities of carbon into the atmosphere.
6. See Macedo (2011) and Macedo (2012).
7. The continuing importance of Kant and Grotius is emphasized in Risse (2012a).
8. Sidgwick discusses this in his *Elements of Politics*, section XV. Sidgwick (2013) [1891].
9. Walzer (1986) 46–47.
10. Blake (2003).
11. Risse (2012a) 154.
12. Risse (2012a) 165.
13. Blake and Risse (2009).
14. These trends are likely to continue for the foreseeable future. See http://www.un.org/en/development/desa/news/population/world-urbanization-prospects-2014.html.
15. The story of Elisha Otis is told in Bernard (2014).
16. A discussion of Manhattan's population density can be found at https://wagner.nyu.edu/files/rudincenter/dynamic_pop_manhattan.pdf. Information about Mongolia's density can be found at https://data.worldbank.org/indicator/EN.POP.DNST.
17. Risse (2016) 268–269.
18. See, most importantly, Miller (1995).
19. Miller (2016) 12–13.
20. These ideas are defended in different ways in Kymlicka (1995) and Walzer (1986).
21. Song (2012). See also Song (forthcoming), and Song (2017).
22. The case is made in several places, but Collier (1999) in particularly important.
23. Song (2009) discusses how solidarity might emerge from diversity.
24. Pevnick (2011) 38.
25. Okin does not think that Locke is unique in this; she notes how any number of philosophical positions court absurdity when they look at reproductive labor. Okin (1989a).
26. Walzer (1986) 295.
27. *People ex rel. Moloney v. Pullman's Palace-Car Co.*, 175 Ill. 125, 51 N.E. 664, 1898 (Ill. January 1, 1898).
28. Coakley (1985).
29. Pevnick (2011) 63.

30. See, for instance, Fine (2010) and Blake (2012a).
31. *Roberts v. United States Jaycees*, 468 U.S. 609 (1984).
32. Lister (2010).

Chapter 4

1. Robert Nozick (1974) provides detail on this methodology.
2. The text of the Montevideo Convention on the Rights and Duties of States is available at http://www.cfr.org/sovereignty/montevideo-convention-rights-duties-states/p15897.
3. Montevideo Convention, Article IX.
4. States also claim jurisdiction over their own citizens, as well, when those individuals travel abroad; they claim the right to defend the rights of those citizens, when those individuals are threatened. This complication, however important in practice, can be ignored in the present context. That there is more than one way of establishing jurisdictional authority does not diminish the fact that those who cross territorial borders impose new obligations on others in virtue of their crossing.
5. A few answers to these questions: Beitz (2001), Ignatieff (2003), and Talbott (2005).
6. For a historical introduction to the development of this trichotomy, see Kock (2012).
7. It is true that some crimes are of sufficient gravity that they can be pursued anywhere; universal jurisdiction is a long-standing concept within international law, and recent scholars have urged an expanded view of this concept. The concept, however, exists as an exception to a general rule of territorial jurisdiction; no one, to my knowledge, has ever thought to extend this concept to cover crimes other than the most gross violations of human rights. See, on this, the Outcome Document of the 2005 United Nations World Summit, /RES/601/1, available at http://www.un.org/en/preventgenocide/adviser/responsibility.shtml.
8. It is worth noting, however, that all this assumes that the particularity of the relationship between the state and those within its jurisdiction is itself morally permissible. I have assumed that it is, but have not argued to that effect. A. John Simmons's analysis of the particularity problem might therefore be a necessary precursor to the discussion I provide here; Simmons questions whether or not the particular relationships defended between particular states and particular citizens can be adequately grounded in any general account of moral duties (such as, most centrally, a duty to uphold just institutions). I assume here that some solution can be found to this problem; if one cannot, then we may have reason to believe that what I say in this paper is morally problematic as well. See Simmons (1979).
9. The strongest statement of this principle is found in the International Convention on the Protection of the Rights of All Migrant Workers and Members of Their Families, GA Res. 45/158 of December 18, 1990, which forbids discrimination against those present in a jurisdiction without legal documentation. Most Western countries have refused to sign the Convention. The rights of those present within a jurisdiction to be protected by that jurisdiction's institutions, however, is less controversial, finding a

home in both the Montevideo Convention and in the International Covenant on Civil and Political Rights, Part II, Article 2.

10. *Plyler v. Doe*, 457 U.S. 202 (1982) at 215.

11. One interesting exception to this is Jeremy Waldron, who critiques John Locke's account of property in virtue of its ability to impose obligations on others without their consent. See Waldron (1990). I am grateful to Wayne Sumner for discussion of this point.

12. The example appears in Thomson (1971).

13. Terry Pratchett introduced the concept of an anti-crime to cover cases such as these: they include such possibilities as breaking-and-decorating, and whitemail (such as threatening to publicize a mobster's secret donations to charity). Terry Pratchett insists that an anti-crime must include the desire to bother or embarrass the victim; my own use of this concept does not contain this restriction. See Pratchett (2002).

14. Kates and Pevnick (2014). A similar point is made in Arrildt (2016).

15. I discuss this case in Blake (2003).

16. One possible response to this argument would be to say that my right to pursue my career was a sufficient reason for the United States to take itself as under an obligation to allow me entry. I do not think this is entirely adequate as a response; the right to occupational choice is not best construed as the right to the maximization of the occupational options open to me. There are, after all, excellent graduate programs in philosophy in Canada; a United States that insisted I choose from among those programs would not have interfered with the freedoms that comprise my moral rights. I discuss these ideas more in chapter 7.

17. A good discussion of the limits that might emerge from such ideas is found in Mendoza (2011).

18. I discuss some of these ideas in Blake (2008).

19. This is a reinterpretation of Arash Abizadeh's argument in Abizadeh (2008).

20. *Edwards v. California*, 314 U.S. 160 (1941), at 173–174, citing *Baldwin v. Seelig*, 294 U.S. 511 (1935) at 522.

21. Stephenson (1992).

22. *Saenz v. Roe*, 526 U.S. 489 (1999).

23. See generally Dinan (2010).

24. The promise—and peril—of this sort of financial intervention is discussed in Wellman and Cole (2011) and in Lister (2013).

25. Rawls (1971).

26. The Dublin II Regulation is available at http://europa.eu/legislation_summaries/justice_freedom_security/free_movement_of_persons_asylum_immigration/l33153_en.htm.

27. Gillian Brock, for example, defends the legitimacy of states keeping their own high-talent individuals from leaving for other countries. See Brock (2009) 190–212.

28. For a contrary view, see Miller (2007).

29. I have not, for instance, examined the notion of family reunification. I believe the approach I give here is compatible with a right to something like family reunification;

the right, however, would have to be derived from the illegitimacy of a domestic state using its political rights to undermine the familial interests of a current member of that state. Even if states have the right to exclude, that is, they have to answer to their own members about how that right is exercised. I regret that I do not have space to consider these matters more fully in the present context.

30. Kates and Pevnick (2014) 192.

31. Oberman (2016a).

32. Brezger and Cassee (2016) 368; see also Hidalgo (2014).

33. Volker Heins, in discussing this case with me, has emphasized that my view stands in need of a theory of weighting, on which I can demonstrate that the right to bodily integrity is more weighty than the right to be free from imposed obligations. I think he might be right; but I would prefer to think of these two rights as distinct not only in weight, but in kind. We might avoid having to discuss the relative weights of different rights, I think, if we are able to identify some rights as having priority in virtue of the kind of right they are. I am grateful to Heins for his discussion on this point.

34. See, on the rights of same-sex couples, Macedo (2015).

35. Lamey (2016).

36. Lamey (2016).

37. My reading of Kant is informed by Murphy (1994).

38. In 1724, an author generally believed to have been a pirate published a description of pirate habits and mores, under the pseudonym Charles Johnson. See Johnson (1724).

39. Johnson (1724).

Chapter 5

1. Many accounts of the contemporary regime of refugee protection have some historic detail; see Maley (2016) and Gibney (2004). Price (2009) is exceptional in how much historical detail it provides from the premodern and early modern experience of sanctuary and asylum.

2. The arguments of these figures are neatly summarized in Price (2009) 24–58.

3. Jefferson's words are cited in *American State Papers, vol. 1, (1789–1852)* at 258.

4. It is worth noting that the relationship between the Convention and domestic law is not a simple one. The United States, for instance, was not originally a signatory to the Convention but has adopted its definition into its domestic legislation. The interpretation of the Convention, moreover, is neither static nor without its difficulties. The Convention was intended to apply only to those displaced prior to 1951, but has come to be regarded as having force in the legal analyses of later migration crises. These complexities are nicely discussed in Maley (2016).

5. The scope of non-refoulement as a norm is also somewhat unsettled. While originally held to apply only to those who qualified for status under the Convention, the norm is now taken to apply to a wider variety of migrants. See DeAngelo (2009) on the scope of non-refoulement.

6. Critics include Gibney (2004), Shacknove (1985), and Shue (1980).

7. Betts proposes this term to overcome the difficulties with the legal concept of the refugee. See Betts (2013); see also Collier and Betts (2017).

8. See Lister (2013) and Price (2009).

9. I make an earlier attempt at this distinction in Blake (2016).

10. The story is given, vividly, in Lewis (1965).

11. Pogge does not endorse the distinction; he simply acknowledges that something like that distinction is held by most of his interlocutors. See Pogge (2008).

12. Carens (2013) 235.

13. This is one of many ways of reducing the flow. Italy may have recently offered financial incentives to Libyan agents—on condition that those agents cease helping migrants pass through Libyan territory on their way to Italy. The status of this act as coercive seems complex; much depends on whether those paid are simply people who will no longer go out of their way to help prospective migrants—or warlords, who are being paid to hinder the onward journey of the one seeking emigration. See Walsh and Horowitz (2017).

14. See Yenginsu and Hartocollis (2015). Prices for those with visas can be verified at ferrybodrum.com.

15. Similar reasoning is behind the Trump administration's efforts to prevent Mexican citizens from presenting themselves at the border and claiming the rights of asylum. See Meyer (2018).

16. Bloom and Risse (2014).

17. See Miller (2016), Miller (2010), Abizadeh (2010), and Abizadeh (2008).

18. My agreement is only partial, since I would argue that coercion can occur when even one option is taken away; when guards are placed on a line in the earth and given guns to fire upon those who walk over that line, I believe that it would be fair to regard what they do as coercive, even if a great many options remain to me on my side of that line. I cannot adequately defend this thought at present, though.

19. Several important legal documents have helped increase the scope—including the Convention Against Torture, and the International Covenant on Civil and Political Rights. See generally Maley (2016) and Gibney (2004).

20. David Owen, for one, has written on the vexed question of integrating refugees into societies of refuge; I do not examine these questions here. See Owen (forthcoming).

21. McAdam and Chong (2014) discuss the Australian practices and find them to be deeply hostile to both the text and the spirit of international human rights law.

22. Benner and Dickerson (2018).

23. Bier (2016).

24. A description of the proposal can be found at https://www.voanews.com/a/trump-border-wall-proposal/4194974.html.

25. See Axelrod (2018).

26. Rawls (1999b).

27. Blake (2013).

28. I should note that the line here is often subject to change; the European Union has begun to pressure the United States to change its death penalty practice and has recently restricted the exports of lethal drugs to the United States. See Ford (2014). It

should be noted that the response by at least one state to an absence of execution drugs has been to reintroduce death by electrocution. See Raymond (2018).

29. Rawls relies here on Soper (1984).

30. The documents setting up the R2P framework can be found at http://www.un.org/en/genocideprevention/about-responsibility-to-protect.html. I am not the first to note how these concepts might relate to migration; see Welsh (2014) and Straehle (2012).

31. Lister (2013). Max Cherem makes a similar point: "Refugees flee the persecutory peril of repudiated membership, which can often only be durably solved by new membership." Cherem (2016) 192.

32. Améry (1980) 49–50.

33. For an introduction to how difficult it will be to adjust to climate change, see Gardiner (2011). On the relationship between climate change and migration, see Lister (2014).

34. Operation Provision: http://www.forces.gc.ca/en/operations-abroad/op-provision.page§.

Chapter 6

1. The Australian points system is unusually clear; it gives points for education, linguistic ability, age, and other desired characteristics—and entirely precludes the migration of those over the age of forty-five. See the Australian government's website at http://www.visabureau.com/australia/immigration-points-test.aspx.

2. The idea is presented in Scanlon (2000).

3. Bump (2018) provides an overview of the dangers of Trump's rhetoric.

4. The White House document, which repeats the word "animals" rather more than might be expected, is called "What You Need to Know about the Violent Animals of MS-13." It is available at https://www.whitehouse.gov/articles/need-know-violent-animals-ms-13/.

5. https://www.whitehouse.gov/briefings-statements/remarks-president-trump-members-angel-families-immigration/.

6. http://www.presidency.ucsb.edu/ws/index.php?pid=29627&st=Chinese&st1=.

7. The government of Dominica is fairly up front about its requirements; one has to provide a "donation" of $100,000 to the Economic Diversification Fund in order to obtain citizenship. See https://cbiu.gov.dm. The United States, in contrast, is somewhat complex—but one can generally obtain the right to permanent residency, under the EB-5 program, with a business investment of over one million dollars and ten employees in the United States. See https://www.uscis.gov/working-united-states/permanent-workers/employment-based-immigration-fifth-preference-eb-5/about-eb-5-visa-classification.

8. http://www.lbjlibrary.org/lyndon-baines-johnson/timeline/lbj-on-immigration.

9. Guerrero (2014) defends what he calls "lottocracy"—in which rulers are chosen not by votes, but by some form of random selection.

10. See Lewis (1989) for a David Lewis's analysis of the relation between randomness and criminal justice.

11. See Coogan (2002) 261–269.

12. Phillip Pettit has done more than anyone to defend and describe this approach to political theorizing. See Pettit (2012).

13. Margalit uses the notion of humiliation to describe a particular form of social evil—one not easily reduced to language about justice. See Margalit (1996).

14. Carens (2013) 174.

15. Reed-Sandoval (2005).

16. Romero (2017).

17. *Yick Wo v. Hopkins*, 118 U.S. 356 (1886) at 375.

18. Holmes (1881) 3.

19. The history of the travel ban can be found in Lowery and Dawsey (2018).

20. *Trump v. Hawaii*, 585 U.S. __ (2018) at 34.

21. *Trump v. Hawaii*, 585 U.S. __ (2018), Sotomayor, dissenting, at 1.

22. An early analysis of the purposes of the group can be found in Wudunn (1995).

23. See Kennedy (1999); see also Hosein (2018).

24. The Jackson-Varner Amendment refused to grant the Soviet Union status as most-favored nation in trade until the refuseniks were allowed to emigrate to Israel.

25. Sorkin (2015) describes Cruz's remarks.

26. This is the EB-1 program, and the various categories used can be found at https://www.uscis.gov/working-united-states/permanent-workers/employment-based-immigration-first-preference-eb-1.

27. Brock and Blake (2014).

28. Bacon (2009).

29. Watson (2008).

30. There is a tremendous amount of research on understanding whether and how democracy is in decline. A useful survey of this literature is found in Lührman and Wilson (2018).

31. Harris and Lieberman (2017).

32. This program has, of course, received a great deal of criticism. See Berry and Sorenson (2018).

33. Schultheis (2018) discusses the prospects for Swedish politics.

34. The Pew Research Center has summarized some of its recent findings at http://www.people-press.org/2018/04/26/the-public-the-political-system-and-american-democracy/.

35. Carens (2013) 235.

36. Pratchett (1996).

37. Wintour (2018).

38. There is some limited evidence that simply watching television shows featuring gay men and women might reduce feelings of homophobia. See Schiappa et al. (2006).

Chapter 7

1. See Walzer (1986); Walzer's views about the Vietnam War are laid out in Walzer (1977).

2. For this concept, see Stilz (2013).

3. I should note, of course, that while a graduate student, I was not a migrant; the F-1 visa one gets as a student is quite explicitly temporary. But doing the PhD takes enough time that it is poorly analogized to such temporary statuses as that of a tourist—and I have, at any rate, never resided outside the United States since arriving there as a graduate student.

4. Makino (2004).

5. Pai (2014).

6. Carens (2010) 17.

7. The argument is laid out in Carens (2010).

8. Hosein (2014). Hosein (2016) provides a very useful taxonomy of other forms of argument that might be used.

9. The case is that of Eugen Karl Mullerschon, whose overstay was described as being for 7,059 days. See the report at https://www.bangkokpost.com/news/general/1509898/35-foreigners-nabbed-for-visa-offences.

10. See "Council Orders Banksy Art Removal." BBC News, October 24, 2008. Available at http://news.bbc.co.uk/2/hi/uk_news/england/london/7688251.stm.

11. I should emphasize, in case any of my employers are reading this, that this is a hypothetical.

12. The case is described in Slovic (2008).

13. The distinction is found in several places in Ronald Dworkin's work; see, most notably, Dworkin (2000).

14. Rep. King's words can be found at https://steveking.house.gov/issues/immigration

15. Arendt's analysis has been influential, and I cannot explore all the complexities of her analysis here. The original concepts are found in Arendt (1958).

16. Barbash (2015).

17. Bort (2018) discusses these facilities.

18. See Maley (2016).

19. Carens (2013) 147–149.

20. The case is described in Warikoo (2018).

21. The law and morality of family life are quite complex. I have learned a great deal from Brake and Miller (2018), Brake (2012), Macedo (2015), and Lister (2010).

22. Carens (2013) 78–80.

23. Ferracioli (2016).

24. The decision can be found at http://cdn.ca9.uscourts.gov/datastore/opinions/2017/09/07/17-16426.pdf.

25. This analysis is informed by that of Macedo (2015).

26. See Lister (2010).

Chapter 8

1. The fateful words are discussed in O'Keefe (2014).

2. This line is frequently invoked in such informal argumentation sites as social media and letters to the editor. See, again, Chomsky (2014) and Gambino (2015).

3. I should note that this reply focuses, in part, on the linguistic reduction that takes the term *illegal* to apply to a person as a whole; as one activist notes, we tend not to refer to those who have broken jaywalking statutes as *illegal pedestrians*.

4. Lister uses these ideas to discuss the nature of justice; I use them here to discuss the related notion of how (and why) we are obligated to *do* justice. See Lister (2011). I should note that these are not, by any means, the only views on how to understand the obligation to obey. I will not consider, for instance, the anarchism of A. John Simmons, nor the normal justification view of Joseph Raz. See Simmons (1979) and Raz (1988).

5. The law of the United States makes entry or attempted entry into the United States without inspection a crime punishable by up to two years' imprisonment. See 8 U.S.C. §1325(a). In contrast, being resident in the United States without right—as is common with those who have entered legally and have overstayed their visa terms—is a civil offense. 8 U.S.C. §1324d(a)(2).

6. These cases are distinct. Joseph Carens defends a version of the former, and David Bacon a version of the latter. See Carens (2010) and Bacon (2009).

7. Abizadeh (2008).

8. John Rawls (1999a).

9. John Rawls (2001) 126–127.

10. A. John Simmons discusses—and rejects—such a view, which he calls the "transactional reciprocation" view of obligation. He notes that such a view might be grounded on either an obligation to be fair or an obligation of gratitude for benefits received. Since nothing I say here depends upon these distinctions, I am ignoring them in the present context. Wellman and Simmons (2005) 118–120.

11. Murphy (1973) 242.

12. The thought that those migrants ought to be grateful for past benefits is only one vision of reciprocity, one which takes this idea to be strongly associated with mutual advantage. I do not claim that this is the only, or even the best, interpretation of reciprocity, which generally understands advantage to be rightly measured with reference to some moralized baseline, rather than with reference to historic distributions. See Lister (2017).

13. See, for example, Nussbaum (2006) 96–154.

14. See, for instance, Richardson (2006) 419–462.

15. Ramsay (2007). Available at https://www.gamespot.com/articles/blitz-banned-in-australia/1100-6164484/.

16. Jonathan Quong's account of cooperative activity would entail this—although he would derive no conclusions about the moral obligations that follow. Quong (2007) 75–105.

17. In his early work John Rawls describes a natural duty to "support and comply with just institutions that exist and apply to us." Rawls (1971) 115.

18. See, for instance, Valentini (2017), James (2012), Buchanan (2003).

19. Sharp and Gonzalez (2013).

20. See Song (2017).

21. Rawls (1999b).

22. McAdam and Chong (2014).

23. Oberman (2016b).
24. Cole (2002).
25. Peter Hoeg (1993).
26. This increase is sensitive to alterations in enforcement policy and in demand for migrant labor. See Borjas (2017).
27. There exists in Mexico a thriving community of wealthy expatriates, coming from countries ranging from South Korea to the United States. See Cave (2013).
28. *R. v. Dudley and Stephens*, 14 QBD 273 (Queen's Bench Division, 1884), emphasis added.
29. Famously, the judges sentenced the killers to death, with a recommendation that the sentence be commuted as unmerciful. Rawson (2000).
30. The Kobayashi Maru test, featured in *Star Trek II: The Wrath of Khan*, similarly involves an inevitable failure; James T. Kirk "wins" only by cheating and rewriting the test's code. See Stemwedel (2015). Available at https://www.forbes.com/sites/janetstemwedel/2015/08/23/the-philosophy-of-star-trek-the-kobayashi-maru-no-win-scenarios-and-ethical-leadership/#268205fd5f48.
31. Littell (2006). It must be said that the narrator's line becomes less convincing over the course of the novel.
32. Rawls (1989) 17.
33. Warren (2015).
34. Rubin (2016).
35. Feinberg (1965).
36. In 2012, Human Rights First prepared a report for the United Nations special papporteur on the human rights of migrants, detailing the ways in which many industrialized nations were merging their prison systems with their systems of migration control. The report is available at https://www.humanrightsfirst.org/wp-content/uploads/pdf/Submission-Immigration_Detention-to_Special_Rapporteur_on_the_Human_Rights_of_Migrants.pdf. See also Parekh (2016).
37. Tom Tancredo, while chairman of the House Immigration Caucus, defended mandatory detention for undocumented immigrants, coupled with the elimination of birthright citizenship for the children of the undocumented. The interview is available at http://www.washingtonpost.com/wp-dyn/content/discussion/2006/03/29/DI2006032901468.html.
38. Nixon and Robins (2017).
39. Tibbetts (2018).
40. Sachetti (2018).
41. Thus, Kishore Mahbubani's prophetic words from 1992: "In the eyes of the North African population, the Mediterranean, which once divided civilizations, has now become a mere pond. What human being would not cross a pond if thereby he could improve his livelihood?" Mahbubani (2001) 60.

Chapter 9

1. Rawls (1971).
2. See Murphy's account, in Murphy and Hampton (1988).

3. His own account, however, focuses on the change of mind in the agent showing mercy; my own account does not do this.

4. Perry (2018). There is now a relatively well-developed literature on mercy, although the majority of that literature applies this virtue primarily to the criminal law. I have been influenced by Murphy and Hampton (1988), Card (1972), Rainbolt (1990), and Staihar and Macedo (2011).

5. See, for instance, the Christian approaches to migration in such works as Kerwin and Gerschutz (2009) and Myers and Colwell (2012).

6. See generally Rose (2012), which describes the struggles of the early sanctuary movement.

7. The statement of the bishops can be found at http://www.usccb.org/issues-and-action/human-life-and-dignity/immigration/catholic-teaching-on-immigration-and-the-movement-of-peoples.cfm.

8. *Fong Yue Ting v. U. S.*, 149 U.S. 698 (1893).

9. Brecht wrote these words in 1931. Available at https://rihlajourney.wordpress.com/2013/02/03/a-bed-for-the-night-bertolt-brecht/.

10. Rawls (1989).

11. Rawls (1989) 194.

12. The text of the encyclical can be found at http://w2.vatican.va/content/john-paul-ii/en/encyclicals/documents/hf_jp-ii_enc_30111980_dives-in-misericordia.html.

13. Mielke (2016).

14. Holy Mass for Migrants, Homily of His Holiness Pope Francis, July 6, 2018. http://w2.vatican.va/content/francesco/en/homilies/2018/documents/papa-francesco_20180706_omelia-migranti.html.

15. Sara Ruddick (1989), whose work is sometimes taken to begin the tradition of care ethics, does not present that ethic as potentially replacing the ethics of justice. Slote (2007), in contrast, is willing to consider that care might be all that ethics requires.

16. Held (2006).

17. Kittay (2009).

18. "What should be resisted is the traditional inclination to expand the reach of justice in such a way that it is mistakenly imagined to give us a comprehensive morality suitable for all moral questions." Held (2006) 17.

19. This dichotomy is likely overstated; Kant was not what his critics have felt him to be, and much the same is true for those writing in the tradition of care. But the core of the dichotomy is rightly pressed, and it is hard to deny that Kant is less willing than Virginia Held to acknowledge the ethical relevance of emotional ties.

20. I rely, in much of my analysis here, on Murphy's reconstruction of Kant. See Murphy (1994).

21. The notion of a "playroom" is discussed in Gilabert (2010).

22. Kant (1998) 4:432.

23. Kant (1998) 4:399.

24. The language here is borrowed from Baier (2013).

25. See James (1992). It is worth noting that the character of Xan is somewhat distinct in the movie and in the book version of the story.

26. Okin (1989a).
27. Okin (1989b) expands on this and discusses how the practice of empathy might be required for social justice.
28. Healy and Martin (2016).
29. Rawls (1989) 157.
30. In this, the law might have something in common with Christian tradition: the notion of *lex orandi, lex credenda* argued that belief might sometimes emerge from practice, rather than preceding it.
31. Costa and Philips (2015) discuss the coordinated effort by Republican governors to refuse admission of Syrian refugees into their states.
32. Rowling (2000).

Chapter 10

1. These new forms of value are discussed in Brock and Blake (2014).
2. The Canadian film *Roadkill*, released in 1989, featured a character who was a serial killer, but who resented the fact that any Canadian with ambition ended up moving to the United States; he was a patriot, he announced, and wanted to stay at home and kill Canadians.
3. The H1-B program is described at https://www.uscis.gov/working-united-states/temporary-workers/h-1b-specialty-occupations-and-fashion-models/h-1b-fiscal-year-fy-2019-cap-season.
4. Davis (2018).
5. Ronald Reagan, in *Public Papers of the Presidents of the United States: Ronald Reagan, June 30 to December 31, 1984*, at 1600.
6. The text of the IRCA is available at https://www.uscis.gov/sites/default/files/ocomm/ilink/0-0-0-15.html.
7. King's words can be found at https://www.gpo.gov/fdsys/pkg/CREC-2013-07-24/html/CREC-2013-07-24-pt1-PgH5044.htm.
8. Clarke (2014) tells the story of Denise Harvey.
9. Brake (2012) and Macedo (2015) provide distinct visions of whether or not a democratic society can defend monogamy without injustice.
10. See Bush (2018).
11. Obama's words are reported in Winston (2015).
12. Williams (1995) introduces the thought that two-level forms of utilitarianism run afoul of the equality of persons.
13. Rawls (1989).
14. As I write, a caravan of migrants fleeing violence in Honduras is walking through Mexico, with the intention of entering the United States. The president has promised to send troops to the border. More troubling, a significant number of paramilitary groups may be going to the border to prevent that caravan from crossing. The US Border Patrol has become worried that this may lead to violence, as the two sides come together. See Merchant (2018).

15. The history of sanctuary, of course, is vastly more complex than I thought—or even than I present here. See Shoemaker (2011).
16. See Lister (2014) for some reflections on climate change and refuge; see Collier and Betts (2017) for some thoughts about how the present framework of protection might fail in the face of such threats.
17. Vonnegut (1965).

Bibliography

Abizadeh, Arash. 2010. "Democratic Legitimacy and State Coercion: A Reply to David Miller." 38(1) *Political Theory*: 121–130.

Abizadeh, Arash. 2008. "Democratic Theory and Border Coercion: No Right to Unilaterally Control Your Own Borders." 36(1) *Political Theory*: 37–65.

Adler, Margot. 2007. "Churches May Help in Fight against Deportations." *National Public Radio*, May 9. Available at https://www.npr.org/templates/story/story.php?storyId=10098237.

Alexievich, Svetlana. 2016. *Secondhand Time: The Last of the Soviets*. New York: Random House.

American State Papers: Documents, Legislative and Executive, of the Congress of the United States, vol. 1 (1789–1815). 1832. Washington: Gales and Seaton.

Améry, Jean. 1980. *At the Mind's Limits: Contemplations by a Survivor of Auschwitz and Its Realities*. Translated by Stanley Rosenfeld and Stella P. Rosenfeld. Bloomington: Indiana University Press.

Arendt, Hannah. 1958. *The Origins of Totalitarianism*. 2nd edition. New York: World Publishing Company.

Arrildt, Julie. 2016. "State Borders as Defining Lines of Justice: Why the Right to Exclude Cannot Be Justified." 21(4) *Critical Review of International Social and Political Philosophy*: 500–520.

Axelrod, Tal. 2018. "Trump: Border Troops Authorized to Use Lethal Force 'If They Have To.'" *The Hill*, November 22.

Bacon, David. 2009. *Illegal People: How Globalization Creates Migration and Criminalizes Immigrants*. Boston: Beacon Press.

Baier, Annette. 2013. "The Need for More Than Justice." *Canadian Journal of Philosophy*, supplementary volume 13: 41–56.

Barbash, Fred. 2015. "Federal Judge in Texas Blocks Obama Immigration Orders." *Washington Post*, February 18.

Bauböck, Rainer, ed. 2018a. *Debating European Citizenship*. New York: Springer.

Bauböck, Rainer, ed. 2018b. *Debating Transformations of National Citizenship*. New York: Springer.

Bauböck, Rainer. 2011. "Citizenship and Freedom of Movement." In *Citizenship, Borders, and Human Needs*, edited by Roger Smith, 343–376. Philadelphia: University of Pennsylvania Press.

Beitz, Charles. 2001. *The Idea of Human Rights*. Princeton: Princeton University Press.

Beitz, Charles. 1999. *Political Theory and International Relations*. Revised edition. Princeton: Princeton University Press.

Benner, Katie, and Caitlin Dickerson. 2018. "Sessions Says Domestic and Gang Violence Are Not Grounds for Asylum." *New York Times*, June 11.

Bernard, Andreas. 2014. *Lifted: A Cultural History of the Elevator*. New York: New York University Press.

Berry, Ellen, and Martin Selsoe Sorensen. 2018. "In Denmark, Harsh New Laws for Immigrant 'Ghettos.'" *New York Times*, July 1.

Bertram, Chris. 2018. *Do States Have the Right to Exclude Immigrants?* Cambridge: Polity Press.

Betts, Alexander. 2013. *Survival Migration, Failed Governance, and the Crisis of Migration*. Ithaca: Cornell University Press.

Bier, David. 2016. "A Wall Is an Impractical, Expensive, and Ineffective Border Plan." *Cato at Liberty*, November 26. Available at https://www.cato.org/blog/border-wall-impractical-expensive-ineffective-plan.

Bioxham, Donald. 2005. *The Great Game of Genocide: Imperialism, Nationalism, and the Destruction of the Ottoman Armenians*. New York: Oxford University Press.

Blake, Michael. 2016. "Positive and Negative Rights of Migration: A Reply to My Critics." 9(1) *Ethics and Global Politics*. Available at https://doi.org/10.3402/egp.v9.33553

Blake, Michael. 2014. "The Costs of War: Justice, Liability, and the Pottery Barn Rule." In *The Ethics of Armed Humanitarian Intervention*, edited by Don Scheid, 133–147. Cambridge University Press.

Blake, Michael. 2013. *Justice and Foreign Policy*. Oxford: Oxford University Press.

Blake, Michael. 2012a. "Immigration, Association, and Anti-discrimination." 122(4) *Ethics* (July): 1–16.

Blake, Michael. 2012b. "Equality without Documents: Political Justice and the Right to Amnesty." *Canadian Journal of Philosophy*, supplementary volume 36: 99–122.

Blake, Michael. 2008. "Immigration and Political Equality." 45(4) *San Diego Law Review*: 963–980.

Blake, Michael. 2003. "Immigration." In *The Blackwell Companion to Applied Ethics*, edited by Christopher Wellman and R. G. Frey, 224–237. Oxford: Blackwell.

Blake, Michael. 2001. "Distributive Justice, State Coercion, and Autonomy." 30(3) *Philosophy & Public Affairs*: 257–296.

Blake, Michael, and Mathias Risse. 2009. "Immigration and Original Ownership of the Earth." 23(1) *Notre Dame Journal of Law, Ethics and Public Policy*: 133–167.

Bloom, Tendayi, and Verena Risse. 2014. "Examining Hidden Coercion at the Borders: Why Carrier Sanctions Cannot Be Justified." 7(2) *Ethics & Global Politics*: 65–82.

Borjas, George. 2017. "The Earnings of Undocumented Immigrants." NBER Working Paper Number 23236. Available at www.nber.org/papers/w23236.

Borjas, George. 2001. *Heaven's Door: Immigration Policy and the American Economy*. Princeton: Princeton University Press.

Bort, Ryan. 2018. "This Is the Prison-Like Border Facility Holding Migrant Children." *Rolling Stone*, June 14.

Brake, Elizabeth. 2012. *Minimizing Marriage: Marriage, Morality, and the Law*. New York: Oxford University Press.

Brake, Elizabeth, and Lucinda Ferguson, eds. 2018. *Philosophical Foundations of Children's and Family Law*. New York: Oxford University Press.

Bratman, Michael. 1987. *Intentions, Plans, and Practical Reasons*. Stanford: Center for the Study of Language and Information.

Brezger, Jan, and Andreas Cassee. "Debate: Immigrants and Newcomers by Birth—Do Statist Arguments Imply a Right to Exclude Both?" 24(1) *Journal of Political Philosophy*: 367–378.

Brock, Gillian. 2009. *Global Justice*. New York: Oxford University Press.

Brock, Gillian, and Michael Blake. 2014. *Debating Brain Drain: May Governments Restrict Emigration?* New York: Oxford University Press.

Buchanan, Allen. 2003. *Justice, Legitimacy, and Self-Determination.* New York: Oxford University Press.

Bump, Philip. 2018. "The Slippery Slope of the Trump Administration's Political Embrace of Calling MS-13 'Animals.'" *Washington Post*, May 21.

Bush, Laura. 2018. "Laura Bush: Separating Children from Their Parents at the Border 'Breaks My Heart.'" *Washington Post*, June 17.

Cabrera, Luis. 2004. *Political Theory of Global Justice: A Cosmopolitan Case for the World State.* Abingdon: Routledge.

Cafaro, Philip. 2014. *How Many Is Too Many? The Progressive Argument for Reducing Migration to the United States.* Chicago: University of Chicago Press.

Calhoun, Cheshire. 2018. *Doing Valuable Time.* New York: Oxford University Press.

Calhoun, Cheshire. 2015. *Getting It Right.* New York: Oxford University Press.

Caney, Simon. 2006. *Justice beyond Borders.* New York: Oxford University Press.

Card, Claudia. 1972. "On Mercy." 81(2) *Philosophical Review* (April): 182–207.

Card, David. 1990. "The Impact of the Mariel Boatlift on the Miami Labor Market." 43(2) *Industrial and Labor Relations Review* (January): 245–257.

Carens, Joseph H. 2013. *The Ethics of Immigration.* New York: Oxford University Press.

Carens, Joseph H. 2010. *Immigrants and the Right to Stay.* Boston: MIT Press.

Carens, Joseph H. 1987. "Aliens and Citizens: The Case for Open Borders." 49(2) *Review of Politics*: 251–273.

Cave, Damien. 2013. "For Migrants, New Land of Opportunity Is Mexico." *New York Times*, September 23.

Cherem, Max. 2016. "Refugee Rights: Against Expanding the Definition of a 'Refugee' and Unilateral Protection Elsewhere." 24(2) *Journal of Political Philosophy* (June) 183–205.

Chiswick, Barry R. 1988. "Illegal Immigration and Immigration Control." 2(3) *Journal of Economic Perspectives* (Summer): 101–115.

Chomsky, Aviva. 2014. *Undocumented: How Immigration Became Illegal.* Boston: Beacon Press.

Clarke, Katrina. 2014. "Florida Sex-Offender Who Had Relations with 16-Year-Old Granted Refugee Status in Canada." *National Post*, May 14.

Clemens, Michael. 2011. "Economics and Emigration: Trillion-Dollar Bills on the Sidewalk?" 25 *Journal of Economic Perspectives*: 83–106.

Coakley, Michael. 1985. "Mayflower Descendants a Breed Apart." *Chicago Tribune*, September 5.

Cohen, Elizabeth F. 2009. *Semi-citizenship in Democratic Politics.* Cambridge: Cambridge University Press.

Cole, Phillip. 2002. *Philosophies of Exclusion.* Edinburgh: Edinburgh University Press.

Collier, Paul. 2013. *Exodus: How Migration Is Changing Our World.* New York: Oxford University Press.

Collier, Paul. 1999. "Why Has Africa Grown Slowly?" 13(3) *Journal of Economic Perspectives* (Summer 1999): 3–22.

Collier, Paul, and Alexander Betts. 2017. *Refuge: Rethinking Refugee Policy in a Changing World.* New York: Oxford University Press.

Coogan, Tim Pat. 2002. *Wherever Green Is Worn: The Story of the Irish Diaspora.* Basingstroke: Palgrave Macmillan.

Costa, Robert, and Abby Philips. 2015. "Republican Governors and Candidates Move to Keep Muslim Immigrants Out." *Washington Post*, November 16.

"Council Orders Banksy Art Removal." 2008. *BBC News*, October 24. Available at http://news.bbc.co.uk/2/hi/uk_news/england/london/7688251.stm.

Davis, Julie Hirschfeld. 2018. "Trump to Cap Refugees Allowed into U.S. at 30,000, a Record Low." *New York Times*, September 17.

DeAngelo, Ellen. 2009. "Non-refoulement: The Search for a Consistent Interpretation of Article 33." 42 *Vanderbilt Journal of Transnational Law*: 279–315.

Dinan, Desmond. 2010. *Ever Closer Union: An Introduction to European Integration*. Boulder: Lynne Rienner.

Dummett, Michael. 2001. *On Immigration and Refugees*. Abingdon: Routledge.

Dworkin, Ronald. 2000. *Sovereign Virtue: The Theory and Practice of Equality*. Cambridge: Harvard University Press.

"Europe Is Coddling Arab Strongmen to Keep Out Refugees." 2018. *The Economist*, August 16.

Faux, Jeff. 2017. "How U. S. Foreign Policy Helped Create the Immigration Crisis." *The Nation*, October 18.

Feinberg, Joel. 1965. "The Expressive Function of Punishment." 49(3) *The Monist* (July): 397–423.

Ferracioli, Luara. 2016. "Family Migration Schemes and Liberal Neutrality: A Dilemma." 13(5) *Journal of Moral Philosophy*: 553–575.

Fine, Sarah. 2010. "Freedom of Association Is Not the Answer." 120(2) *Ethics* (January): 338–356.

Fisher, Michael H. 2013. *Migration: A New World History*. New York: Oxford University Press.

Ford, Matt. 2014. "Can Europe End the Death Penalty in America?" *The Atlantic*, February 18.

Freiman, Christopher, and Javier Hidalgo. 2013. "Liberalism or Immigration Restrictions, but Not Both." 10(2) *Journal of Ethics and Social Philosophy* (May): 1–22.

French, Howard. 2014. *China's Second Continent: How a Million Migrants Are Building a New Empire in Africa*. New York: Random House.

Gambino, Lauren. 2015. "'No Human Being Is Illegal': Linguists Argue against Mislabeling of Immigrants." *The Guardian*, December 6.

Gardiner, Stephen M. 2011. *A Perfect Moral Storm: The Ethical Tragedy of Climate Change*. New York: Oxford University Press.

Gibney, Matthew. 2018. "The Ethics of Refugees." 13(10) *Philosophy Compass* (October). Available at https://onlinelibrary.wiley.com/doi/full/10.1111/phc3.12521.

Gibney, Matthew. 2004. *The Ethics and Politics of Asylum*. Cambridge: Cambridge University Press.

Gilabert, Pablo. 2010. "Kant and the Claims of the Poor." 81(2) *Philosophy and Phenomenological Research* (September): 382–418.

Gilgan, Chloë M. 2017. "Exploring the Link between R2P and Refugee Protection: Arriving at Resettlement." 9(4) *Global Responsibility to Protect*: 366–394.

Grotius, Hugo. 1979. *Rights of War and Peace*. Translated by A. C. Campbell. New York: Hyperion Press.

Guerrero, Alexander A. 2014. "Against Elections: The Lottocratic Alternative." 42(2) *Philosophy and Public Affairs* (Spring): 125–178.

Harris, Frederick C., and Robert C. Lieberman. 2017. "The Return of Racism?" *Foreign Affairs*, August 21.

Hassoun, Nicole. 2012. *Globalization and Global Justice: Shrinking Distance, Expanding Obligations*. Cambridge: Cambridge University Press.

Healy, Patrick, and Jonathan Martin. 2016. "Donald Trump Won't Say If He'll Accept Result of Election." *New York Times*, October 19.

Held, Virginia. 2006. *The Ethics of Care and Empathy*. New York: Oxford University Press.

Hidalgo, Javier. 2014. "Immigration Restrictions and the Right to Avoid Unwanted Obligations." Discussion Note, 8(2) *Journal of Ethics and Social Philosophy*: 1-9.

Higgins, Peter. 2013. *Immigration Justice*. New York: Oxford University Press.

Hightower, Jim. 1997. *There's Nothing in the Middle of the Road but Yellow Stripes and Dead Armadillos*. New York: HarperCollins.

Hill, Thomas. 1973. "Servility and Self-Respect." 57(1) *The Monist* (January): 87-104.

Hoeg, Peter. 1993. *Smilla's Sense of Snow*. Translated by Tiina Nunnally. New York: Farrar, Straus and Giroux.

Holmes, Oliver Wendell. 1881. *The Common Law*. New York: Little, Brown.

Hosein, Adam. 2018. "Racial Profiling and a Reasonable Sense of Inferior Political Status." 26(3) *Journal of Political Philosophy*: 1-20.

Hosein, Adam. 2016. "Arguments for Regularization." In *The Ethics and Politics of Immigration: Core Issues and Emerging Trends*, edited by Alex Sager, 159-179. Lanham, MD: Rowman and Littlefield.

Hosein, Adam. 2014. "Immigration: The Case for Legalization." 40(4) *Social Theory and Practice*: 609-630.

Hosein, Adam. 2013. "Immigration and Freedom of Movement." 6(1) *Ethics and Global Politics*: 25-37.

Huemer, Michael. 2010. "Is There a Right to Immigrate?" 36(3) *Social Theory and Practice*: 429-461.

Ignatieff, Michael. 2003. *Human Rights as Politics and Idolatry*. Princeton: Princeton University Press.

James, Aaron. 2012. *Fairness in Practice: A Social Contract for a Global Economy*. New York: Oxford University Press.

James, P. D. 1992. *Children of Men*. London: Faber and Faber.

Johnson, Charles. 1724. *A General History of the Pyrates*. London: Charles Rivington.

Kant, Immanuel. 1998. *Groundwork of the Metaphysics of Morals*. Translated by Mary Gregor. Cambridge: Cambridge University Press.

Kant, Immanuel. 1991. *Political Writings*. Translated and edited by Hans Reiss. Cambridge: Cambridge University Press.

Kates, Michael, and Ryan Pevnick. 2014. "Immigration, Jurisdiction, and History." 42(2) *Philosophy and Public Affairs* (Spring): 179-194.

Kennedy, Randall. 1999. "Suspect Policy." *New Republic*, September 13.

Kerwin, Donald, and Jill Marie Gerschutz, eds. 2009. *And You Welcomed Me: Migration and Catholic Social Teaching*. Lanham, MD: Lexington Press.

Kittay, Eva. 2009. "The Moral Harm of Migrant Carework: Realizing a Global Right to Care." 37(2) *Philosophical Topics*: 53-73.

Kock, Ida Elizabeth. 2012. "Dichotomies, Trichotomies, or Waves of Duties?" 12(3) *Human Rights Law Review*: 81-103.

Korsgaard, Christine. 1996. *Creating the Kingdom of Ends.* Cambridge: Cambridge University Press.

Kukathas, Chandran. 2012. "Why Open Borders?" 19(3) *Ethical Perspectives*: 649–675.

Kukathas, Chandran. 2010. "Expatriatism: The Theory and Practice of Open Borders." In *Citizenship, Borders and Human Needs*, edited by Roger M. Smith, 324–342. Philadelphia: University of Pennsylvania Press.

Kukathas, Chandran. 2005. "The Case for Open Immigration." In *Contemporary Debates in Applied Ethics*, edited by Andrew I. Cohen and Christopher Heath Wellman, 207–220. Oxford: Blackwell.

Kullgren, Ian. 2016. "Trump Misrepresents Clinton's Position on 'Open Borders.'" *Politico*, October 10. Available at https://www.politico.com/blogs/2016-presidential-debate-fact-check/2016/10/trump-misrepresents-clintons-position-on-open-borders-230045.

Kymlicka, Will. 1995. *Multicultural Citizenship.* New York: Oxford University Press.

Lamey, Andy. 2016. "The Jurisdiction Argument for Migration Control: A Critique." 42(3) *Social Theory and Practice* (July): 581–604.

Lenard, Patti, and Christine Straehle, eds. 2012. *Legislated Inequality: Temporary Labour Migration in Canada.* Montreal: McGill-Queens University Press.

Lenard, Patti, and Christine Straehle. 2010. "Temporary Labour Migration: Exploitation, Tool for Development, or Both?" 29(4) *Policy and Society*: 283–294.

Lewis, Anthony. 1964. *Gideon's Trumpet.* New York: Random House.

Lewis, David. 1989. "The Punishment That Leaves Something to Chance." 18(1) *Philosophy and Public Affairs*: 53–67.

Lister, Andrew. 2017. "Public Reason and Reciprocity." 25(2) *Journal of Political Philosophy* (June): 155–172.

Lister, Andrew. 2011. "Justice as Fairness and Reciprocity." *Analyze & Kritik*: 93–112.

Lister, Matthew. 2014. "Climate change refugees." 17(5) *Critical Review of International Social and Political Philosophy*: 618–634.

Lister, Matthew. 2013. "Who Are Refugees?" 32(2) *Law and Philosophy*: 645–651.

Lister, Matthew. 2010. "Immigration, Association and the Family." 29 *Law and Philosophy*: 717–745.

Littell, Jonathan. 2006. *The Kindly Ones.* Translated by Charlotte Mandell. New York: HarperCollins.

Lowery, Wesley, and Josh Dawsey. 2018. "Early Chaos of Trump's Travel Ban Set Stage for a Year of Immigration Policy Debates." *Washington Post*, February 6.

Lu, Catherine. 2017. *Justice and Reconciliation in World Politics.* Cambridge: Cambridge University Press.

Lührmann, Anna, and Matthew Wilson. 2018. "One-Third of the World's Population Lives in a Declining Democracy. That Includes the United States." *Washington Post*, July 4.

Macedo, Stephen. 2015. *Just Married: Same-Sex Couples, Monogamy, and the Future of Marriage.* Princeton: Princeton University Press.

Macedo, Stephen. 2012. "The Moral Dilemma of U. S. Immigration Policy Revised." In *Debating Immigration*, edited by Carol Swaim, second edition, 286–310. Cambridge: Cambridge University Press.

Macedo, Stephen. 2011. "When and Why Should Liberal Democracies Restrict Immigration?" In *Citizenship, Borders, and Human Needs*, edited by Rogers M. Smith, 301–323. Philadelphia: University of Pennsylvania Press.

Mahbubani, Kishore. 2001. *Can Asians Think?* Hanover: Steerforth Publishing.

Makino, Catherine. 2004. "Japan Gets Tough on Visa Violators. 1-Day Overstay Can Bring Time in Cell, 5-Year Banishment." *San Francisco Chronicle*, May 10.

Maley, William. 2016. *What Is a Refugee?* New York: Oxford University Press.

Mandle, Jon. 2009. *Rawls's "A Theory of Justice"*. Cambridge: Cambridge University Press.

Margalit, Avishai. 1996. *The Decent Society*. Cambridge: Harvard University Press.

Massey, Douglas, and Kerstin Gentsch. 2014. "Undocumented Migration and the Wages of Mexican Immigrants." 48(2) *International Migration Review* (Summer): 482–499.

McAdam, Jane, and Fiona Chong. 2014. *Refugees: Why Seeking Asylum Is Legal and Australia's Policies Are Not*. Randwick: University of New South Wales Press.

McWhorter, Diane. 2012. "The Strange Career of Juan Crow." *New York Times*, June 16.

Mead, Walter Russell. 2018. "Why Italy Dares to Turn Away Refugees." *Wall Street Journal*, June 18.

Mendoza, José Jorge. 2017. *The Moral and Political Philosophy of Immigration: Liberty, Security, and Equality*. Lanham, MD: Lexington Press.

Mendoza, José Jorge. 2015. "Enforcement Matters: Reframing the Philosophical Debate over Immigration." 29(1) *Journal of Speculative Philosophy*: 73–90.

Mendoza, José Jorge. 2011. "The Political Philosophy of Unauthorized Immigration." *APA Newsletter on Hispanic/Latino Issues in Philosophy* 10.2: 1–6.

Merchant, Nomaan. 2018. "Border Patrol Warns Landowners of 'Armed Civilians' after Militia Offers to Help Stop Caravan." *Chicago Tribune*, October 26.

Meyer, David. 2018. "Trump Moves to Limit Asylum Claims at U.S.-Mexico Border." *Fortune*, November 9.

Mielke, Roger. 2016. "Stewarding Mercy: The Role of Churches in the Refugee Crisis." 10 *Plough Quarterly* (Autumn). Available at https://www.plough.com/en/topics/justice/social-justice/immigration/stewarding-mercy

Miller, David. 2016. *Strangers in Our Midst: The Political Philosophy of Immigration*. Cambridge: Harvard University Press.

Miller, David. 2010. "Why Immigration Controls Are Not Coercive: A Reply to Arash Abizadeh." 38(1) *Political Theory*: 111–120.

Miller, David. 2007. *National Responsibility and Global Justice*. New York: Oxford University Press.

Miller, David. 2005. "Immigration: The Case for Limits." In *Contemporary Debates in Applied Ethics*, edited by Andrew I. Cohen and Christopher Heath Wellman, 193–206. Oxford: Blackwell.

Miller, David. 1995. *On Nationality*. New York: Oxford University Press.

"Morecambe Bay Cockling Disaster's Lasting Impact." 2014. *BBC News*, February 3. Available at https://www.bbc.com/news/uk-england-lancashire-25986388.

Moyn, Samuel. 2010. *The Last Utopia: Human Rights in History*. Cambridge: Harvard University Press.

Murphy, Jeffrie. 1994. *Kant: The Philosophy of Right*. Reprint edition. Macon, GA: Mercer University Press.

Murphy, Jeffrie G. 1973. "Marxism and Retribution." 2(3) *Philosophy and Public Affairs* (Spring): 217–243.

Murphy, Jeffrie G., and Jean Hampton. 1988. *Forgiveness and Mercy*. Cambridge: Cambridge University Press.

Myers, Ched, and Matthew Colwell. 2012. *Our God Is Undocumented: Faith and Immigrant Justice*. Maryknoll, NY: Orbis Publishing.

Nett, Roger. 1971. "The Civil Right We Are Not Ready For: The Right of Free Movement of People on the Face of the Earth." 81(3) *Ethics*: 212–227.

Ngai, Mae. 2010. "The Civil Rights Origin of Illegal Immigration." 78 *International Labor and Working Class History* (Fall): 93–99.

Nixon, Ron, and Liz Robbins. 2017. "Office to Aid Crime Victims Is Latest Step in Crackdown on Immigrants." *New York Times*, April 26.

Nozick, Robert. 1974. *Anarchy, State and Utopia*. New York: Basic Books.

Nussbaum, Martha. 2006. *Frontiers of Justice: Disability, Nationality, Species Membership*. Cambridge: Harvard University Press.

O'Keefe, Ed. 2014. "Jeb Bush: Many Illegal Immigrants Come out of an 'Act of Love.'" *Washington Post*, April 6.

Oberman, Kieran. 2016a. "Immigration as a Human Right." In Sarah Fine and Lea Ypi, eds., *Migration in Political Theory*, 32–56. New York: Oxford University Press.

Oberman, Kieran. 2016b. "Refugees and Economic Migrants: A Morally Spurious Distinction." *The Critique*, January 6.

Oberman, Kieran. 2015. "Poverty and Immigration Policy." 109(2) *American Political Science Review* (May): 239–251.

Oberman, Kieran. 2011. "Immigration, Global Poverty and the Right to Stay." 59 *Political Studies*, 253–268.

Okin, Susan Moller. 1989a. *Justice, gender and the family*. New York: Basic books.

Okin, Susan Moller. 1989b. "Reason and Feeling in Thinking about Justice." 99(2) *Ethics* (January): 229–249.

Osterloh, Margit, and Bruno S. Frey. Forthcoming. "Cooperatives Instead of Migration Partnerships." *Analyse & Kritik*.

Owen, David. Forthcoming. *Migration and Political Theory*. Abingdon: Routledge.

Owen, David. 2013. "Citizenship and the marginalities of migrants." 16(3) *Critical Review of International Social and Political Philosophy*: 326–343.

Pai, Hsiao-Hung. 2014. "The lessons of Morecambe Bay have not been learned." *The Guardian*, February 3, 2014.

Parekh, Serena. 2016. *Refugees and the Ethics of Forced Displacement*. Abingdon: New York: Routledge.

Pérez-Peña, Richard. 2017. "Former Arizona Sheriff Joe Arpaio Convicted of Criminal Contempt." *New York Times*, July 31.

Perry, Adam. 2018. "Mercy." 46(1) *Philosophy and Public Affairs* (Winter): 60–89.

Pettit, Philip. 2012. *On the People's Terms: A Republican Theory and Model of Democracy*. New York: Oxford University Press.

Pevnick, Ryan. 2011. *Immigration and the Constraints of Justice*. Cambridge: Cambridge University Press.

Pogge, Thomas. 2008. *World Poverty and Human Rights*. Second edition. London: Polity Press.

Pogge, Thomas. 2007. *John Rawls: His Life and Theory of Justice*. Trans. Michelle Kosch. New York: Oxford University Press.

Pogge, Thomas W. 1997. "Migration and Poverty." In *Citizenship and Exclusion*, edited by Veit Bader, 12–27. London: Macmillan.

Pratchett, Terry. 2002. *Reaper Man*. New York: Harper Torch.

Pratchett, Terry. 1996. *Feet of Clay*. London: Victor Gollancz.

Price, Matthew E. 2009. *Rethinking Asylum: History, Purpose, and Limits*. Cambridge: Cambridge University Press.

Public Papers of the Presidents of the United States: Ronald Reagan, June 30 to December 31, 1984. Available at https://www.reaganlibrary.gov/sspeeches

Pufendorf, Samuel. 1934. *De Jure Naturae et Gentium*, trans. C. H. Oldfather and W. A. Oldfather. Oxford: Clarendon Press.

Quong, Jonathan. "Contractualism, reciprocity, and egalitarian justice." 6(1) *Philosophy, Politics, and Economics* (February): 75–105.

Rainbolt, George. 1990. "Mercy: An Independent, Imperfect Virtue." 27(2) *American Philosophical Quarterly* (April): 169–173.

Ramsay, Rudolph. 2007. "Blitz Banned in Australia." *Gamespot*, January 22. Available at https://www.gamespot.com/articles/blitz-banned-in-australia/1100-6164484/.

Raymond, Adam K. 2018. "Tennessee Man Is First U.S. Inmate Killed by Electric Chair in Five Years." *New York Magazine*, November 2.

Rawls, John. 2001. *Justice as Fairness: A Restatement,* edited by Erin Kelly. Cambridge: Belknap Press of Harvard University Press.

Rawls, John. 1999a. *Collected Papers.* Edited by Samuel Freeman. Cambridge: Harvard University Press.

Rawls, John. 1999b. *The Law of Peoples.* Cambridge: Harvard University Press.

Rawls, John. 1989. *Political Liberalism.* 2nd edition. New York: Columbia University Press.

Rawls, John. 1971. *A Theory of Justice.* Cambridge: Belknap Press of Harvard University Press.

Rawson, Claude. 2000. "The Ultimate Taboo." *New York Times*, April 13.

Raz, Joseph. 1988. *The Morality of Freedom.* New York: Oxford University Press.

Reed-Sandoval. Forthcoming. *Socially Undocumented: Identity and Immigration Justice.* New York: Oxford University Press.

Reed-Sandoval, Amy. 2015. "Deportations as Theaters of Inequality." 29(2) *Public Affairs Quarterly* (April): 201–215.

Reed-Sandoval, Amy. 2013. "Locating the Injustice of Undocumented Migrant Oppression." 47(4) *Journal of Social Philosophy*: 372–398.

Richardson, Henry S. "Rawlsian social-contract severely disabled." 10(4) *Journal of Ethics* (December): 419–462.

Risse, Mathias. 2016. "On Where We Differ: Sites Versus Grounds of Justice, and Some Other Reflections on Michael Blake's *Justice and Foreign Policy.*" 35(3) *Law and Philosophy* (June): 251–270.

Risse, Mathias. 2012a. *On Global Justice.* Princeton: Princeton University Press.

Risse, Mathias. 2012b. *Global Political Philosophy.* Basingstoke: Palgrave Publishing.

Rodríguez, Cristina M. 2013. "Immigration, Civil Rights, and the Evolution of the People." 142(3) *Daedalus* (Summer) 228–241.

Romero, Simon. 2017. "Latinos Express Outrage as Trump Pardons Arpaio." *New York Times*, August 25.

Rose, Ananda. 2012. *Showdown in the Sonoran Desert: Religion, Law, and the Immigration Controversy.* New York: Oxford University Press.

Ross, Janell. 2016. "From Mexican rapists to bad hombres: the Trump campaign in two moments." *Washington Post*, October 20.

Rowling, J. K. 2000. *Harry Potter and the Goblet of Fire.* London: Bloomsbury.

Rubin, Jennifer. 2016. "Don't forget that, for a year, Trump called for deporting all illegal immigrants." *Washington Post*, August 23.

Ruddick, Sara. 1989. *Maternal Thinking: Towards a Politics of Peace.* New York: Ballentyne Books.

Sacchetti, Maria. 2018. "Top Homeland Security officials urge criminal prosecution of parents crossing border with children." *Washington Post*, April 26.

Sager, Alex. 2018. *Toward a Cosmopolitan Ethics of Mobility: The Migrant's-Eye View of the World*. New York: Springer.

Scanlon, T. M. 2000. *What We Owe to Each Other*. Cambridge: Harvard University Press.

Scarry, Elaine. 1985. *The Body in Pain*. New York: Oxford University Press.

Schiappa, E., et al. 2006. "Can one TV show make a difference? Will & Grace and the Parasocial Contact Hypothesis." 52(4) *Journal of Homosexuality*: 15–37.

Schotel, Bas. 2012. *On the Right of Exclusion: Law, Ethics and Immigration Policy*. Abingdon: Routledge Press.

Schulteis, Emily. 2018. "Is Sweden Ungovernable?" *Foreign Policy*, October 10.

Scoones, Ian, et al. 2018. "Emancipatory rural politics: confronting authoritarian populism." 45(1) *Journal of Peasant Studies*: 1–20.

Sen, Amartya. 1992. *Inequality Re-examined*. New York: The Russell Sage Foundation.

Shachar, Ayelet. 2009. *The Birthright Lottery: Citizenship and Global Inequality*. Cambridge: Harvard University Press.

Shacknove, Andrew. 1985. "Who Is a Refugee?" 95(2) *Ethics* 95: 274–284.

Shariatmadari, David. 2015. "Swarms, floods, and marauders: the toxic metaphors of the migration debate." *The Guardian*, August 10.

Sharp, Gene, and Jaime Gonzalez. 2013. *How Nonviolent Struggle Works*. Boston: Albert Einstein Institution.

Shoemaker, Karl. 2011. *Sanctuary and Crime in the Middle Ages*. New York: Fordham University Press.

Shue, Henry. 1980. *Basic Right: Subsistence, Affluence, and U. S. Foreign Policy*. Princeton: Princeton University Press.

Sidgwick, Henry. 2013. *The Elements of Politics*. Cambridge: Cambridge University Press.

Simmons, A. John. 1979. *Moral Principles and Political Obligations*. Princeton: Princeton University Press.

Singer, Peter. 1971. "Famine, Affluence, and Morality." 1(3) *Philosophy and Public Affairs* 229–243.

Slote, Michael. 2007. *The Ethics of Care and Empathy*. Routledge.

Slovic, Beth. 2008. "He's an illegal eh-lien." *Willamette Week*, January 19.

Song, Sarah. Forthcoming. *Immigration and Democracy*. New York: Oxford University Press.

Song, Sarah. 2017. "Why Does the State Have the Right to Control Immigration?" In *NOMOS LVII: Immigration, Emigration, and Migration*, edited by Jack Knight, 3–50. New York University Press.

Song, Sarah. 2012. "The Boundary Problem in Democratic Theory: Why the Demos Should Be Bounded by the State." 4(1) *International Theory*: 39–68.

Song, Sarah. 2009. "What Does It Mean to Be an American?" 138(2) *Daedalus* (Spring): 31–40.

Soper, Philip 1984. *A Theory of Law*. Cambridge: Harvard University Press.

Sorkin, Amy Davidson. 2015. "Ted Cruz's Religious Test for Syrian Refugees." *New Yorker*, November 16.

Staihar, Jim, and Stephen Macedo. 2011. "Defending a Role for Mercy in a Criminal Justice System." In *Merciful Judgments and Contemporary Society*, edited by Austin Sarat, 138–194. Cambridge: Cambridge University Press.

Stemwedel, Janet T. 2015. "The Philosophy of Star Trek: The Kobayashi Maru, No-Win Scenarios, and Ethical Leadership." *Forbes*, August 23.

Stephenson, Neal. 1992. *Snow Crash*. New York: Bantam Books.

Stilz, Anna. 2016. "Is There an Unqualified Right to Leave?" In *Migration in Political Theory: The Ethics of Movement and Membership*, edited by Lea Ypi and Sarah Fine, 57–79. New York: Oxford University Press.

Stilz, Anna. 2013. "Occupancy Rights and the Wrong of Removal." 41(4) *Philosophy and Public Affairs* (Winter): 324–356.

Straehle, Christine. 2012. "Thinking about Protecting the Vulnerable When Thinking about Immigration: Is There a 'Responsibility to Protect' in Immigration Regimes?" 8(1–2) *Journal of International Political Theory*: 159–171.

Talbott, William. 2005. *Which Rights Should Be Universal?* New York: Oxford University Press.

Tan, Kok-Chor. 2014. *Justice, Institutions, and Luck*. New York: Oxford University Press.

Tan, Kok-Chor. 2000. *Toleration, Diversity, and Global Justice*. University Park, PA: Penn State University Press.

"Thirty-Five Foreigners Nabbed for Visa Offenses." 2018. *Bankgok Post*, July 25. Available at https://www.bangkokpost.com/news/general/1509898/35-foreigners-nabbed-for-visa-offences.

Thomson, Judith Jarvis. 1971. "A Defense of Abortion." 1(1) *Philosophy and Public Affairs* (Fall): 47–66.

Tibbetts, Ron. 2018. "From Mollie Tibbett's Father: Don't Distort Her Death to Advance Racist Views." *Des Moines Register*, September 1.

United States Commission on Civil Rights. 1980. *The Tarnished Golden Door: Civil Rights Issues in Immigration*. US Government Printing Office.

Valentini, Laura. 2017. "The Natural Duty of Justice in Non-ideal Circumstances: On the Moral Demands of Institution-Building and Reform." *European Journal of Political Theory*. Online early available at http://eprints.lse.ac.uk/85948/1/EJPT%20_%20Final.pdf.

Valentini, Laura. 2012. *Justice in a Globalized World: A Normative Framework*. New York: Oxford University Press.

Vonnegut, Kurt. 1965. *God Bless You, Mr. Rosewater, or Pearls before Swine*. New York: Holt McDougal.

Waldron, Jeremy. 1990. *The Right to Private Property*. Oxford: Clarendon Press.

Walsh, Declan, and Jason Horowitz. 2017. "Italy, Going It Alone, Stalls the Flow of Migrants. But at What Cost?" *New York Times*, September 17.

Walzer, Michael. 1986. *Spheres of Justice*. New York: Basic Books.

Walzer, Michael. 1977. *Just and Unjust Wars*. New York: Basic Books.

Warikoo, Niraj. 2018. "Disabled Detroit Immigrant in US for 34 Years Faces Deportation." *Detroit Free Press*, September 8.

Warren, Michael. 2015. "Trump Hits Jeb on 'Act of Love.'" *Weekly Standard*, August 31.

Watson, Lori. 2008. "Equal Justice: A Commentary on Michael Blake's 'Immigration and Political Equality.'" 45(4) *San Diego Law Review* (Fall): 981–988.

Wellman, Christopher H. 2008. "Immigration and Freedom of Association." 119 *Ethics*: 109–141.

Wellman, Christopher H., and Phillip Cole. 2011. *Debating the Ethics of Immigration: Is There a Right to Exclude?* New York: Oxford University Press.

Wellman, Christopher H., and A. John Simmons. 2005. *Is There a Duty to Obey the Law?* Cambridge: Cambridge University Press.

Welsh, Jennifer. 2014. "Fortress Europe and the Responsibility to Protect: Framing the Issue." *EUI Forum*, European University Institute, Florence, November. Available at www.eui.eu/Documents/RSCAS/Papers Lampedusa/FORUM-Welshfinal.pdf.

Wenar, Leif. 2017. *Blood Oil.* New York: Oxford University Press.

Wilcox, Shelly. 2009. "The Open Borders Debate on Immigration." 4(5) *Philosophy Compass* (September): 813–821.

Williams, Bernard. 1995. "The Point of View of the Universe: Sidgwick and the Ambitions of Ethics." *Cambridge Review*, May 7.

Winston, Kimberly. 2015. "Obama Denounces Religious Test for Refugees: 'That's Not Who We Are.'" *Washington Post*, November 16.

Wintour, Patrick. 2018. "Hillary Clinton: Europe Must Curb Immigration to Stop Rightwing Populists." *The Guardian*, November 22.

WuDunn, Sheryl. 1995. "Secretive Japan Sect Evokes Both Loyalty and Hostility." *New York Times*, March 24.

Yenginsu, Ceylan, and Anemona Hartocollis. 2015. "Amid Perilous Mediterranean Crossings, Migrants Find a Relatively Easy Path to Greece." *New York Times*, August 15.

Yong, Caleb. 2018. "Caring Relationships and Family Migration Schemes." In *The Ethics and Politics of Immigration: Core Issues and Emerging Trends*, edited by Alex Sager, 61–84. Lanham, MD: Rowman and Littlefield.

Ypi, Lea. 2013. "What's Wrong with Colonialism." 41(2) *Philosophy and Public Affairs*: 158–191.

Ypi, Lea. 2008. "Justice in Migration: A Closed Borders Utopia?" 16(4) *Journal of Political Philosophy*: 391–418.

Index